Winnie Davis

Winnie Davis

Daughter of the Lost Cause

HEATH HARDAGE LEE

Foreword by J.E.B. Stuart IV

Epilogue coauthored by Bertram Hayes-Davis

POTOMAC BOOKS

An imprint of the University of Nebraska Press

Potomac Books is an imprint of the University of Nebraska Press. Manufactured in the United States of America.

♾

Library of Congress Cataloging-in-Publication Data
Lee, Heath Hardage.
Winnie Davis: daughter of the lost cause / Heath Hardage Lee; foreword by J.E.B. Stuart IV; epilogue coauthored by Bertram Hayes-Davis.
pages cm
Includes bibliographical references and index.
ISBN 978-1-61234-637-3 (cloth: alk. paper) —
ISBN 978-1-61234-638-0 (ebook) 1. Davis, Varina Anne, 1864–1898. 2. Children of presidents—Confederate States of America—Biography.
3. Davis, Jefferson, 1808–1889—Family.
4. Confederate States of America—Biography.
I. Title.
E467.1.D28L44 2014
973.713092—DC23
[B] 2014001161

Set in Adobe Caslon Pro by L. Auten.
Designed by A. Shahan.

Contents

Illustrations

Foreword

Poor Jeb Stuart was shot through the kidneys and his liver grazed also. He lay in the bloom of youth and apparently in high health strong in voice and patience and resigned to his fate at eleven o'clock in the morning, at five that evening was dead without seeing his wife who was traveling to get to him. Poor young man the city he did so much to save mourned him sincerely.

Confederate first lady Varina Howell Davis to her mother, Margaret Kempe Howell, May 22, 1864

Gen. J.E.B. Stuart, so memorable for his twinkling blue eyes, his roguish sense of humor, his famous plumed hat, and his remarkable leadership skills as the commander of the Cavalry of the Army of Northern Virginia, was only thirty-one when he died. Stuart, like so many others who fought in that war, could not escape feeling a sense of mortality. Several lines from a letter dated March 2, 1862, that he wrote to his wife, Flora, speak to his dedication as a soldier and to the uncertainty of the future. "I, for one, though I stood alone in the Confederacy, without countenance or aid, would uphold the banner of Southern Independence as long as I had a hand left to grasp the staff, and then die before submitting . . . Tell my boy when I am gone how I felt and wrote and tell him . . . never to forget the principles for which his father struggled."[1]

The young general was fatally wounded at the Battle of Yellow Tavern, north of Richmond, in May 1864, joining thousands of others as martyrs of the South. Stuart was thus transformed into a representative of all the proud, resourceful young men of the South who had died in battle. Confederate president Jefferson Davis visited J.E.B. on his deathbed in Richmond on May 12, 1864. Davis realized that he was losing one of his most accomplished commanders, and he wanted to express his personal appreciation for Stuart's dedicated service to the Confederacy.

After Stuart's death, Confederate troops' morale was crushed. How would this devastating war end? There seemed to be little hope left. Ironically, however, the death of this beloved general became a defining moment in the life of Varina Anne "Winnie" Davis, the daughter of Jefferson and Varina Davis. When Winnie was born in the White House of the Confederacy on June 27, 1864, she became the bright spot that Stuart had been.

The human condition compels us to search for the positive in the midst of the negative, for a light in the darkness. Confederate troops, grasping for something to be optimistic about, considered Winnie's birth a good omen. The baton had passed from one youthful figure to another. In their time of desperation southern troops needed someone to believe in. A transfer of affection occurred, from a young popular general to a little baby. In the middle of the hell of war, there was a new reason to keep fighting, someone worth saving.

A magazine article from the 1940s imagined what life would have been like for Stuart had he survived the war. The fanciful story woven by the author was that Stuart would have become ambassador to Cuba, riding rough there with Teddy Roosevelt.[2] This perhaps is a stretch. Yet I do think he would have cautioned us not to forget the past or try to expunge parts of our southern history. He would have been intensely supportive of preserving our past so that we all may learn from it.

In this respect he and Winnie would have been on the same page. The two came from similar backgrounds. Both made great sacrifices at tremendous personal cost. Both were ultimately casualties of the war. I feel sure they would have understood each other well had they met as adults.

Kudos to the author, Heath Lee, for opening the doors to fully understanding the last child of Confederate president Jefferson Davis.

J.E.B. Stuart IV
Colonel, U.S. Army, Retired
October 21, 2012

Preface

What is it about Varina Anne "Winnie" Davis, youngest daughter of Confederate president Jefferson Davis and Varina Howell Davis and appointed "Daughter of the Confederacy," that has had such a hold on me for the past twenty-odd years? Even in Richmond, Virginia, where Winnie and I were both born, she is a half-forgotten symbol of the Lost Cause known primarily for her scandalous romance with the northern grandson of a famous abolitionist following the Civil War.

Winnie's 1897 portrait by Virginia artist John P. Walker has hung in various clubs and museums in Richmond for many years. I remember seeing this image as a teenager and wondering about this beautiful lady: who was she, and why was her expression so melancholy? In the painting Winnie is dressed in a white lace gown that drapes beautifully over her slim figure. She is portrayed with dark hair and deep blue eyes with a diamond tiara in her hair and a red ribbon badge pinned to her bodice. Her regal bearing suggested to me that she was nineteenth-century royalty of some sort. I wondered for a number of years about her in an offhand way, not bothering to do any research on her until college.

By my senior year at Davidson College in 1991, I began to outgrow the confines of the academic cage. Having spent the spring of my junior year abroad in France, taken all the required classes, had my share of failed romances, and exhausted the limited shopping options in downtown Davidson, North Carolina, I decided to devote myself entirely to my thesis on Winnie Davis. As I began to delve into Winnie's background through personal letters, diaries, newspaper accounts, and brief references to her in southern history books, I became fascinated with her tragic story. As part of my thesis work, I convinced my professors to send me to an academic conference being held at her family home,

Beauvoir, in Mississippi. I do not remember much about the conference I attended there, but I do remember the dresses.

Beauvoir had a collection of Winnie's dresses—elaborate nineteenth-century gowns for both day and evening. The docent leading the tour that day picked me out of the crowd and said, "Now you could wear her clothes easily—you are just her exact same size!" Of course, nothing would have pleased me more that day than to be able to try on all her clothes, just to see how they fit. In a sense that is exactly what I have been doing the past twenty years.

Trying on Winnie's metaphorical clothes through researching her life, motivations, and passions has made me realize why I am so drawn to her. We are both Richmonders from similar social backgrounds. We both grew up perhaps a bit overprotected by well-meaning parents. We were both partially educated in Europe, both schooled in all-female environments. We both have a deep-rooted relationship with Richmond. Working on Winnie's life story was like seeing what my life could have been if I had been raised in the late-nineteenth-century South.

Richmond itself is not so very different now than it was during Winnie's day. It is a still a small village, with its provincial, gossipy side and its highly cultured sophisticated side. It has an infinitely strong hold on those who are born here, even if they later live far away. The White House of the Confederacy, where Winnie was born, still stands on Clay Street. Gracious homes from the Civil War and Reconstruction periods still line the streets. The ghosts of the Confederacy, including those of the Davis family, still flit through Hollywood Cemetery.

If you visit the Davis family graves at Hollywood, you will find the entire clan there. You will see the graves of Jefferson and Varina, the patriarch and matriarch; oldest daughter Margaret "Maggie" Hayes, her husband, Addison, and some of their children; and the four Davis sons: Samuel, little Joe, Billy, and Jeff Jr. Moss covers all tombs, and you can barely make out the names of the younger Davis boys, with their tiny crumbling grave markers.

Winnie's grave, however, stands out. Well-tended, with blooming red geraniums at its base, her tomb is guarded by a sculpture of a beautiful granite angel, sculpted by Hungarian artist George Julian Zolnay, with an appropriately melancholy expression. She clearly represents the public's image of the former Daughter of the Confederacy. The angel is tendering a wreath—perhaps attempting to heal the breach between North and South caused by the Civil War. In my mind, though, the angel, Winnie herself, is trying to reconcile her private life with her public image. The contrast between the two, as illustrated by her life story, is striking.

Most telling of all is the dedication marker next to the grave. Erected in 1899, one year after Winnie's death, one might expect it would have been placed there by Richmonders. Instead, the marker on the grave reads, UNITED DAUGHTERS OF THE CONFEDERACY: NEW YORK CHAPTER. Only in death was Winnie able to help reconcile the breach between North and the South, a wound that festered and refused to heal during her short lifetime.

Winnie Davis

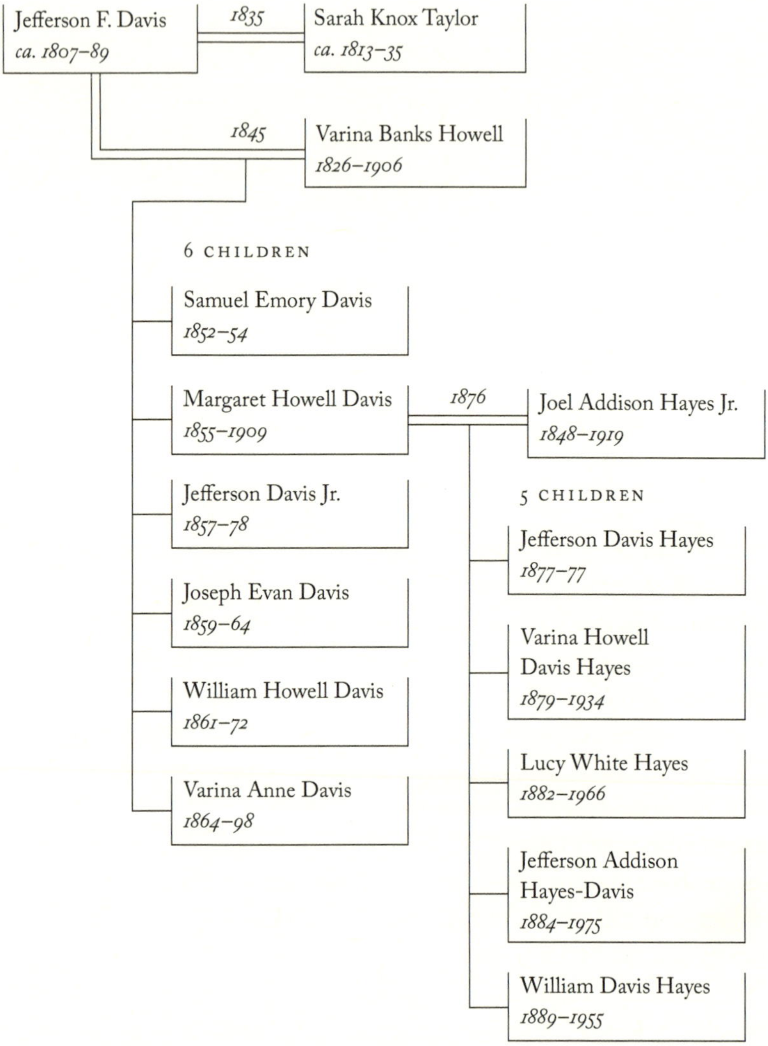

Jefferson F. Davis Family Tree

Source: *Papers of Jefferson Davis* online, Rice University, https://jeffersondavis.rice.edu/. Additional research provided by John Putnam. Chart design by Deena Coutant.

Introduction

> The girls who loved the boys in gray,
> The girls to country true,
> Can ne'er in wedlock give their hands,
> To those who wore the blue.
>
> Fragment from a southern poem, "True to the Gray," late 1860s–1870s

It was April 1864 in Richmond, Virginia. The northern and southern United States were locked in an epic battle for dominance over states' rights and slavery. Thousands were being slaughtered every day, and Richmond was literally surrounded by rivers of blood. Depressed and downtrodden, Confederate troops prayed for deliverance, for a sign that something good was to come out of all this bitter warfare.

Confederate president Jefferson Davis was struggling to salvage the remnants of his army, beat the odds, and win the war. A workaholic who could not separate his home life from his political and work obligations, Jefferson used the home's gorgeous dining room as a conference room. George Washington's portrait watched over the president of the Confederacy and his generals, such as Robert E. Lee, while they planned strategy and held their councils.[1]

The Confederate first lady, Varina, was heavily pregnant with their sixth child and worried about her husband, whose delicate constitution was not bearing up well under his enormous responsibilities. She noticed his angular, sharp features becoming more prominent by the day. The stress had begun to take a severe toll on the Confederacy's anxious president, who had recently begun to look much older than his fifty-six years.

Varina watched carefully over their four young children: Margaret ("Maggie," also known in the family as "Pollie"), Jefferson Davis Jr.

("Jeff"), William Howell ("Billy"), and the youngest, Joseph Emory ("Joe"). Although she could hear gunfire in the distance, Varina fervently wished that she could keep her children safe at the Executive Mansion, which had been her one oasis of peace since they moved into the residence in August 1861.

The mansion was a stately and gracious home originally built in 1818 for John Brockenbrough, an aristocratic Virginian who was president of the Bank of Virginia, and his wife, Gabriella. Lewis Crenshaw, a wealthy flour merchant and the second owner of the house, had just added a third floor to the mansion and redecorated it entirely. He sold the house to the city of Richmond for forty-three thousand dollars so it might serve as the Executive Mansion for the Confederate president. The city then rented the house to Jefferson and his family.[2]

Crenshaw had outfitted the house with luxury items such as gas lighting and a water closet. One of the Richmond newspapers declared that the Confederate "First Family was getting a residence with 'all the modern conveniences.'" The home also boasted the very latest fabrics and carpets from England to show off the previous owner's fine taste and sophistication. The grand front entrance hall boasted faux-marble wallpaper and custom-made floor cloths. Two imposing plaster statues representing the Greek figures Comedy and Tragedy flanked both sides of the entry hall and served as gas lamps.[3]

By all reports the Davis family enjoyed living at the Executive Mansion, spending much of their time in a small library known within the household as the "Snuggery," which was the warmest room in the house. Another popular gathering spot for the family was the imposing drawing room featuring an Italian Carrera marble fireplace with two beautiful mythological women on either side, which the Davises' two little boys often kissed good night.[4] Richmonders called the striking home both the "Brockenbrough Mansion" and the "Gray House," due to the home's gray stucco facade.[5]

Although in public Jefferson was known to be reserved, he was a far different person at home with his family. He adored all his children and was attentive and affectionate with them. He always set aside time to play with his brood, and he made sure to engage with them on their level. Varina was constantly scolding him for ruining his fine clothes rolling around with Maggie, Jeff Jr., and Joe. "He had worn out many pairs of expensive dress pants crawling around on all fours playing with the children."[6]

While Jefferson preferred to be with his family and was not fond of socializing, Varina loved a good party. She was well known for her soirees, playing the piano in the drawing room to entertain her guests and serving "coffee made from chestnuts and chicory along with cakes baked with molasses." In the early days of the war, glittering balls and parties still flourished, but by 1863 "starvation parties" were all the rage, and wartime food deprivations necessitated such substitutions.

Music and dancing continued on these occasions, but no food was served.[7] The young ladies of Richmond would often wear old gowns that had previously belonged to their mothers or grandmothers. They would rarely wear jewelry, as they had given it all to support the Confederate cause.[8]

Jefferson and Varina held weekly receptions at the Executive Mansion that continued for almost the entire duration of the war. The public was admitted, but frequent esteemed guests included Confederate Cabinet member Judah P. Benjamin; vice president of the Confederacy Alexander Stephens; former president of Virginia John Tyler; and General J.E.B. Stuart. Jefferson was said to have a cordial and unpretentious manner, welcoming all who came to his door.

These presidential receptions, starvation parties, and even amateur theatricals contributed to a lively and flourishing social life in Richmond during the war. Although Richmonders might have had barely enough to eat, they adhered to these amusements as a bulwark against the horrors of war. Rome might soon be burning, but parties in the southern capital would continue until the bitter end.[9]

Varina was a gracious hostess, a highly educated woman, and a superb conversationalist. These skills had served her well during her time with her husband in Washington DC in the 1850s, when they had been among the city's most popular political couples. One of Varina's early biographers flatteringly summed up Varina's character by sketching her as "a combination of Queen Elizabeth, Queen Victoria, and Andromache. Queen Elizabeth for her wit, shrewdness, tart epigram, haughtiness, and statesmanship; Victoria for her dignity, propriety, conservatism, and practice of homely virtues; Andromache for the Trojan lady's unselfish absorption in fatherland, husband, and children."[10] Richmonders often used the word *queen* to describe Varina, but it was not always employed in such a flattering manner.

Constance "Connie" Cary Harrison, wife of Jefferson's private secretary, Burton Harrison, knew the first lady well. She described Varina as "a woman of warm heart and impetuous tongue, witty and caustic, with a sensitive nature underlying all; a devoted wife and mother, and most gracious mistress of a salon." Varina's sister, Margaret Howell, also lived with the Davises' in the Executive Mansion and was well known for her mischievous nature and sparkling wit.[11]

Richmond, however, was not Washington DC. The Confederate capital was a far more conservative and provincial place. Here the "First Lady of the Confederacy" was looked down upon for her intellect. Varina was accustomed to the warmer manners of the Deep South of Mississippi, and she found many Richmonders to be cold and snobbish. In her study *Civil War Wives* Carol Berkin writes: "The elite women of the Old Dominion condemned her as coarse and unpolished. To these women of impeccable genealogy, Varina represented the crass, nouveau cotton society."[12]

Women from old Richmond families often snubbed her, while the men called her "Empress Eugenie," an allusion to Eugenie de Montijo, the imperious Spanish-born wife of Emperor Napoleon III. The Richmond newspapers echoed the sentiments of the town's socialites and took potshots at Varina's appearance, criticizing her as "portly and middle-aged."[13]

The nursery was home base for the four Davis children and Catherine, their Irish nanny. Mary Chesnut, the South Carolina diarist and great friend of the family, described the Davis children as "wonderfully clever and precocious children—but unbroken wills. At one time there was a sudden uprising of the nursery contingent. They fought, screamed, and laughed. It was bedlam broke loose."[14] Jefferson and Varina's room was separate but nearby and decorated in grand Victorian style, with a massive carved bed in the center.[15]

Maggie was the Davises' only girl at this time. She had sparkling black eyes, glossy brown hair, and good, even features. She also had the Howell family's olive skin, a trait inherited from their Welsh forebears.[16] Rambunctious Jeff Jr., the oldest Davis boy, led the nursery gang. "Jeffy" was indulged by the staff and aides at the White House, who also called him "the General."[17] He was always described as a handsome child, "well-made, with dark hair, dark eyes, and good features." Like his sister Maggie, "his skin is a rich brown, like that of all his family."[18]

Billy and Joe typically followed Jeffy's lead. Billy had been born deaf and was the most sensitive of all the Davis children. He was paler than his sister and other brothers, with gray eyes, light hair, and an aquiline nose.[19] The youngest Davis child, Joe Jr., was gentle and sweet but also extremely curious and full of energy. His favorite toy was a miniature cannon that actually fired. He and his brothers spent many happy hours dressing up in miniature Confederate and Zouave uniforms, blowing up imaginary Union soldiers.[20] He was described by many as an extremely intelligent, affectionate little boy and also the best behaved of all the Davis children.[21] He was also perhaps the most beloved by his parents. Jefferson and Varina had high hopes for his future.

The children were joined in their revels by a black friend, James Limber, who was the orphan of a free black woman. Varina had rescued the child after she spied a black man beating him on a carriage ride around Richmond one day. He joined the household as a free black and became a playmate and companion to the Davis children.[22]

Despite the battles around Richmond, life for the Davises went on much as it had before the war. The seeming normalcy of day-to-day routines in the home lulled the Davis clan into a false sense of security. Little did Jefferson and Varina know that the figure of Tragedy guarding the front hall portended extreme misfortune for their family. The horrors of war were becoming well known outside the confines of the mansion, but terror would soon spring unexpectedly from within.

CHAPTER ONE

A Tragic Fall

Despite the comforting routines of day-to-day life within the Executive Mansion, it was fast becoming impossible for Varina to ignore the increasing sounds of not-so-distant gunfire just outside of Richmond. The noise made the Confederate first lady extremely nervous, and rightly so, as a breach of the city by the Union army was a constant threat. Author Mary P. Couling describes that time: "The early glitter of extravagant parties had given way to the fear and panic at the frequent tolling of the tocsin—the warning bell—in Capitol Square and the frightening sound of the Federal cannon less than ten miles away."[1]

Despite the looming shadow of Union invasion, the southern spring of 1864 arrived fragrant and fresh. At the end of April azaleas and dogwoods, with their pink and white petals, were bursting into bloom, though the weather over the past week had been rainy and much cooler than usual.[2]

On the afternoon of April 30 a heavily pregnant Varina left the Executive Mansion on 12th and Clay Streets to take her husband lunch at his Custom House office. The Confederate first lady was a born nurturer and known to stay up all night with her husband nursing him through various illnesses. Jefferson, often too busy to eat, had grown weak and thin, so his wife had made it part of her daily ritual to take him his lunch and often dinner as well.[3]

Scarcely had Varina rushed out to make this important delivery when a messenger from the Executive Mansion approached her with awful news. Her youngest child, Joe Jr., had fallen from the mansion's high balcony to the pavement below.

Apparently, the children's nanny, Catherine, was not watching her charges as the five-year-old Joe was able to make his way out the window to play on an outdoor portico. The open balcony was just too enticing for the two young boys to ignore. Older brother Jeff was reportedly walking from pillar to pillar. Little Joe tried to imitate him but failed, falling twenty feet to the ground below.

The fall was over in a second, but poor Joe lived on, breathing shallowly. His left thigh was broken, his small skull was crushed, and blood oozed from the corner of his mouth. Jeff reached him first, and he was beside himself with fear and frustration. He may have felt that the accident was his fault.

Two men happened to pass by the Executive Mansion at this moment, one of whom was a Confederate officer. In the officer's eyewitness account he noticed Maggie crying and running to the neighbors next door for help.[4] The two men rushed over to offer their aid, joined by Jeff Jr. and Billy. They found little Joe "in the arms of a Negro man, insensible and almost dead."[5] The men rubbed camphor and brandy on the unconscious child. Their attempts revived him momentarily, and he began to breathe better.

Medical aid was sent for immediately, and the badly injured boy was brought into the Executive Mansion. Four local physicians were all in attendance in short order.[6] Meanwhile, a servant was dispatched to the Custom House with the news. He communicated his story to Jefferson's messenger, Mr. William Davies, a young man of only eighteen.

Davies had the terrible task of informing Jefferson and Varina of the accident. Davies tried to soften the blow temporarily by concealing its potentially fatal nature from Varina. In a whispered aside, however, Davies alerted Jefferson to the serious nature of the fall. The meal forgotten, the frantic parents jumped into their waiting carriage and rushed home, tearing through the back streets, desperate to reach their young son.

As Varina and Jefferson reached little Joe's side, they realized they had little time left with him. The Confederate officer who had come to the small child's aid remembered that Joe opened his eyes once more, and the crowd around him hoped he was reviving. Alas, as it was reported in the *Richmond Sentinel* a month later, "it was the last bright gleaming of the wick in the socket before the light was extinguished forever."[7]

Forty-five minutes later the small child died, and then both parents unraveled, Varina completely and immediately, shrieking with grief and utter disbelief. The Confederate officer witnessed the terrible shock his president was experiencing firsthand, and he would never forget it. As Jefferson watched his favorite little son die before him, the officer told the newspaper, "such a look of petrified unbearable anguish I never saw. His pale intellectual face, already oppressed with a thousand national troubles, that now so imminently threaten our existence, seemed suddenly ready to burst with unspeakable grief, and thus transfixed into a stony rigidity."[8]

Jefferson broke down later. Varina recalled that her husband was numb. "I saw his mind was momentarily paralyzed by the blow . . . [he] called out, in a heart-broken tone, 'I must have this day with my little child.'"[9] This was the one time known on record when Jefferson stayed home from his work for the Confederacy. For just one day during the war he left behind his role as president of the Confederate States and allowed himself to be simply a bereaved father who had lost his favorite son.

Close family friend Mary Chesnut was in Richmond at the time of the accident and went directly to the White House to help the Davises' on that awful day. Her eyewitness account painted a gloomy picture of this tragic event: "Mrs. Semmes [a family friend] said when she got there, little Jeff was kneeling down by his brother. And he called out to her in great distress, 'Mrs. Semmes, I have said all the prayers I know how, but God will not wake little Joe.'"

Mary continued: "Poor little Joe, the good child of the family, so gentle and affectionate, he used to run in to say his prayers at his father's knee. Before I left the house I saw him lying there, white and beautiful as an angel—covered with flowers. Catherine, his nurse, lying flat on the floor by his side and weeping and wailing as only an Irish woman can."[10] In her diary Mary remembered the Confederate president's heavy footsteps reflecting his heavy heart that evening: "That night with no sound but the tramp of his [Jefferson Davis's] foot overhead, the curtains flapping in the wind, the gas flaring, I was numb—stupid—half-dead with grief and terror."[11]

Jefferson's only consolation seemed to be that he was sending his son to heaven. His mantra, repeated over and over silently to himself and behind closed doors, was "Not mine, O Lord, but thine."[12] Joe had been his father's favorite, adored by his family and the staff alike. Burton Harrison's wife, Constance Cary Harrison, wrote of the boy as "little, merry, happy Joe, petted by all visitors to the Executive Mansion—he who when his father was in the act of receiving official visitors, once pushed his way into the study and, clad only in an abbreviated night-gown, insisted upon saying his evening prayer at the President's knee."[13]

The popular little boy's unexpected death inflicted great psychological damage on the family. Varina's letter to Brig. Gen. Richard Griffith's widow summed up her sorrow: "One week ago I should have been able to tell of my most beautiful and promising child. Now I can only tell you that I have three left—none so bright, none so beautiful, but all infinitely precious."[14]

Joe Jr. was the second son Jefferson and Varina had lost. The Davises' first son, Samuel Emory, had been an unexpected blessing to the couple. After seven years without a pregnancy, Varina and Jefferson had given up hope of ever having a family. When he was born, in July 1852, they could scarcely believe their good fortune. Davis proudly called him "le man," a Celtic nickname, and enjoyed showing him off whenever he had the opportunity. The boy was a charming and lively infant, and the couple was overjoyed and relieved at his arrival.[15]

Sadly, the joy was not to last. In 1854 their adored son died just before his second birthday from measles. Samuel's illness was especially gruesome: "His mouth had swelled and blistered and bled. His eyes had turned bloodred. Sores spread over his entire face, and though Varina managed to cure them, it left his head 'a perfect mat of scabs.'" After a brief recovery, Samuel died. Both parents were devastated.[16]

Samuel's death, like the death of his first wife, Sarah Knox-Taylor, was life changing for Jefferson. The tragic and early demise of these adored individuals took away a great deal of his ability to love and be loved by others. After these two traumatic events, a hard and unyielding shell formed around his heart—a self-protective mechanism to be sure but one that would later critically hobble his marriage to Varina.

To lose one child to an illness is horrific, but sadly, this was not an uncommon occurrence in the mid-nineteenth century. The shadow of death lurked around every nursery corner at this time: antibiotics such as penicillin had not yet been discovered. Not until World War II was penicillin widely available and used to treat infections, thanks to its discovery in 1928 by Scottish bacteriologist Alexander Fleming. Thus, Samuel, like so many wounded later in the Civil War, had very little chance of survival when faced with such an illness.

While Samuel's death may have devastated Jefferson the most, Joe's death was perhaps more painful for Varina. Losing a second child in such a tragic and potentially avoidable accident must have cut both parents to the core. All night long Varina and Jefferson mourned their son. The lights burned in the Executive Mansion through the darkness as they sat with his little body and prepared themselves for a bleak future without him. A massive funeral was held on May 1, at Richmond's Hollywood cemetery. The other Davis children were witnesses to this terrible grief.

Mary Chesnut stayed in Richmond a day longer than planned to attend the funeral and provided a firsthand account of the sad event: "Immense crowd at the funeral. Sympathetic but shoving and pushing rudely, thousands of children. Each child had a green bough or a bunch of flowers to throw on little Joe's grave, which was already a mass of white flowers, crosses &c&c."[17]

Mary also recalled that Jefferson seemed to have aged overnight following his son's death and that Varina had lost her vigor. "The dominant figure, that poor, old gray-haired man. Standing bare-headed, straight as an arrow, clear against the sky by the open grave of his son. She stood in her heavy black wrappings and her tall figure drooped. The flowers, the children, the procession as it moved, comes and goes. But these two dark, sorrow-stricken figures stand."[18] Prophetically, Mary questioned the reader, "Who will they kill next of that devoted household?"[19]

Maggie was the oldest child of the Davises and nine years old at the time of Joe's death. Jeff Jr., who had found his brother lying on the pavement outside the Executive Mansion, was seven. Billy was scarcely three. Winnie's birth was just weeks away. Her mother's emotional state was precarious and volatile. Varina was grieving for one child while simultaneously preparing for the birth of another. Despite the gratifying outpouring of support from Richmonders, family, and other friends after Joe's death, the scars left on the Davis parents and their children were deep and had far-reaching repercussions. Sadness would hallmark each and every member of this prominent southern family.

CHAPTER TWO

My Name Is a Heritage of Woe

May 1864 witnessed the death of beloved Confederate major general James Ewell Brown "J.E.B." Stuart, a great loss for Confederate troops and a heavy blow to their already sinking morale. The young military hero was well known to all Southerners for his extreme bravery, witty banter, and dashing sartorial sense. A peer of J.E.B. wrote: "His fighting jacket shone with dazzling buttons and was covered with gold braid; his hat was sloped up with a gold star and decorated with an ostrich plume; his fine buff gauntlets reached to the elbows; around his waist was tied a splendid yellow silk sash; and the spurs were of pure gold.' He had piercing blue eyes, a full beard, an athletic figure and a zest for life."[1]

The young general loved parties, dances, and theatricals. He often came to Richmond in between battle engagements to partake of Confederate society. As Connie Harrison, diarist and wife of Jefferson's private secretary, Burton Harrison, noted in regards to J.E.B. and his socializing, however, "In all our parties and pleasurings, there seemed to lurk a foreshadowing of tragedy, as in the Greek plays where the gloomy end is ever kept in sight."[2]

This bright, handsome young man was mortally wounded in the Battle of Yellow Tavern north of Richmond on May 11, 1864. In an ironic twist of fate, J.E.B. was struck down by the troops of his old enemy from his student days at West Point, Union cavalry commander Maj. Gen. Philip Sheridan. As he was carried from the battlefield, J.E.B. propped himself up and called to his men, saying: "Go back! Go back! Do your duty as I have done and our country will be saved. I would rather die than be whipped!"[3]

In the late afternoon of May 11, the seriously wounded soldier was taken by ambulance to Richmond, jolted mercilessly during the long journey. He would not allow his suffering to be mitigated by brandy the doctor tried to give him: J.E.B. had promised his mother twenty years ago that he would not touch alcohol.

The ambulance finally reached the home of his brother-in-law, a Confederate surgeon general, Dr. Charles Brewer—the husband of Flora's sister Maria—at 206 East Grace Street in Richmond.[4] This gracious home with yellow roses blooming behind a low red brick wall was the scene of J.E.B.'s last hours. The bullet wounds to his belly would produce a slow, excruciating death.

After a long, painful night, May 12 dawned, full of ominous thunder and lightning.[5] Word of J.E.B.s fatal injury had spread quickly around Richmond, and a huge crowd was already gathered outside the Brewers' home weeping for their fallen soldier. John B. Jones, the famous Confederate war clerk, kept a diary (published after the war, in 1866) that offered his firsthand observations from the War Office. A sense of gloom pervaded his diary entry on this stormy day. "Major Gen. J.E.B. Stuart was wounded last evening through the kidney, and now lies in the city, in a dying condition! Our best generals thus fall around us."[6]

The grieving crowd suddenly parted to let through a distinguished visitor. The tall, gaunt Confederate president had arrived to say his good-byes to his most beloved general. Jefferson "took his [J.E.B.'s] hand in there, and asked how he felt. Easy, he said, but willing to die if God and his country felt that he had fulfilled his destiny and done his duty." Later that day his doctor, Dr. Brewer, told him the end is near. Stuart nodded his head and said, "I am resigned, if it be God's will; but I would like to see my wife."[7]

Flora was staying with friends in Beaver Dam Station, about twenty-five miles from Richmond. She received a telegram the morning of May 12 that J.E.B. had been gravely wounded—a message that she had probably been expecting, and dreading, for months. Flora had always known that J.E.B. would fight to the death if needed, with no regard for his personal safety. The telegram read: "General Stuart has been seriously wounded. Come at once."

Flora and her two children, J.E.B. "Jimmy" Stuart II, age three, and seven-month-old Virginia Pelham Stuart, accompanied by a nurse named Tilda and the Reverend Woodbridge as their escort, set out that afternoon by train to reach the fallen general.[8] Flora was frantic to see her husband. When she and the children reached Ashland, Virginia, around three o'clock, they found the rails destroyed.

The reverend then accepted the offer of a mule-drawn ambulance wagon for the rest of the journey on Flora's behalf. When the family finally reached Richmond, late that evening, it was during the peak of a violent thunderstorm. Terrible lightening lit up the muddy, rutted road to Richmond. The winds that evening were so strong that the steeple of historic St. John's Church was blown away.[9] Flora Stuart and her children at last arrived at the Brewers' house late in the evening, but by then there was no time for a parting embrace. J.E.B. was gone.

Varina wrote to her mother on May 22, 1864, telling her about Stuart's tragic death and the general atmosphere of panic and chaos that reigned in Richmond at the time. In her letter Varina noted that her husband had displayed a total lack of regard for personal safety: "Jefferson . . . has been forced from home constantly, and in the various battles around Richmond had been pretty constantly on the field. I hear that at Drewry's Bluff he was very much exposed [—] a man's drum was taken off by a shell in five feet of him."[10]

Varina also clearly saw the mental toll the war was taking on her husband, who had always had a nervous temperament. "Jeff is much worn by anxiety, he seems to have got nearly as bad as I am and I hear the roar of artillery and the crack of musketry it seems to me all the time." She concludes with a gloomy description of Richmond in crisis: "There is an immense deal of suffering here now, so much so that they are impressing servants in the street to nurse the wounded."[11]

Winnie was born into this war-torn environment on June 27, 1864, in her parent's ornate mahogany bed, draped with filmy mosquito netting.[12] The baby arrived not simply in the midst of Civil war battles and political maneuvers but also during a very personal period of parental grief. Both parents were still deep in mourning for little Joe. Emotions and stress were running high throughout the Davis household. Surely as a result of this tense environment, Winnie was always hyper-attuned to her parents' needs and moods.

Winnie partially filled a gap in both her mother's and her father's hearts. While she could not totally bridge the voids left by the deaths of her two brothers, her presence still helped both parents tremendously.

Before Winnie was even conscious of her surroundings, she became a salve to her parents' psychic wounds as well as the spirits of beleaguered Confederate troops. Superstitious southern soldiers viewed the passing of J.E.B. Stuart as an ominous sign. The arrival of Winnie, however, seemed to counteract their feelings of dread, at least temporarily.

The birth of the last child of Confederate president Jefferson Davis was thought to be a good omen for the Confederate forces battling the Union soldiers. Winnie's arrival was heralded by one and all as a blessing to southerners weary of war. In the late 1920s Eron Opha Moore Rowland, Varina's first biographer, wrote of the child's birth, "Born amid the victories that had saved the city [Richmond] from the enemy, it was thought to be a happy augury, and General Lee came and held the infant in his arms."[13]

As the object of much hero worship, Gen. Robert E. Lee bestowed a special status upon the newborn that would remain with her throughout her life. The fact that she was born during a short period of southern victories was especially significant. Confederate troops, by now completely desperate for positive signs, took Winnie's birth as a sign that the South might still triumph, despite increasingly negative odds.

Winnie had the distinction of being born in Richmond's White House of the Confederacy during the war. Rowland noted of Winnie, "Since she had been born in the White House of the Confederacy, she should be set apart as a kind of shrine at which those below the Mason-Dixon Line should worship."[14] Winnie always retained this special distinction, which fostered a deep sense of camaraderie between her and her father. The baby's nickname "Winnie" was chosen with a view toward a happier future. An Indian name meaning bright or sunny, it was perhaps chosen in an attempt to shed some light on a dark time. It also was her father's pet name for her mother.[15]

Although Winnie bore her nickname from birth, Varina and Jefferson took almost a year to give their youngest child her formal name of Varina Anne Davis. In contrast to the family's upbeat view of the child's nickname, Varina expressed regret that Winnie's formal name reflected her own. "*My name is a heritage of woe*, but as no one is exempt now, the chances are greater for her than in the days when some were happy."[16]

Varina adored Winnie, and she would eventually bond with her the most completely of all her children. Throughout Winnie's life Varina would brag about her youngest to friends and acquaintances. In a letter to Mary Chesnut, Varina gushed: "She is so soft, so good, so very *ladylike*—and knows me so well. She is white as a lily and has such exquisite hands and feet and such bright blue eyes."[17] The description seems to be one of a much more mature child or even a grown woman. The emphasis her mother put on Winnie being "ladylike" was a label that would stick with her throughout her life. Even as an infant, Winnie already represented so many of the virtues and traits held in high regard by southerners and the Confederate culture.

The pre–Civil War "Cult of Domesticity and True Womanhood" had four ideals to which southern women especially were expected to adhere: piety, purity, submissiveness, and domesticity.[18] Winnie would eventually become an interesting mix of these ideals—a fusion of the True Woman and the New Woman. But for now she was just an infant with the hopes and dreams of those around her projected onto her tiny countenance.

A brighter future seemed within reach for the new baby lying snug in her cradle in the Executive Mansion at 12th and Clay Streets. She was soon ensconced with her loving Irish nurse, Mary Ahern, who was to become an adored member of the Davis household and would remain with Winnie and her family for ten years.[19] Her godmother, noted beauty Imogene Penn Lyons, lived close to her goddaughter in a mansion on Grace Street.[20] The experience of living in the capital of the Confederacy with her family and friends nearby, however, was not to last long for Winnie.

Richmond was seen as "the spiritual center of Virginia's aristocracy and of the rebellion."[21] Unlike other southern cities (such as Atlanta, Charleston, Mobile, New Orleans, Savannah, and Vicksburg) that had fallen to the Union army, Richmond had proudly survived. By 1865, despite the fierce battles that raged close to the southern capital between Union and Confederate troops, no invaders had been able to break through the city's defenses. The headquarters of the Confederacy had "been spared the horrors of war, the physical devastation, and humiliating enemy occupation that had befallen many of the great cities of the South."[22] This feeling of invincibility, of being above the fray, lasted for Richmonders, and indeed for Jefferson Davis, until almost the end of the war.

On a bright and beautiful early spring Sunday, however, while Jefferson was attending St. Paul's Church, a telegram from General Lee arrived.[23] The message was addressed to secretary of war Gen. J. C. Breckenridge, but the fateful document soon made its way into the hands of the highest-ranking Confederate. The president of the Confederacy turned gray as he read the devastating news.

> HEADQUARTERS
> April 2, 1865
>
> *General J. C. Breckenridge:*
>
> I see no prospect of doing more than holding our position here till night. I am not certain that I can do that. If I can I shall withdraw tonight north of the Appomattox, and if possible, it will be better to withdraw the whole line tonight from James River. Brigades on Hatcher's Run are cut off from us. Enemy have broken through our lines and intercepted between us and them, and there is no bridge over which they can cross the Appomattox this side of Goode's or Beaver's, which are not very far from the Danville Railroad. Our only chance, then of concentrating our forces, is to do so near Danville Railroad, which I shall endeavor to do at once. *I advise all preparation be made for leaving Richmond tonight. I will advise later, according to circumstances.*
>
> —R. E. Lee[24]

With this news Jefferson and his fellow cabinet members made plans to leave the city that evening. They would evacuate Richmond and establish a new Confederate capital in Danville, Virginia, which lay 140 miles to the southwest.

But what of Varina and the Jefferson's four remaining children? As any good leader knows, your family is your most vulnerable spot. Find and capture the wife and children, and you can be exploited and manipulated into decisions that will not be beneficial to your political cause. Jefferson would be forced to give himself up to Union forces if the children and Varina were captured.[25]

Anticipating this possibility, Jefferson had sent Varina, Maggie, Jeff Jr., Billy, and the infant Winnie away to Charlotte, North Carolina, three days earlier, on Friday, March 31. Naturally, Varina was terrified, but she begged to stay with her husband, as did their children. Varina recalled: "Mr. Davis almost gave way, when our little Jeff begged to remain with him. And Maggie clung to him convulsively; for it was evident he thought he was looking his last upon us."[26] Winnie mostly slept in her mother's arms. Ever loyal, Varina did not want to leave her husband alone to face the Union invasion.

Jefferson gave his wife scarce provisions, some gold and other money to bribe her way South, and a loaded percussion cap, black powder .32 or .36 caliber revolver. He knew Varina would fight to the death to protect their family, telling her, "You can at least, if reduced to the last extremity, force your assailants to kill you."[27]

Although she had been selling and giving away her possessions for weeks, she was still forced to leave many sentimental items at the Executive Mansion. The women of Richmond knew long before most of the city's men of the Davis family's plan to flee town. "The upper-crust ladies of St. Paul's [Church] had known through their own grapevine that Mrs. Davis had been planning an evacuation for weeks before she actually left. She had put her finest possessions such as her collection of silk dresses and leather gloves on consignment in the shops in the city that specialized in fine ladies attire."[28] Such worldly goods were excess baggage, and she had much more precious cargo, her four children, to protect and transport. Facing a long journey as refugees, hunted and wanted by the Union army, Varina and her brood were desperate to get away.

Jefferson's private secretary, Col. Burton Harrison, and two daughters of the secretary of the treasury, George Trenholm, accompanied the Confederate first lady and her children on their escape route. Varina's sister, Margaret, the free black boy James Limber, and two trusted black servants, Ellen and James Jones, rounded out their entourage. The group's sole armed escort was James Morgan, a young midshipman.[29]

Varina was a woman of rare courage and resolve—for this her children and Jefferson were extremely lucky. She would keep a cool head and guard her children fiercely. There is no doubt the Confederate first lady would have given her life for any one of her offspring or for her husband without hesitation. This proud and refined woman would soon walk miles in the mud, carrying baby Winnie in her arms with her children trailing behind her as she fled toward Charlotte, North Carolina, then further South and hopefully beyond Yankee reach.

For days the bedraggled Davis family and their companions had only scant knowledge regarding the fate and whereabouts of Jefferson. On May 2 President Andrew Johnson proclaimed a $100,000 bounty on the Confederate president's head (equivalent to almost $8 million today).[30] This husband, father, and rebel leader was soon to become the most wanted and vilified man of the Confederate cause. Even worse, he was considered by many to be the probable assassin of beloved President Abraham Lincoln. "In the emotional aftermath of Abraham Lincoln's assassination an angry northern public opinion and an antagonistic, suspicious government assumed Davis's complicity, even to the point of orchestrating, in that horrific act."[31]

CHAPTER THREE

Escape, Capture, and Fort Monroe

Her loving and generous nature as exhibited when she was an infant and I a prisoner is to be a blessed memory & gives high hopes of what she will be in her maturity.

Jefferson Davis to Varina Howell Davis,
January 17, 1870, regarding Winnie

Varina and her party arrived in Charlotte, North Carolina, mentally spent but physically unharmed on April 1 or 2, 1865.[1] After spending several days there, she learned that on the night of April 2, Richmond had been evacuated and that the city had been burned and looted. The thought of her household treasures and domestic goods being pawed by Yankee invaders must have endlessly tortured Varina. She may have also vaguely wondered who among the ladies of St. Paul's Episcopal Church might be wearing her fine silks now.

Because Richmond had served as the mobilization and supply center for the Confederacy during the majority of the war, its ultimate fate if the Confederates had to evacuate was not unexpected. Ironically, it was the Confederate troops themselves who set fire to part of the business district, vowing that nothing valuable would fall into Union hands. A first-person account of the burning of Richmond on April 2 vividly illustrated a catastrophe of biblical proportions. The author, Oscar F. Weisiger, lived and worked there and was told by Gen. Richard S. Ewell, Richmond's military commander, that the city was to be evacuated at midnight.

Weisiger recalled: "I cannot begin to describe to you the terrors of the day. It can only be likened to my conception of the Judgment Day.

At no time during the war did the fiercest artillery duel equal in bursting of shell the firing of the Laboratory [building] . . . The whole business part of the City from 9 to 15th St. is in ashes." The author went on to note the ultimate implications of the fire: "The result has been just what I predicted three years ago, that when Richmond was given up it would be the death blow of the Confederacy."[2]

Although parts of Richmond's downtown were reduced to cinders, the Confederate capital escaped the total destruction that characterized so many other southern cities. Yet the capture and burning of Richmond was a psychologically potent symbol and a massive victory for the northern troops, whose rallying cry over the past three years had been "On to Richmond!"[3] Photographers flocked to the city while it still burned to document its ruins. "These views were stamped into the national memory, and for a long time to come Richmond in ashes signified irretrievable loss to the South and the fruits of failed rebellion to the North."[4]

Another image made famous by the northern press was that of President Abraham Lincoln touring the White House of the Confederacy in Richmond on April 4, 1865. Abraham and his young son Tad had sailed up the James River from Petersburg that day and disembarked from Rockett's Landing. From there the pair made their way on foot to the Executive Mansion, at the intersection of 12th and Clay Streets.[5] April 4 happened to be Tad's twelfth birthday.

The Davises' housekeeper showed the president and his son into the mansion. Abraham soon was sitting in Jefferson's padded leather chair and surveying the place where his archrival had lived and worked against him, and the Union, for the past four years. Not surprisingly, the office was almost obsessively orderly.[6] As Nelson Lankford writes in his study of the destruction of Richmond, "For the few first days, before too many souvenir hunters had passed through, the house retained the air of having just been abandoned by its residents."[7] It must have been an eerie sight, this gorgeous southern mansion remaining almost untouched amid the charred remains of downtown Richmond.

While Abraham was inspecting her former home, Varina was strung tight with terror and worry for her husband, her children, and herself. By mid-April the former first lady of the Confederacy was forced to flee farther south, nomadically wandering and seeking shelter from Confederate sympathizers and old friends along the way. To fall so far so fast must have been humiliating to Varina, though she herself had predicted such a turn of events for months.

The southern first lady and her children eventually joined the Confederate "treasure train," which carried the remains of the administration's treasury. When the cache originally left Richmond, it contained "Mexican silver dollars, American golden double eagles, ingots, nuggets, and silver bricks, millions of dollars in Confederate banknotes and bonds, 16,000 to 18,000 pounds sterling in Liverpool Acceptances, negotiable in England, and chest full of jewels—diamonds, emeralds, rubies, sapphires, and pearls—donated by Southern women to buy a warship."[8]

Over the course of its transport, large sums were paid out to Confederate troops for their services. Davis and his Cabinet were given $35,000 to keep the Confederate government afloat. All these funds were eventually disbursed or handed over to federal troops. Contrary to reports in the northern press, Jefferson retained nothing for himself.[9]

On April 9, 1865, a few months before Winnie's first birthday, General Lee surrendered to Gen. Ulysses S. Grant, after losing the Battle of Appomattox Court House, which effectively ended the war in Virginia. While the nightmare of war was finally over, Varina and her brood were still struggling desperately through the mud and muck toward Chester, South Carolina, with the Confederate treasure. When the railroad tracks ended, Varina and the children were forced to get off the train, and the treasure guards had to reload the valuable cargo onto wagons.

The exhausted Davis children were frightened and fearful for their father's safety. Maggie, Jeff Jr., and Billy were "tired, scared, and hungry," writes historian Retta D. Tindal. "The ambulance that was transporting the Davis family was too heavy for the muddy roads that had turned into quagmires from the rain, so Mrs. Davis, carrying her baby Winnie in her arms, walked through the darkness one long night."[10] Varina, her silk skirts filthy with mud, trudged onward toward an uncertain future. Was her wanted husband dead or alive? His enemies were howling for his blood. Union soldiers across the country were chanting, "Hang Jeff Davis from the Sour Apple Tree," set to the tune of the popular marching song "John Brown's Body":

They will hang Jeff Davis to a sour apple tree!
They will hang Jeff Davis to a sour apple tree!

They will hang Jeff Davis to a sour apple tree!
As they march along![11]

On the heels of Lee's spectacular defeat at Appomattox came more shocking news. John Wilkes Booth, the famous American actor, who was also a Confederate sympathizer and agent, had shot and killed President Lincoln during a performance of *Our American Cousin* at Ford's Theatre in Washington DC on the night of April 14.[12] Booth hoped that by killing Lincoln, he could help rally the remaining Confederate troops to continue fighting against the Union. Lincoln's death was far from welcome news for the Confederacy. The murder, meant to help the Confederate cause, effectively rendered Jefferson Davis and his remaining Cabinet members prime suspects in the case.

Varina Davis broke down upon hearing the news of Lincoln's death. She later wrote about her reaction in her memoir of her husband: "I burst into tears, tears which flowed from the mingling of sorrow for the family of Mr. Lincoln and a thorough realization of the inevitable results to the Confederates, now that they were at the mercy of the Federals."[13] With this tragic turn of events, hopes for mercy upon the rebels and their leader were dimming.

The Davis camp, upon hearing news of the assassination, despaired both for the fallen leader and for the fate of the South. Burton Harrison reported to his wife, Connie, that these were "tidings universally regretted by the [Confederate] staff and following. 'Everybody's remark . . . was that in Lincoln the Southern states had lost their only refuge in their then emergency. There was no expression other than of surprise and regret. As yet, we knew none of the particulars of the crime.'"[14]

Although there was absolutely no evidence that Jefferson had committed this heinous crime, northerners and the federal government used the supposition as a pretext to reel in the rebel leader, offering a reward of $100,000 for his capture. Thus began a manhunt that lasted for several weeks. Jefferson rode through the Carolinas, often just miles behind Varina and her party as they fled further and further south. The fugitive finally caught up with his family near Irwinville, Georgia. He decided to stay the night of May 9 with them, planning next to continue on to Texas alone.

Varina, though a practical and sensible woman, also had a superstitious side to her. She often had detailed and prophetical dreams and seemed able to forecast disasters. Her good friend Mary Chesnut was among those who noted Varina's gift or curse in this area: "At West Point the year before the war began, Mrs. Davis said to Mrs. Huger sadly: 'The South will secede if Lincoln is made president. They will make Mr. Davis president of the Southern side. And the whole thing is bound to be a failure.'"[15]

On the night of May 9 Varina told her younger sister, Margaret, who was traveling with her party, that "she dreamed they would be caught at a campsite in Georgia, and that this was the place in her dream."[16] Despite Varina's intuitive sense of danger, the group set up camp at the site anyway. Exhausted, both mentally and physically, after almost six weeks of living like refugees, they collapsed and slept deeply and dreamlessly. What next ensued was truly the stuff of nightmares for the Davis family. The event has been endlessly reported, analyzed, and dissected. In the end neither Jefferson Davis nor Varina were portrayed in a flattering light, despite heroic efforts on the part of Varina to save her husband and herculean efforts on Jefferson's part to escape in order to keep defending the Confederate cause.

The *New York Times* on Sunday, May 14, 1865, trumpeted the headline, "DAVIS TAKEN." The article's subheads included "Cowardly Behavior of the Head of Southern Chivalry" and, even more humiliating, "He Puts on His Wife's Petticoats and Tries to Sneak into the Woods." The story was based upon capturing federal general James H. Wilson's May 13 telegram to Secretary of War Edwin Stanton, which read, "The captors report that he [Jefferson] hastily put on one of his wife's dresses and started for the woods, closely followed by one of our men, who at first thought him a woman, but seeing his boots while he was running, they suspected his sex at once."[17] Jefferson Davis thus became the butt of many a cruel joke because of these rumors. He was caricatured frequently in newspapers of the time wearing women's clothing.

Yet the idea circulated gleefully by the capturing federal troops, aided and abetted by the northern press, that the former Confederate president was wearing his wife's dress in a deliberate attempt to elude capture is patently false. As Clint Johnson notes in his study of Davis's capture and imprisonment, "Not only would it have been physically impossible for Davis to put on one of Varina's dresses in the short amount of time he had before trying to escape, he would not have done it. He would rather have died."[18] In truth Jefferson had apparently thrown on, or Varina had thrown on him, her raglan (a short-sleeved cloak) as he attempted to escape from their encampment near Irwinville, Georgia. By the mid-1860s both upper-class women and men were wearing variations of the raglan cloak, originally developed by the British baron Lord Raglan during the Crimean War.[19]

A 2012 exhibition entitled *President in Petticoats! Civil War Propaganda in Photographs* at the International Center of Photography (ICP) in New York supports this view of Jefferson's capture and the related false reports. The exhibition closely examined the portrayal of these deliberately false images of Jefferson in the northern media. ICP assistant curator Erin Barnett noted that the feminized caricatures of Jefferson in the northern press "circulated in the newspapers, illustrated periodicals, and prints as well as cartes de visite" and that "these vengeance-fueled caricatures of Davis in a dress further damaged his reputation and that of the Confederate States just as Lincoln was being hailed as a martyr. These images allowed Northerners to emphasize their own manliness by feminizing Davis, celebrate their victory over the South, and laugh."[20]

As soon as Jefferson was captured, Varina threw her arms around her husband to save him from a Union soldier who had trained his gun directly on Davis. Although Varina probably saved her husband's life by doing so, Davis became angry with her for interfering. The northern press also chose to present this detail in a derisive manner. Suggestions were made that Varina was more masculine than her husband and that she was the one who truly was the head of the Davis family. As historian Nina Silber noted in *The Romance of Reunion*, "To underscore the transformation of [gender] roles and the loss of the male aristocrat's power, the *Herald* [a New York City newspaper] informed its readers that Mrs. Davis's actions proved her to be 'more of a man than her husband.'"[21]

The humiliating story that Davis tried to escape in a woman's disguise, along with the suggestion that Varina was the family protector and not he, deeply wounded both Jefferson's pride and that of his men.[22] To call a southern soldier's manhood into question was the most shameful taunt imaginable at the time: southern soldiers took the insinuation that the leader of the Confederacy had fled his camp in full woman's costume as an insult to the entire Confederate army. The accusation underlined the total demise of the southern cause. According to historian William C. Davis, "There could be no more fitting end to punctuate the utter defeat of the Confederacy than to . . . [have] its president run in ignominy with skirts about his heels."[23]

Although Winnie was just an infant in 1865, carried in her mother's arms as the family fled a falling Confederate capital, this incident would seriously impact her much later in life. Her very existence reinforced the masculinity of her father and of all former Confederates. Their deeply rooted insecurities, stemming from the southern defeat in the Civil War, ultimately became an issue Winnie was forced to defend. Indeed, as Silber has pointed out, "numerous southern leaders squirmed at the implications of the capture accounts, as well as the other assaults on southern manliness, and launched their own reaffirmation of southern virility in their protection and idealization of Davis's daughter Winnie."[24]

On May 19, 1865, Davis arrived at Fort Monroe in Hampton Roads, Virginia, where he was to spend the next two years in prison. Thus began a dark period of confinement resulting in illness, emaciation, and deep depression for Davis. For the first year in prison Davis was confined to a very small cell. Only in May 1866 was he finally allowed more spacious quarters, exercise, and generally better treatment. At this point Varina took up permanent residence at Fort Monroe and was allowed to see her husband on a more frequent basis.

Winnie, at this point a toddler, was the only one of Davis's children allowed to visit with him. During the two horrific years of 1865–67, Charles Clifton Ferrell wrote in 1899, Winnie was "the only sunshine that came to him."[25] For Davis his young daughter was one of the few links to the outside world and to a past in which he was revered by many and empowered to control his own fate. In later years her father remembered that it was this shared experience at Fort Monroe that, despite Winnie's young age, bound daughter and father together inextricably.

Although she was probably barely conscious of her visits at the time, Winnie was forever marked by the remembrances of this period provided to her by other witnesses. Winnie was fussed over by officers and their wives at Fortress Monroe, where she played with their children and attended parties and musical entertainments.[26] In her infancy and toddlerhood she became the receptacle for her family's nostalgic memories of the past.

Jefferson had shown his family and the nation by example that he was willing to sacrifice his own material comforts as well as his life, if necessary, for the Confederate cause. During his time at Fort Monroe, the former Confederate leader reportedly endured terrible treatment, all the while refusing to ask for a pardon for his leadership of the South in the Civil War. He steadfastly and staunchly endured all these ordeals without complaint. The end result, according to historian Cita Cook, was that "people who had questioned the judgment of the President of the Confederacy in the midst of a bloody war had begun to consider him a Confederate George Washington once he was sent to prison."[27] Jefferson's terrible treatment at Fort Monroe transformed him from master to martyr of the Confederacy.

Although Jefferson was prepared and fully willing to forgo almost everything for the cause, he tried to distance his actions from his family so that they would not also have to suffer his fate. In an 1862 letter from Richmond to Varina he declared that "the heroism which could lay my wife and children on any sacrificial altar is not mine."[28] Yet, however noble this desire, it was impossible for Jefferson to separate himself from Varina and the children. For better or for worse, the entire family, its legacy and its reputation, were staked on his fate. Particularly in the nineteenth century, when a woman's fate was so closely tied to her husband's, Jefferson's wish was a futile one, and his suffering became his family's suffering. It was a public fate and one that created permanent psychic scars on his children.

Thus, the ideal of personal sacrifice was imprinted upon Winnie even as a small child. The Davis legacy of self-sacrifice was nationally known and discussed continually. It would have been practically impossible for an approval-oriented young girl, as Winnie turned out to be, to miss such vivid cues. The stamp of martyrdom, so visible in her father's story, was internalized by Winnie at Fort Monroe and would be regularly reinforced throughout her girlhood. Even so, her father hoped for better things for his youngest child, asking Varina, in a letter sent from Fort Monroe, to "kiss the Baby for me, may her sunny face never be clouded, though dark the morning of her life has been."[29]

CHAPTER FOUR

A Fatal Romance

The stoic, long-suffering father Winnie first knew at Fort Monroe was a personality forged as a result of severe political upheavals and personal tragedies, including the death of his beloved first wife. The marriage Winnie observed between her mother, Varina, and her father, Jefferson, in the 1860s was stable and at times affectionate but by no means a fairy tale. Although Varina adored Jefferson, she resisted his controlling nature. He in turn resented Varina for her lack of submission to his will and decisions.

Jefferson had not always been such a hardened figure. He grew up the adored son and tenth child of Samuel Davis and Jane Cook, who were married in 1783 in Georgia. The couple soon moved to Kentucky and then later to Woodville, Mississippi. Jefferson respected his parents, who were well educated for their time. His mother and sisters were very loving toward the boy, but Jefferson characterized his father as cold and distant.

Education was important in the Davis family. Jefferson was a standout in ancient languages such as Latin and Greek. His father insisted he attend Transylvania University in Lexington Kentucky, a well-known and distinguished school, where he did extremely well. After Samuel suffered major financial difficulties and then died, Joseph, Jefferson's much older brother, assumed the paternal role in the Davis family. He insisted Jefferson either go on to West Point as a cadet or attend the University of Virginia to study law. Surprisingly, despite his clear disdain for those who did not agree with him, Jefferson chose life at West Point. There he became known for his willful and spirited behavior.

The young and mischievous cadet frequently disobeyed orders, stayed out late at parties, drank too much, skipped drills, and generally thumbed his nose at authority. Although he briefly became a soldier in the frontier territories after graduation and enjoyed soldiering, he had a strong dislike of authority, and in 1835 he decided to leave the military. He then dove straight into marriage and the life of a southern plantation owner.[1]

Jefferson's first wife, Sarah Knox "Knoxie" Taylor, was the daughter of Lt. Col. Zachary Taylor, who was later to become president of the United States. Zachary, who knew Jefferson through their military service together at Fort Taylor in the Michigan territories in the 1830s, forbade the match for several years. Although a career soldier himself, he did not wish for his adored daughter to suffer the life of a military wife. He also clashed with Jefferson during their time soldiering together. Zachary eventually consented to the match, but he and his wife did not attend the wedding on June 17, 1835, at Sarah's aunt and uncle's house, Beechland, in Kentucky.[2]

Knoxie was feisty and pretty and accustomed to the good things in life. Mrs. Anna Magee Robinson, a cousin of Sarah who was present at her marriage, describes a young, striking couple madly in love on their wedding day: "My cousin Knox Taylor was very beautiful, slight and not very tall, with brown, wavy hair and clear gray eyes, very lovely and lovable, and a young woman of decided spirit. Lieutenant Davis was of slender build, and had polished manners, and was of a quiet intellectual countenance."[3]

The new couple had originally planned to delay their move to Brierfield, Jefferson's Mississippi plantation, due to the summer sicknesses such as malaria and yellow fever that annually claimed hundreds of lives across the Deep South. But Davis insisted that he and Sarah move to his Mississippi residence immediately. As historian William C. Davis describes it, the impulsive young man was "looking ahead to a new life, with the anxiety and impetuosity of youth, he wanted Sarah for his wife now, his wife in his bed, and his bed at Brierfield."[4]

After spending time with Jefferson's older brother Joe at Hurricane Plantation in Mississippi, the newlyweds made their way to Locust Grove, Louisiana, to visit Jefferson's sister and brother-in law, thinking the hill climate healthier. It was a fatal mistake. Both Jefferson and Sarah contracted malaria in short order. Jefferson, who was the hardier of the two, survived, but Sarah was not so lucky. She died in her husband's arms, singing "Fairy Bells" while her young life ebbed away. They had been married for less than three months. Sarah was only twenty-one years old when she was laid in the ground at Locust Grove.[5]

William Davis notes that this event marked a significant turning point for Jefferson. The cadet who had delighted in parties, pretty girls, and drinking became a more sober, serious character. Although there is no record that shows he expressed guilt or remorse for Sarah's untimely demise,[6] the tragedy completely crushed Jefferson. As he was often wont to do, he had made a quick decision and never looked back. His ill-advised choice had cost him his beloved first wife[7]

Once his adored Knoxie was gone, the grieving husband locked his deepest emotions away for good. The more joyful and emotional version of the young Davis was never to be glimpsed again by another woman. His young wife's tragic death diminished his capacity for marital affection and love. He would never love a woman so deeply again. Nearly one hundred years after Sarah's death, the historian Burton J. Hendrick wrote: "So vanished the one human being who was able to arouse the deepest emotions of this silent, undemonstrative man. Though Jefferson Davis married a second time . . . he never recovered from the shock of his first and lasting love affair."[8]

Jefferson Davis's second marriage to Varina Howell has been analyzed many times by historians but far too often only superficially. The two Mississippians had much in common: Welsh progenitors, family ties, and superior educations for their time. Both became doting parents whose great mutual love was that of their children. On paper the couple seemed to be well suited, if not destined for each other. Yet their commonalities would work against them as each struggled to control the other.

Varina Howell's family was a boisterous, open-minded, and emotional clan. Her family first settled in Delaware, then New Jersey. Varina's grandfather Richard Howell served with distinction under General Washington and later became governor of New Jersey.[9] Her own parents, William Howell and Margaret Kempe, settled in Natchez, Mississippi. They were married in 1823, with Joseph Davis, Jefferson's older brother, attending the wedding as best man.

Varina's father made a good living in merchandising for a time. As a child, Varina lived in a well-off household and was one of eleven children. Margaret insisted Varina be well educated, with an emphasis on literature, languages, and music. She hired an at-home tutor for her daughter named George Winchester, who schooled Varina from the time she was a young girl until she married. She was his only student, and the two became lifelong friends. She also briefly attended a girls' academy near Philadelphia.[10]

In addition to being well educated, Varina's views on life were not limited to the provincial South. She had cousins in New Jersey with whom she was close and therefore had ties to both North and South. For this she later famously termed herself a "half-breed."[11] She also knew both wealth and poverty. Her father's financial collapse in the 1830s forced her to experience life without material wealth. Her ability to empathize with different constituencies: rich and poor, South and North, would both aid her struggles later in life and hurt her reputation as the first lady of the Confederacy.

Varina Howell met Jefferson Davis almost eight years after Sarah's death through his brother Joseph and mutual friends in Mississippi. Varina fell quickly for Davis, telling friends that he was her first love and the only man she had ever loved.[12] The couple's courtship took a speedy path, and they were soon engaged. The wedding itself was put off for months, however, due to a lingering fever that afflicted Varina. When she recovered, she was determined they should be wed with little delay, and the ceremony took place on February 26, 1845.[13]

It is telling to note that the day after their wedding Jefferson and Varina made a visit to Sarah Knox Davis's grave in Locust Grove. They were visiting Jefferson's family there, where Knoxie was buried in the family graveyard. The cemetery visit could not have been too palatable to the newlywed Varina.[14] It would be understandable if this incident planted a seed of jealousy and competition within her. How could a flesh-and-blood wife compete with a sentimentalized ghost?

Jefferson, while attracted to the young Varina, never considered her the equal of his first wife. "The Sainted Sarah," as Varina called her, had also been a strong-willed character. Unlike Varina, however, Sarah had not lived long enough to offend her husband, to nag him or do anything but enjoy his company.[15] Jefferson was a southern gentleman, with lovely manners, attractive looks, and a melodic voice. But he expected nothing less from his wife than complete submission and acquiescence to his commands.

Both Varina and Jefferson were extremely strong personalities with a pronounced contempt for those who tried to control them. This tendency would make life with her husband especially difficult for Varina. The mold for southern wives of the era required total acceptance of male authority. Successful wives were, as historian Anne Firor Scott notes, "obedient, faithful, submissive women [who] strengthened the image of men who thought themselves vigorous, intelligent, commanding leaders."[16] Young Varina did not fit comfortably into this role. Jefferson's inability to admit fault caused problems in his second marriage from the start. He and Varina fought both during their courtship and within months of their marriage.[17]

Jefferson and his new wife spent their honeymoon in New Orleans and then settled at his plantation. The couple did not enjoy much time together, as Jefferson's political duties often kept him on the road. He had started his political career as a Democratic delegate representing Mississippi's Warren County in 1842 and quickly ascended up the political ranks. In 1844 Davis made an advantageous reconciliation when he randomly ran into his former father-in-law, Zachary Taylor, on a riverboat. Taylor and Jefferson's clash in the 1830s and Sarah's tragic end did not prevent the men from now becoming fast friends. One wonders what they said to each other on that riverboat. Did they talk about Sarah and their mutual loss? More than likely they did not, as both tended to keep their deepest emotions to themselves, but they both seemed to be ready to put their past behind them. From that point on the friendship deepened, and Jefferson and Zachary developed a clear sense of mutual trust and respect.[18]

When Jefferson took his place in the House of Representatives in the fall of 1845, he left Varina behind in Mississippi. He would move even farther away from her when he resigned from Congress in 1846 to join Zachary Taylor in the Mexican War. There Jefferson led a regiment of Mississippi volunteers and fought bravely alongside his former father-in-law. This time together cemented the friendship between the two men. But the time apart further damaged Jefferson's relationship with his new wife.[19]

Even early in their marriage, Jefferson spoke of his "need for separation." The couple would live apart again and again during the course of their relationship. "In the end," according to William C. Davis "it is quite probable that the only reason the marriage lasted as long as it did is that Varina finally was willing to subordinate her own strong will to her husband's."[20] Perhaps the long separations also made their hearts grow fonder of each other. By 1849 both he and Varina moved together to Washington DC for the congressional session.

Zachary Taylor was now President Taylor, and his connection to the nation's leader began to produce political dividends for Jefferson. The young senator from Mississippi and his second wife had instant entrée to the White House and its social life.[21] Columnist Retta D. Tindall writes, "The Davises spent a great deal of time at the White House in their official capacity by virtue of Jefferson's Senate seat and also as esteemed members of the extended Taylor family."[22]

The political connection with Taylor and other relationships the couple developed during their time in the nation's capital further encouraged the young senator's political ambitions. In 1851 Jefferson resigned his Senate seat to run as the Democratic candidate for governor of Mississippi. When Jefferson lost to opponent Henry Foote, however, he and his wife moved back to Brierfield.

This residency was not to last for long. When Franklin Pierce became the president in 1852, he asked Jefferson to become his secretary of war, and the Davises returned to Washington DC in the spring of 1853. Throughout the 1850s Varina was occupied with being a mother and the social whirl and intrigue of the nation's capital.

Washington DC was a power center in the 1850s, just as it is today. The cultural, political, and social life there was rich and varied. Women tried to outdo one another with their fabulous ball gowns and fashionable accessories. Elaborate balls, parties, dinners, and receptions were regular parts of life, and congressional wives had a full and even exhausting social calendar. Virginia Clay remembered that in 1850s Washington DC, "it was no uncommon thing for society women to find themselves completely exhausted ere bedtime arrived."[23]

Varina might enjoy Washington DC's exhilarating social life and exercising her sharp wit among the city's high society. But she also relished her time at home with her children. The young matron "enjoyed the social life in Washington," writes Tindall, "but her family took precedence over any other obligations. She was a 'hands-on' mother, tending to her children's needs, overseeing their meals, teaching them Bible stories, and reading to them at bedtime."[24] Jeff Jr. was born in the winter of 1857 during the couple's time in the capital, joining his older sister, Maggie.

Although Jefferson was a loving father and always interested in his children and their doings, the young senator was often tied up with his political career and his obligations to Brierfield plantation in Mississippi. During his four years as secretary of war under Pierce, Jefferson had many significant achievements, including the establishment of the Smithsonian Institution, the beginnings of the movement to build the Panama Canal, and the introduction of a humanities program at his old school, West Point.[25] Although Jefferson was often far away from his family, he always kept in close touch through his letters. The written word allowed him to express emotions he could not or would not show when he was physically present.[26]

By the summer of 1860 political talk of the southern states seceding from the Union began to solidify. Lincoln was elected president in November 1860, and Jefferson resigned his Senate seat in January 1861. By February he had been chosen as provisional president of the Confederacy.[27] The couple's marriage then took a backseat to the epic political drama of the approaching Civil War beginning to unfold around them.

Joan Cashin, one of Varina's recent biographers, eloquently summarizes the Davis union: "They had a difficult relationship, fraught with passionate outbursts of love, regret, and resentment and marked by terrific power struggles, most of which she lost. She did not have the companionate marriage she wanted, but she tried to accommodate, to overlook, and to forgive, as did most women of her generation."[28]

Both partners in the Davis marriage wanted control over the other. Neither one, however, would ever be able fully to achieve this dominance. Varina and Jefferson were doomed to perpetually misunderstand the other's motivations and actions. The Davis children were witness to this constant power struggle, and it undoubtedly affected Winnie's views of marriage, perhaps contributing to her reluctance to wed later in life. Her personal views of marriage, expressed in her writings, reflected her ambivalent stance toward this institution.

Yet Winnie also observed the survival of the Davis marriage despite the overwhelming forces of war, death, homelessness, and their ultimate loss of wealth and status. This model meshed well with her father's example of self-sacrifice of the individual for the good of the whole. Keeping the family intact within a marriage was the couple's top priority, divorce was almost unthinkable, but happiness within marriage? That was an entirely separate affair.

CHAPTER FIVE

Scandal and Sickness

After Jefferson's release from Fort Monroe in 1867, the Davis family reunited in Montreal, where Varina, her mother, and her sister, Margaret, had been living with the four Davis children. Varina notes that when Jefferson was finally released, "we were pecuniarily prostrate, our plantations had been laid waste and seized . . . we turned our faces to the world and cast about for a way to maintain our little children, four in number, Margaret, Jefferson, William, and Varina."[1]

The family was overjoyed to be back together again, yet their happiness was temporary. Like many former soldiers, Jefferson seemed to suffer from what might now be termed "post-traumatic stress disorder," the result in particular of his experiences in the war and at Fort Monroe. The Canadian winters also proved too harsh for Jefferson's enfeebled frame, so the family spent some time in Cuba after hearing that a Confederate agent had deposited money in an account there on behalf of the Davis children.[2] The rumor proved false, and the family soon journeyed on to Mississippi.

When the family returned to the South, their first order of business was to check on the former Davis family plantations. Jefferson became even more depressed upon witnessing what he described as "the desolation of our country."[3] Both the Brierfield and Hurricane plantations were completely ruined, echoing the fate of countless other family homes throughout the region. The federal government had confiscated both plantations several years earlier, in 1865.[4]

The physical destruction of the war was mirrored by the psychological damage done to many white southerners, like the Davis family. Historian Bertram Wyatt-Brown describes the widespread affliction: "Demoralization of Southern white families was a serious consequence of the war—the mourning for lost kindred and neighbors, the wrenching adjustments to be made in race relations, the woes of lost investments and treasure, ruined homesteads." Utter desolation of the spirit remained in southern communities long after the military conflict had ceased.[5]

The politics of this new Reconstruction era were clearly inhospitable to the Davis family. Seen as the ultimate perpetrator of slavery and all its evils, Jefferson received many death threats; rumors of plots to hurt him and his family were never far from his ears. Given the great political animus they faced in the post–Civil War world, Varina and Jefferson were always terrified that some harm would come to their children.

Two political schools of thought ruled the United States directly after the Civil War. The Radical Reconstructionists demanded a complete overhaul of the South in the North's image, while the Moderates preached reconciliation between North and South and an end to Reconstruction in the southern states.[6]

The emancipation and integration of former slaves in this postwar environment was not easy. Freed slaves often experienced their new lives as a nomadic existence, wandering from place to place in search of food and work. The Freedman's Bureau, established in 1865 to manage the transition of blacks from slavery to freedom, had mixed results. The bureau's responsibilities included the provision of medical care, funds, and education to both white and black refugees.

During its seven-year existence, white southerners angrily fought back against the bureau and its policies, particularly the redistribution of former Confederate-owned lands. In response to this national political effort, vigilante groups such as the Ku Klux Klan (KKK) first appeared in the South. The KKK persecuted and terrorized blacks while intimidating any whites who might try to help them.[7]

Despite institutions such as the Freedman's Bureau and the prevailing winds of national politics, many southerners still refused to accept the changes thrust upon them by the North. Historian Drew Gilpin Faust explains the subversion that many southerners subscribed to as a way of fighting back against the new political regime. Faust cites a postwar letter from Mary Lee of Winchester, Virginia, in which Lee explains: "Political reconstruction is inevitable now, but social reconstruction, we have in our hands and we can prevent."[8] This statement would prove prophetic for Davis daughter Winnie, in particular.

Although many in the North saw Jefferson Davis and his family as the embodiment of such southern subversion, at this point in their lives

Jefferson and Varina were more focused on personal and family matters. Their total loss of income was the couple's primary preoccupation in the postwar world. How would they feed, clothe, and educate their brood? What would Jefferson do for a living that was both worthy of his status as former president of the Confederacy and could produce enough income to maintain his wife and children sufficiently? In which corner of the world could they be received and protected without death threats descending upon their doorstep? For many years after the war these questions would remain frustratingly unresolved.

In late 1867 the Davis family moved again to Lennoxville, a small town near Montreal. Here Davis, still in terrible physical shape, fell down a long flight of stairs with the three-year-old Winnie in his arms. Varina noted: "While vexed by every anxiety that could torture us, in coming down a long flight of stairs with baby Winnie in his arms, Mr. Davis fell from top to bottom, breaking three of his ribs. His first question after he came out of the fainting fit into which he sank was for the baby."[9] There was never any question that Jefferson adored Winnie; the bond they had formed at Fort Monroe was unbreakable. Luckily, Winnie was unharmed by the accident.

Impoverished and in very poor health, Jefferson and his family then made their way to Quebec from Lennoxville and sailed on to Liverpool in the summer of 1868. The family then spent time in London and Paris and were for the most part well received by English and French friends and sympathizers as well as former Confederate colleagues such as former Cabinet member Judah P. Benjamin who were also living abroad.[10] The couple somehow still had some money. Friends had likely stashed some away for the couple during the war, southern sympathizers gave them monetary gifts, and British friends even paid their boys' tuition for a time.[11] Letters that survive also note that Benjamin let Varina know about $12,500 remaining Confederate funds in England that were earmarked for her family. He ultimately invested a portion of this money for her in British government securities.[12]

Although Varina loved England and would have been content to stay there long term, Jefferson missed the American South and found he could not make an adequate living in London. In 1869 he was offered a job as president of the Carolina Insurance Company, which he gladly accepted.

Winnie and the other children remained in England with their mother while Jefferson became established in his new job. They all missed their father deeply and fervently wished for his return. Jefferson wrote Varina from Memphis on November 23, 1869, replying to a previous comment from his youngest daughter: "Tell Winnie Anne I am trying to get 'a good home and stop wandering about' as she had advised."[13]

In another letter to Varina, Jefferson worried about the precocious Winnie and her many questions to her mother on a variety of subjects: "I fear from your account of Winnie Anne's extraordinary conversations that her brain has been much too excited. She is too old for her years, pray keep her back that her constitution may be such as to bear study when she can better profit by it."[14] This remark notes a recurring theme in the Davis family: concern that intellectual "fever" may wear the physical body out. Jefferson often applied this nineteenth-century psychology to his curious and intellectually gifted youngest daughter.

During his time alone in Memphis, Jefferson developed a deep admiration for and perhaps an infatuation with the lively Virginia Clay, whose husband, Clement, had been a friend and colleague of Jefferson in the U.S. Senate. Clement had also been imprisoned with him in Fortress Monroe for his Confederate activity, so the two men knew each other well. Virginia and Clement were childless, so after her marriage to him in 1843, she continued to collect beaux. This attractive and vivacious woman was "ambitious, self-centered, energetic, attractive, and sociable"; according to historians Carol Bleser and Frederick M. Heath, she "attempted for over twenty years to be a married belle, a role through which she enjoyed some of the delights of her single days and achieved both recognition and influence."[15]

According to Varina's biographer Joan Cashin, Jefferson suggested to Varina at this time that she would not like Memphis and that with his new job he could provide her with the means to "live elsewhere."[16] He seemed to be content at this point to live in Memphis alone. Varina was understandably bewildered and upset by this suggestion. Finally, in the fall of 1870 Jefferson returned to England to retrieve his family and sail with them back to Memphis. The former Confederate first family rented a lovely home on fashionable Court Street in downtown Memphis. They tried to settle into a consistent routine and to lead as normal a life as possible after years of searching for financial and geographic stability. Ugly rumors about his personal life surfaced, however, on July 15, 1871, when the *Louisville Daily Commercial* newspaper published an account accusing Jefferson of having an adulterous tryst on a train with another woman. The newspaper identified the woman as a former Memphis actress by the name of Mrs. Bowers,[17] while other accounts claimed the woman in question was Virginia Clay.[18]

Jefferson denied the incident, as did Virginia. Varina never acknowledged the accusations, but it surely cut her deeply. Voluminous correspondence suggests a deep emotional relationship between Jefferson and Virginia that continued long after and despite the scandal of the train affair. His letter of October 1871 confirms his attachment to Virginia, whom he often called "Ginnie": "I wish to come to you in this season of gorgeous colors and do love you not little but long."[19]

Scholars of the Jefferson Davis papers at Rice University who have analyzed all the Jefferson Davis–Clement and Virginia Clay correspondence have offered another conclusion. Jefferson, while alone in Memphis and trying to adjust to his new job, reached out to both Clays, who entertained him and corresponded with him often. Clement was asthmatic and often ill, so it was primarily Virginia who responded to Jefferson's letters and hosted him. According to these scholars: "Although he never hid his abiding affection for Ginnie, he always thought of the two Clays, not just one. He told them of his daydreams for the three of them—a good ship, good cigars, and a good library."[20]

Ginnie was probably attractive to Jefferson as she had no children to care for, no dependents to divert her attentions from him. She was not nearly so intelligent as his wife and was never in a position to criticize him. Unlike Varina, who had family in the North and therefore divided loyalties, Virginia wholeheartedly supported the Confederate cause. For all these reasons she was the perfect object of his affections. She was also a married "belle" and therefore a somewhat safe choice.[21]

Varina stayed silent on this issue, and in her memoirs of her husband there is absolutely no mention of the scandal or her thoughts about Virginia Clay. She was still in love with her husband, and there is no evidence that she herself ever strayed with another man or even flirted with one. As Jefferson's personal nurse, adoring wife, and tireless lobbyist for her husband's release from prison, to have such rumors floating about must have been humiliating and devastating for Varina, even though the train incident may have been simply vicious gossip.

Yet social scandal would soon pale in comparison to the tragedy about to befall both Davises. In October 1874 the couple's eleven-year-old son Billy died of diphtheria. Like the Davises' first child, Samuel, Billy was the victim of a disease that claimed so many in the nineteenth century prior to the development of penicillin. There was literally nothing the hopeless parents or their physicians could do as the child slowly suffocated.

Varina's grief over Billy's death is still palpable nearly a century and half later. She wrote at the time: "All that sympathy and kindness could do was tempered to us to alleviate our grief, but the death of one whose character, talents, and personal beauty made the joy of our lives, and promised to justify the hope of our old age, was a blow which must leave us mourning until the end."[22]

The agony of Billy's death was devastating to both parents as well as to his remaining siblings. He was the third Davis boy to go to an early grave. Now the only son remaining in the Davis family was Jefferson Davis Jr.. Even in the nineteenth century, the childhood deaths the Davises had suffered were extreme. Both parents tried to remain calm and stoic, but with each child who died, Jefferson retreated further into his interior life. Varina tried harder to interact with her family, but she also was profoundly depressed following her son's death. Winnie was surely intently absorbing the drama that surrounded her, observing silently while her parents suffered yet another almost unbearable blow. Winnie, Maggie, and Jeff Jr. together mourned for Billy, their observant, gentle brother.

Soon after this tragedy, the family faced another major upset. In 1873 the Carolina Life Insurance Company failed and was sold to another company. Jefferson then resigned his post with the company and shortly thereafter left his family alone again as he sailed to England in the early winter of 1874 to seek new employment. Although his job search proved to be unfruitful, perhaps the time alone allowed for some reflection. Jefferson at least temporarily realized the faithfulness his wife had demonstrated to him at this point, as he wrote her from England on their anniversary in February 1874, pledging his love to her and his regret that she had had to deal with so many important responsibilities alone throughout their marriage.[23]

When their father finally returned home to Memphis from this latest trip to England in June 1874, Maggie was a young lady of nineteen, Jeff Jr. a seventeen-year-old, and Winnie ten years of age. Since her brother Billy's death particularly, Winnie, more than Jeff Jr. or Maggie, was the child upon whom both parents focused most of their attention.

Winnie attended school at the Memphis Female Seminary in the early 1870s. The young girl could walk to the school, located just a few blocks from her home. It was a small establishment, with only five teachers, where a group of young women received instruction in music, art, and languages.[24] Education at the seminary was supplemented by instruction at home by Winnie's parents. Varina and Jefferson had more time on their hands now than they had had with their other children to develop Winnie and her education. As a result, Winnie developed extremely close bonds with both parents, bonds that were perhaps a bit too tight.

Victorian child-raising techniques, as historian Sarah Wollfolk Wiggins puts it, held that "the essential issue was that children voluntarily obeyed their parents."[25] Winnie had little problem fitting into this school of thought. A child like Winnie was treated as a small adult who possessed an inherent congruence of interests with her parents. Fortunately, the young girl was eager to please, and she loved classic English literature. Both parents took great pains to ensure that Winnie was well-read.[26] Jefferson was extremely proud of Winnie's developing intellect, and he encouraged and helped shape her serious nature. Conversely, however, the overprotective father worried about intellectual overstimulation in his youngest child.

Although Jefferson and Varina's home instruction was intended to teach the child how to "fit in" in their southern community, in reality it had the opposite effect. Winnie found social interaction with others outside her family to be difficult and awkward at best. Spending so much time with her parents in the adult world from a young age created a child who did not know how to play with her peers. Neither Winnie nor her parents realized that too much time spent with parents obsessed with the past was preventing her from living fully in the present.

The early attention and teachings of Jefferson had affected Winnie in an especially profound manner: she knew what would win her father and mother's attention. Things like parties, clothes, boys, and gossip were seen as frivolous and not worth discussing, while political issues,

CHAPTER SIX

Boarding School Blues and the Dorsey Dilemma

> Trained in the schools, and broadened too,
> By reading, travel, and converse.
>
> Rev. R. M. Tuttle, a fragment of his poem "Miss Winnie Davis, a Tribute," 1905

How strange it must have seemed to those who were aware of the extremely close relationship shared by Winnie and her parents that they would send her off to a German boarding school at the age of thirteen. The child—so sheltered, shy, and fond of both her parents and siblings—was terribly homesick and traumatized about leaving the comforts of home. Several events may have triggered this decision by Jefferson and Varina. Winnie would soon be alone in the Davis household, as her sister wedding to a young and charming Confederate veteran was imminent, and her brother was attending Virginia Military Institute.[1]

In 1875 the Davises' oldest daughter, Maggie, had become engaged to Joel Addison Hayes, "a native Mississippian from an old and distinguished Tennessee family."[2] Addison was a Confederate veteran, well liked by both Jefferson and Varina, who held a good bank job in Memphis. Maggie, more outspoken and independent than her younger sister, had grown into "a pretty woman with soulful eyes, a mass of dark hair and a taste for beautiful clothes."[3]

The oldest Davis girl was known for her sweet singing voice and had been educated at a convent in Paris, where she became friends with two European princesses. A Confederate Veteran magazine article from 1909 noted the friendship: "Margaret of Italy and Princess Margaret of Bavaria were her closest friends. To distinguish her [Maggie Davis] in this trio of 'namesakes,' she was called Pearl, the meaning of her name, and that jewel entered largely into her life pleasures."[4]

Despite the Davis family's lack of funds, Jefferson and Varina made every effort to make sure their oldest girl was married in high style. Lynda L. Crist and Suzanne Scott Gibbs note that "although the family was in difficult financial straits, Maggie wore a gown from Paris." (It is possible that this dress was her Aunt Margaret's Parisian couture wedding gown from 1870.)[5] The event was noted not just in the Memphis and southern papers but in the *New York Times* as well.[6]

In photos of the event Maggie looks every inch the fashionable and sophisticated product of an upper-class family of the era. Her intricately draped lace dress had a fitted bodice that showed off her tiny waist. She wore a crown of orange blossoms in her hair. Looking the part was very important both to her and to her parents, even if money was in scarce supply.

The wedding took place on New Year's Day morning, 1876, at St. Lazarus Episcopal Church in downtown Memphis. Winnie and Jeff Jr., along with Addison's sister Sallie, were in the wedding party. A reception followed at the Davis home, and the newlyweds spent a few days honeymooning in St. Louis.[7] Maggie and Addison seemed to be madly in love, and Jefferson and Varina were both pleased and relieved that their oldest girl had married well with another southern aristocrat.

The Davis girls were typecast from the very beginning. Each had her own role to play: Maggie's wedding set her on the traditional nineteenth-century feminine path of becoming a wife and mother. She was always considered the "pretty one" in the Davis family, while Winnie was the "smart one." Their mother had created this contrast.

While, according to historian Suzanne T. Dolensky, Varina's "written comments about Winnie overwhelmingly outnumbered those about all their other children combined, her only regret was that Winnie was not pretty. She often commented on the beauty of her sons and found Maggie as a young woman 'unusually pretty.'"[8] With the wide age difference and the girls living in different places, this type of labeling did not seem to present a problem. Later in life, however, Maggie would express some jealousy regarding her sister, doubtless exacerbated by her mother's blatant favoritism of her youngest child.[9]

With Maggie safely married off, Varina and Jefferson began more seriously to consider Winnie's future. Sending their youngest, most intellectual child abroad for school seemed like the perfect solution. The parents reasoned that if Winnie were in Europe, where many had favored the Confederate cause, the young girl might escape some of the abuse directed toward her family as well as unflattering commentaries about her father's conduct during the war. Jefferson especially was always solicitous of his daughter's well-being and never wished her to bear the consequences of his actions as the leader of the Confederacy.[10]

Moreover, the traumas Varina had endured over the years, her three sons' tragic deaths, her frequent struggles with Jefferson within her marriage, their loss of fortune, and the collapse of the Confederacy had finally caught up with her. She was suffering from debilitating depression, and Jefferson felt she could not adequately care for their youngest child. Although Varina had pulled herself together for her eldest daughter's wedding, the former Confederate first lady suffered from unidentified physical ailments—probably the result of the crushing mélange of misery that had weighed her down over the years.

As early as 1873, Jefferson himself had perceptively noted the connection between Varina's physical ill health and her mental state in a frank letter to family friend Lucinda Davis Stamps on January 4, 1873: "Varina has for a long time suffered from a numbness in her limbs and her mental depression caused by our domestic bereavement has increased both the frequency and the violence of the attacks. The Doctors seem powerless, and only advise cheerfulness."[11] By 1876 Jefferson decided that Varina could no longer care for Winnie sufficiently. According to historian Carol Berkin, "Modern doctors would conclude that Varina Howell Davis had suffered a nervous breakdown."[12]

The Davises had another reason for sending Winnie away, this one perhaps more surprising. Jefferson was apparently quite worried about his youngest daughter's stubbornness and lack of parental deference.[13] Jefferson did not admire this trait in his wife, and he would certainly not tolerate such displays in his youngest daughter. It seems the parents jointly decided to crush this trait out of Winnie. Perhaps Varina knew how much her own strong will had cost her within her marriage and wished to save Winnie from facing similar problems. Jefferson expected complete deference from all females. So, on this point, at least, the Davises were in agreement.

Consequently, the couple decided to place Winnie in a girls' boarding school known as the Misses Friedlanders' School for Girls in Karlsruhe, Germany. The establishment operated under the patronage of the Grand Duchess Luise of Baden, whose palace was not far from the school.[14] Varina and Jefferson had other friends with children in the school, and Varina's brother-in-law Carl de Wechmar Stoesse, Margaret's husband, a titled Alsatian, may have also recommended the establishment.[15]

Although Maggie had attended boarding school in Paris, at the Convent of the Assumption in Auteuil, 16th Arrondissement,[16] Jefferson vetoed this path for Winnie. He wrote to Varina that he was disgusted by the Parisian open display of "prints and toys of amorous passions, such words and the exhibition of such types of general sentiment cannot be favorable to the cultivation or preservation of modesty."[17] Why the Davises allowed Maggie to go to Paris and not Winnie remains a mystery.

Winnie, her friend Pinnie Meredith, and her parents sailed for Liverpool in late May 1876. Varina and the girls stayed with her sister Margaret and her husband in Liverpool while Jefferson worked in London.[18] Then, in early September 1876 Jefferson took a very apprehensive Winnie and a nervous Pinnie to a London railway station to place them en route to boarding school. Jefferson left them there with a friend of the family, who accompanied them to Karlsruhe.[19] Varina did not see the girls off. She stayed at home in London, too ill to accompany them.

It was Jefferson who answered Winnie's first letter home to her parents. Writing from London on September 21, 1876, he began his letter sympathetically, but Jefferson also chided Winnie for not acknowledging his parting gesture: "I yet see your sad little face as you sat crouching in the corner of the R.R. carriage, too absorbed in your grief to notice my last salutation. The house seemed funereal when we no longer heard the voices of our little ones, and your Mother said she was ever expecting one of you to come in."[20]

He continued, now launching into what was to be a recurring and central theme in both his own life and that of his approval-oriented daughter: "It is true, but not pleasant that duty demands self-sacrifice. Yet it is the highest attribute of humanity to be able to give to a sense of duty, that which it costs pain to surrender."[21] This was the formative lesson that Winnie was to absorb above all others and to reflect dramatically in her adult personal life.

Jefferson soon sailed back home, but Varina stayed on in Liverpool alone, remaining physically and mentally too ill to travel. As she began to feel better, she often visited Winnie in Karlsruhe, but her health still did not permit her to return to the United States. Varina wrote her husband on February 18, 1877, noting, "I am much better last week—I am however afraid to risk travelling yet, so remain near Winnie until I am strong enough to go to England again." In the same letter she relates that her physician Dr. Cartwright had diagnosed her troubles as "misplaced malaise."[22]

While Varina battled depression and illness, Winnie slowly adjusted to convent life. The cold German landscape was a stark contrast to that of the sunbaked warmth of Memphis and the young girl's cozy home on Court Square. A friend described Winnie's German boarding school town of Karlsruhe as "a dreary place, with granite buildings and severe public squares, the school's curriculum was rigorous and the students hailed from elite Continental families."[23]

Life at Karlsruhe proved spartan and regimented. Winnie was a good fit for this type of school, however, despite her pervasive homesickness. This was no place for young socialites-in-training to kick up their heels, shop for the latest fashions, and indulge in parties and gossip. Winnie, always serious and never frivolous, blossomed in such an environment.

Indeed, Winnie was as sequestered at her German school as she had been under the eaves of the Davis household. The discipline Winnie received at the Misses Friedlanders' School was of the strictest and most moral sort: day-to-day existence there was "as secluded and free from gaiety and frivolity as that of a convent."[24] For a cerebral young woman with little or no interest in the beau monde, the choice of school was congruent with both her personality and her interests.

This school was also the perfect fit for Jefferson and Varina's desires for their sheltered youngest child. Jefferson wrote Winnie from Mississippi City on March 17, 1877, about their reasons for sending her to Karlsruhe and his hopes for her future: "We look hopefully forward to your becoming a well-educated young Lady, but most of all to your acquiring systematic habits, to your learning how to study, and last and greatest the formation of a vigorous, healthy constitution."[25]

Winnie's health was something that constantly worried both Varina and Jefferson because of her innate nervousness and her tendency toward stomach ailments. The fact the couple had already lost several children deepened their awareness of the fragility of life in general. Perhaps sending Winnie away in some way helped them fend off anxiety about her health.

Both Varina and Jefferson were pleased that the stubborn streak they had noted in a younger Winnie seemed to be diminishing. Varina wrote to her husband after their daughter had been in school for a number of months that "she is learning self-control and fortitude which is very much for a woman to learn—God grant that she may comfort our old age."[26] Knowing the hard road that lay ahead for women who dared to disagree with male authority, the former first lady of the Confederacy cultivated her youngest daughter to be the type of subservient woman that she herself could never be.

Winnie continued to have periodic bouts of homesickness even though she seemed to enjoy school. She wished fervently for visits from her parents, even calling upon her religious faith in hopes it would persuade her mother or father to come see her. She wrote Varina: "I must take my bibel [*sic*] to bed with me and when it gets warm I put my hand on it and try to think it is you—I have done some thing that gives me great hope. I prayed very hard that you and father would be hear [*sic*] in a month and so I asked the Lord to let me know by the Bible if I saw yes it should be yes if no-no and it came out yes 3 or 4 times."[27]

Despite her longing to see her parents, Winnie benefited immensely from her years living in Germany. Immersion in a new country helped her to develop and inform her critical and artistic eye, a trait she would be lauded for later in her life. Under the auspices of her school, the young girl was able to attend special events such as a concert at the Palace in Karlsruhe, where, she remarked to her mother, she had seen Princess Victoria, who was to become the queen of Sweden. Winnie wrote with childish honesty, "The Princess was a littel [*sic*] girl of about 12 or 13 and was dressed in pink silk and I can't say I thought she was very pretty but she looked good-natured."[28]

Winnie was also fortunate to witness notable European historical events of the time. As she became older and more sophisticated, she provided political commentary for her parents from Germany. Winnie reported to her mother in May 1878 about the assassination attempt on Wilhelm I, king of Prussia and the emperor of Germany: "You know that as the Emperor and the Grand-Dutches [*sic*] of Baden were riding on the 11 of May and someone shot at them that the Grand-Dutches threw herself over her father to protect him."[29]

This event made a deep impression upon Winnie. The image of the daughter sacrificing herself for the father surely resonated with her and reinforced the lessons on this subject she had learned from Jefferson. She even drew pictures of the grand duchess throwing herself over the emperor in the margins of the letter to her mother to illustrate the tale.[30]

Within a few years Winnie was at the top of her class, and "Miss Friedlander considered her 'an example to the school' with her bright and responsive mind." She took advanced classes with a select group of her classmates in her senior year.[31] The Davises' youngest daughter stayed on the straight and narrow path at school, hoping for approval from her absent parents and her teachers.

While Winnie lived within the strict confines of the convent, scandal was once again casting a shadow over the Davis family back in Mississippi. Jefferson had become the subject of more titillating gossip, much to Varina's chagrin. Tales of a wealthy southern widow named Sarah Dorsey and her attentions toward the former president of the Confederacy were beginning to circulate on both sides of the Atlantic. Varina, still living in England because of her poor health, learned from a newspaper article that Sarah Dorsey, her former schoolmate in Philadelphia, had become her husband's landlady in Mississippi. The paper insinuated that this unorthodox arrangement might lead to improper relations. Varina was undoubtedly stunned by the news.[32]

Sarah was an avid admirer of both Jefferson and the Confederacy. She had been born and raised in Natchez, Mississippi, by wealthy parents who, like Varina's parents, made sure their daughter received a superior education.[33] Sarah married Samuel Worthington Dorsey in 1853, but the couple never had children. Instead, she wrote six novels and one nonfiction work between 1862 and 1877. From her writings, her upbringing in Natchez, her marriage, and her strong support of the Confederacy during the Civil War, Sarah developed a sentimental view of the prewar South that led her to idealize both Jefferson Davis and the "Lost Cause" he was so closely associated with.[34]

After learning of Jefferson's financial problems and his desire to write his memoirs, Sarah offered Jefferson the use of a cottage on her coastal Mississippi estate, Beauvoir, in 1877. It was a lovely serene spot built in 1849 in the Louisiana plantation architectural style. The main house was raised on pillars to allow for maximum air circulation and boasted tall ceilings, crushed shell floors, and refreshing breezeways.[35]

Sarah, being an author herself, began to help Jefferson with his memoirs, reading his drafts, taking dictation, and helping with his research. She also organized his life for him, took care of his entertaining, and guarded his privacy fiercely.[36] The widow Dorsey became the former president's handler and manager—and perhaps something more. To many it looked as if she had taken Varina's place as Jefferson's wife.

Varina was at first taken aback and then quickly became incensed to think her old school friend had taken her place at her husband's side. She was the one who had suffered through a series of family tragedies with him and experienced the humiliating defeat of the Confederacy firsthand. Historian Carol Berkin explains: "For Varina this was a betrayal, made more painful by the fact that the history he was writing was *her* history as much as his, her experiences as much as those of her husband. It was as though her autobiography was being stolen from her."[37]

What was Sarah's attraction for Jefferson? She was a well-regarded and published author, an accomplished woman whose intellect rivaled Varina's own. She was three years younger than the former first lady of the Confederacy and had the money and time to coddle Jefferson. Sarah hero-worshipped Jefferson—he could do no wrong in her eyes. This was also a large part of her appeal to Jefferson, who could not bear any criticism and particularly not from his wife. In these respects Sarah very much resembled Virginia Clay, Jefferson's other significant female friend and admirer.

Maggie, the Davises' eldest daughter, was clearly appalled by the situation, taking her mother's side: "I never liked Mrs. Dorsey. I think she is mannish and her conduct to you the very least of it. You will not go there if anything I can say will prevent it. I told Father what I thought of her when he was here, I said I did not think you would enjoy being her guest. She assumes a superiority over all other women which is very disgusting to me."[38]

Sarah apparently was immensely charming, however, and Maggie, like her father, soon fell under the widow's spell. After Maggie lost her infant son to cholera in 1877, she needed some maternal comfort. Varina was still in Europe, and Maggie surprisingly accepted an invitation from Sarah to visit Beauvoir. Maggie and Addison stayed at the Gulf Coast estate for a month. After the vacation the couple was quite won over by their hostess's hospitality. Maggie, like Jefferson, was captivated by Sarah's gracious manner.[39]

It is difficult to understand why Varina, after having lost three of her own sons to early deaths, did not come back immediately to help Maggie. Even more difficult to fathom is why she would let her supposed archenemy, Sarah Dorsey, take her place yet again. Sarah had become a pseudo-wife to Jefferson and now a replacement mother to Maggie. And yet Varina was slow to return home to reestablish her place within the family.

Despite her generosity toward Jefferson, Maggie, and Addison, Sarah's usurpation of Varina's role was gossiped about widely both in England and the United States and was considered unseemly by most observers. "The situation, so odd and titillating, became the subject of gossip all over the region," writes Joan Cashin in her biography of Varina, adding, "Dorsey's own family was aghast."[40]

The biggest shock came in 1878, when Sarah created her will. Any doubts about her close relationship with Jefferson were dispelled immediately. In this document she left Jefferson her entire estate, effectively disinheriting all of her family members. Jefferson was also given Sarah's power of attorney. Winnie unknowingly became Sarah's heir as well. If her father predeceased her, she, not her mother, would become the mistress of Beauvoir.[41] Sarah wrote Jefferson in March 1879 urging him to make a will and leave all he inherited from her to Winnie, even though the widow and the young girl had never met. "I should prefer her to have it after you are done with it."[42] Sarah also left Winnie her portrait.[43] It seems odd, if the relationship with Jefferson was in fact strictly platonic, that Sarah would leave the estate to Jefferson and then Winnie, leaving her old "friend" and schoolmate Varina completely out of the picture. Other accounts claim, however, that Winnie was given a reversionary interest in order to prevent Jefferson from refusing the gift.[44]

Jefferson's own comments toward the end of his life regarding his relationships also provide some evidence that Sarah Dorsey may have ranked above Varina in his estimation. In a brief autobiography dictated in 1889, only a week before his death, according to historian Carol Bleser, he "recalled his first marriage in 1835, commented most favorably on Sarah Dorsey . . . and only in the final paragraph did he mention his second wife. He did not state her first name and about her he commented only, 'she has borne me six children—four sons and two daughters.'"[45]

Although Winnie was far removed from the situation at Beauvoir, she heard whispers of the Dorsey drama while still in boarding school. She wrote Varina, saying, "Motherly do tell me I heard from Pin [Winnie's friend Pinnie Meredith] that Mrs. Dorsey had left Father three plantations and also all her money but I heard the other day that there is still a lawsuite [*sic*] pending about the will." Winnie's main concern in this missive is that the will and lawsuit might deter her parents from visiting her in Germany—she still missed them both intensely. She seemed not to know that she, too, would eventually become Sarah's heir.[46]

In her own memoir of Jefferson, Varina glosses over the entire furor, noting that Sarah was an old school friend and a literary person of note. She also takes pains to assert that there was no impropriety taken between Jefferson and Sarah in her absence. She states that Jefferson had rented a cottage from Sarah on the property and that Sarah also had several female relatives and her brother living with her on the plantation.[47] Her rationalization of such an odd and inappropriate relationship reads as a thinly veiled statement of denial. Varina's memoirs were created with the public in mind. This particular passage is one of emotional fiction disguised as fact.

The situation was extremely upsetting for Varina, a fact that she confirmed many other times in her private correspondence with relatives and friends. She wrote to her husband on September 9, 1877, from London apologizing for not writing to Sarah. The thought of any interaction with her rival clearly made Varina furious, and she let Jefferson know she was humiliated by the situation: "I do not desire ever to see her house . . . Nothing on earth would pain me like living in that kind of community in her house—or in that of another—I am grateful for her kindness to you and my children, but I do not desire to be under any more obligation to her." Varina continued, clearly referring to the rumors about the widow Dorsey and Jefferson that were swirling around her in England: "When people here ask me what part of your work she is writing, and such like things, I feel aggravated nearly to death."[48] The arrangement may have suited Jefferson and Sarah perfectly, but it humiliated Varina and alienated her even further from her husband.

The former first lady of the Confederacy lived with her oldest daughter and son-in-law in Memphis for eight months upon her return from Europe, from the fall of 1877 until May 1878.[49] Maggie had considerately offered her mother a safe haven from the Dorsey drama: "Your room is ready and waiting to receive you," she had written to Varina. "It was built for you and so you will have to take it . . . I have made my house look as near like the Court Street House [the Davis home in Memphis] as I can so that you will feel at home."[50] This deed was brave of Maggie, as she adored her father. Yet she may have felt he had seriously wronged her mother with his impropriety. Appearances were extremely important to Maggie, and the gossip about her father must have upset her.

Still furious at Jefferson for humiliating her by choosing to live with Sarah at Beauvoir, Varina would not be easily persuaded to join them. The gossip she had had to endure both at home and abroad could not have been easy to bear. Eventually, however, Varina conceded to Jefferson's wishes, as she always did. Varina arrived at the estate in May 1878 in the midst of preparations for a garden party Sarah had arranged either in her honor or in the honor of the absent Winnie—sources differ on this point. Varina had barely unpacked when "she flared up in a temper, denounced the widow for alienating her husband, and flew off into the woods." Somehow Sarah managed to calm Varina down in time for the party, allowing both herself and her guest to save face. The former first lady of the Confederacy rose to the occasion, acting cool and collected in front of her guests.[51]

Another development may have also helped Varina to feel more at home in Biloxi. In 1879 Sarah arranged for Jefferson to buy Beauvoir from her. Soon the Davises would finally be able to own a permanent home. True to his nature, Jefferson immediately paid Sarah the first of three installments for the property in February 1879.[52]

One of Varina's great strengths was her ability to cope and to adapt to difficult circumstances. This skill she again put to use while living with Jefferson and Sarah in an uncomfortable ménage. Yet fate arranged things so that Varina did not have to remain long in this awkward position. By June 1879 Sarah Dorsey was dead from breast cancer.[53] When she died, Jefferson insisted on fulfilling his last two payments on Beauvoir, which were then applied to the estate's debts. Ultimately, the proud former president of the Confederacy paid in full for his dream home.[54] Varina paid a high price emotionally for Beauvoir. As a consequence, she would never feel quite at home there. For Varina the estate was always another woman's domain.

Oblivious to most of these events in Mississippi, Winnie blossomed at school. She showed a marked aptitude for artistic pursuits such as drawing, painting, music, and writing. Her parents and her teachers at the Misses Friedlanders' School encouraged all these interests as both appropriate and desirable. Such talents were seen as both ladylike and befitting of a young woman of her social class in the nineteenth century.

When a visitor to Beauvoir commented on one of Winnie's paintings displayed there, Varina seized the opportunity to boast about her daughter's talent: "That is my daughter's work. She has been in Germany being educated and is now in Paris for music. She has a natural taste for drawing, and no matter what studies her teachers impose upon her, she goes back to art for recreation."[55] Jefferson was so pleased with Winnie's progress in this area that he eventually converted a room at Beauvoir into an art studio for her use when she returned home.[56] Winnie's work can still be seen today displayed throughout Beauvoir.

The young girl became more confident and sure of herself and her place at school. She wrote her mother that "the new girls are all fond of me but I am not so fond of them as I ought to be because I cannot agree with their way of thinking."[57] Winnie was on her way to becoming thoroughly European—German in fact. She assimilated almost completely into the culture she had been thrust into by her parents, despite her severe homesickness. Her hot temper had been cooled by Teutonic discipline.

In October 1879 headmistress Rosalie Friedlander wrote to Jefferson that Winnie's disposition had entirely changed since she had enrolled at the school: "Her stay with me . . . has made a different girl of her altogether. I cannot tell you how wonderfully she has improved. Her hot temper is there, but she bravely fights against it. She is not only a general favorite, she is a pattern girl for all the new girls."[58]

Winnie would become known as one of the most educated women of her generation when she returned to the South. Ironically, years later she would write strongly against foreign education for American girls.

The crushing homesickness Winnie experienced while living at the German boarding school, the primitive living conditions there, which she would describe later, and above all the sense of "otherness," of being set apart and isolated from the rest of her peers by her European education, made a deep impression on the sensitive young woman.[59]

This European life, so intellectually and culturally broadening for Winnie despite its flaws, was not to last. Events at home were once again turning ominous. Death and depression, familiar visitors to the Davis household, were about to announce themselves once again.

CHAPTER 7

Yellow Fever

> *God seems to keep green the memory of our solitary little dead children—Whether they lie on a hillside in the midst of enemies or sleep in the earth where their father defended Richmond . . . The past is inexpressibly bitter is it not.*
>
> Letter from Varina Davis to Jefferson Davis, June 20, 1875

While Winnie was still ensconced in her German convent and her father and mother were living at Beauvoir, the family turned its attentions to the last living Davis boy, Jeff Jr. Jeff was handsome and a charming young man, though perhaps lacking a bit in motivation. As a child, Jeff displayed a hot temper and a protectiveness of his family that was unusual in a small boy. When he was just nine, he fought a sixteen-year-old boy who had teased him by repeating the false rumor that Jefferson Sr. had been wearing petticoats when he was captured.[1]

Virginia Clay, whose husband, Clement, was imprisoned with Jefferson Davis at Fort Monroe, recalled in her memoirs that little Jeff had reacted violently when his father was taken to prison. "When I get to be a man, I'm going to kill every Yankee I see!" the child had cried.[2] When Virginia then held him and tried to calm him, he relaxed and reportedly said, "My papa told me to take care of you and my Mamma!"[3] From a young age Jeff Jr. was expected to take on this protective role, becoming the "man of the house" while his father was absent.

Young Jeff's childhood after the Civil War was an itinerant one: he attended schools in Canada, England, and the state of Maryland, moving from place to place as his parents' fortunes waxed and waned. The young man attended military school at the Virginia Military Institute (VMI) in Lexington, beginning in 1873. His father withdrew him from the school two years later, however, fearing the boy's expulsion was imminent due to his poor academic performance.[4]

While Varina's memoirs paint an idealized portrait of Jeff Jr. as a "strong, sober, industrious, and witty young man, who was exceedingly intimate with his father, and loved him devotedly—indeed they were like two young friends together,"[5] Jefferson worried about his oldest son's lack of maturity. Like most boys his age, the young man preferred parties to schoolwork. At twenty years old Jeff Jr. cut a dashing figure in Memphis and was popular with the town belles. He looked like a young, slim Clark Gable with piercing blue eyes and a handsome mustache. He soon fell in love with local beauty Bessie Martin.[6]

Jefferson and Varina were clearly concerned about their eldest son; although they loved Jeff Jr. dearly, they worried he would not amount to much. Sounding much like a frustrated parent of today, Jefferson noted drily, "We do not understand him and fear we never shall."[7] The father had apparently forgotten the troubles of his own youth when he was a cadet at United States Military Academy at West Point.

Jefferson Sr. had constantly been in trouble at school for disobeying orders, not keeping his room clean, being absent from parades, and drinking and fighting. He narrowly avoided dismissal from the school several times. He graduated in the bottom third of his class and racked up an impressive number of demerits during his time at West Point.[8] In this respect father and son had very similar educational experiences. Jefferson had later achieved great renown, despite his lackluster college career. Perhaps Jeff Jr. would follow the same pattern.

By 1877, however, Jefferson Sr. had had enough of his son's gallivanting aimlessly around Memphis, where he had become a familiar presence on the local social scene. Jeff was feted and adored by the young people of Memphis, and he was soon swept up in the social whirl of the city.[9] In January of that year Jefferson insisted that Jeff Jr. move to Beauvoir, where he and Sarah Dorsey were still living, ostensibly so the young man could help him with his memoirs.

Surely the father thought the relative isolation and quiet of the Gulf Coast estate would calm down his son's spirited nature and keep him away from parties, drinking, and other temptations. Jefferson knew his son had no way of marrying and supporting his love, Bessie, until he obtained appropriate and steady employment. The Davis family, wealthy before the Civil War, now had little money to ease their son's transition into adulthood.

Aside from a summer visit to Memphis, Jeff Jr. remained at Beauvoir studying and acting as his father's secretary until October, when Varina finally returned home from England. Father and son greeted Varina in Memphis. Jefferson Sr. soon returned to his coastal retreat, but the younger Jefferson elected to stay in Memphis with his mother and sisters.[10] Naturally, the lure of urban life and society was far too strong for twenty-year-old Jeff Jr. to ignore. He was young, handsome, and sought after in Memphis. Beauvoir and the Gulf Coast were isolated and lacked such entertainments and diversions. His sister Winnie would learn this herself when she returned home from Europe.

In 1878 Jeff Jr.'s new brother-in-law, Addison Hayes, tried to help the directionless young man by finding him a job as a bank clerk in Memphis. Jefferson and Varina were thrilled and hopeful that a respectable job in finance would set young Jeff on the path to an industrious adulthood.[11] Perhaps he could finally marry Bessie and settle down.

Despite the good fortune of finding a promising career, sometime in September 1878 young Jefferson had a strange and prophetic dream about his own death. He seemed to have inherited his mother's ability, or curse, to foresee imminent disaster.[12] A classmate of Jeff's at VMI had noted this trait when Jeff was much younger: "He had a sort of clairvoyant, or sixth sense and had a way of seeing things around the corner which I could never quite understand."[13]

Jeff Jr.'s nightmare would soon come true. A few months after the young man's arrival in Memphis, one of the worst outbreaks in that century of yellow fever overwhelmed the town. Mosquitoes carry this dread disease, and the warm weather of Memphis and its dreadful sanitary conditions provided the perfect breeding ground for the illness to spread.[14] By September 1878 it was as if a medieval bubonic plague had descended on the city. Government offices and businesses were closed, while carts full of dead bodies flooded the streets and funeral bells rung continuously. More lives were lost in this Tennessee city from the disease than in the infamous tragedies of the San Francisco fire, the Johnstown flood, and the Chicago fire combined.[15] Over 5,150 citizens of Memphis eventually died in this particular epidemic.[16]

By mid-October Jeff was among those infected with yellow fever. He quickly showed signs of the "black vomit" that signaled his internal organs were disintegrating. Yellow fever begins suddenly, after a three- to six-day incubation period. Victims often rally and seem to improve, as Jeff Jr. appeared to do. During one of these lulls he reportedly received a letter from Bessie Martin, replying to his recent proposal of marriage. He never opened the letter, telling his brother-in-law, Addison, that he would read it when he was better.[17]

A more intense period of suffering often follows such respites from this illness, with the afflicted person vomiting blood and suffering liver and renal failure. Jeff Jr. and the other Memphians who stayed there during the epidemic died painful and frightening deaths, experiencing symptoms such as fever chills, jaundice, and hemorrhaging.[18]

The last living son of the Davises died on October 16, 1878, the sixth anniversary of his brother Billy's death. Unbelievably, neither parent was present at the time, something Varina apparently regretted deeply until the end of her life.[19] She said she was torn between helping her husband at Beauvoir with his memoirs and tending to her children in Memphis.[20]

Why did the parents not journey as quickly as possible to their dying son's bedside? In a letter to Winnie after Jeff's death, Jefferson explained to her that he and Varina had received multiple assurances that Jeff was fine, until they received a telegram on October 11 stating that he was infected with the dread disease. Jefferson claimed he and Varina were both too ill to travel, so he sent their friend Maj. William T. Walthall to check on Jeff Jr.

The major was present at Jeff Jr.'s deathbed along with Addison and several nurses. Even to the end, the major said, Jeff was able to "talk in a lucid, intelligent and sometimes sparkling way."[21] More than likely, this was just the major's kind lie to ease the bereaved parents' pain. The "Good Death" was a concept that nineteenth-century families clung to as a way to ease their own suffering. If the deceased had declared himself devoted to God and had expressed a lucidity of mind at the time of death, this assured the departed eternal salvation and reassured those family members left behind.[22] The major's unlikely description of Jeff Jr.'s passing was probably fabricated for his parents' peace of mind. The death the major witnessed would not have been a Good Death. It would have been a horribly painful final experience, worsened by the lack of parental support.

Varina's despair over losing their last boy was crushing. She noted in her husband's memoirs: "Our son died of a short, sharp illness in which he knew his danger and expressed his willingness to obey God's will . . . The last of our sons at age twenty-one, was now taken from us, and we had but two children left."[23]

Bessie, Jeff Jr.'s girlfriend and probable fiancée, was also devastated by his early demise. She remained friends with the Davis family all her life, and Varina considered Bessie one of her daughters, writing to the young woman six years after Jeff Jr.'s death, "You will never cease to be mine as well as your Mother's." The bereaved mother often mentioned their mutual loss and the "common grief" that bound the two women together.[24]

Winnie also remained great friends with Bessie and visited her often in New York after the Memphis belle married a doctor and became Mrs. J. Harvey Dew. Varina even called Bessie "Winnie's twin,"[25] thus integrating Bessie further into the family fabric. The young woman who was once a distraction was now a precious link to the past.

Despite moving on with marriage, children, and a move to New York, Bessie apparently never forgot her first love, the witty, fun-loving young Jeff.[26] She kept reams of newspaper clippings about Jeff Jr. and his early death. One friend commented that in her old age Bessie talked often of "her beloved Jeff . . . Mrs. Dew would cry telling of her love for him and how dear he was to her."[27]

How must Jefferson and Varina have felt, after losing their fourth and final son, the one whom they had assumed would take care of them both in their old age? Even by the standards of the day, losing all four sons to accident and illness was the cruelest of blows. Both parents were clearly stunned by this latest turn of events.

Jefferson wrote his son-in-law, Addison, just a few days after Jeff Jr.'s death. The two men had an affectionate relationship. Jefferson treated the young man as if he were a blood relative. Addison appreciated his father-in-law's respect and trust. He would later take over many of Jefferson's financial and business affairs. In Jefferson's heartfelt letter to Addison, the former leader of the Confederacy communicated his utter shock at losing the last of his male heirs. "The last of my four sons has left me, I am crushed under such heavy and repeated blows. I presume not God to scorn, but the many and humble prayers offered before my boy was taken from me, are hushed in the despair of my bereavement."[28]

Jefferson's work on his memoir came to an abrupt halt. According to Varina, he would stare off into space and lose his train of thought, so preoccupied was he with thoughts of his last son's untimely and tragic death.[29] He was utterly and completely depressed, and his health and literary work were quickly undermined by this unexpected tragedy. Yet despite this most recent loss, Jefferson was still concerned with the present and the future of his family. In his letter to Addison he asked about Maggie, now known to all as "Margaret." Jefferson and Varina had forbidden her to nurse Jeff Jr. during the yellow fever epidemic, though she had offered to do so. "Now what of my Daughter, where and how is she?" he asked his son-in-law.[30]

Winnie was far away from yellow fever and her brother's death, still isolated per her parent's wishes in her convent school in Germany. Jefferson wrote to Winnie from Beauvoir on November 27, echoing the sentiments he had displayed for Addison in October. "I only shut my eyes, to what it is not permitted to me to see, and stifling the outward flow, let my wounds bleed inwardly."[31]

The stoic former president of the Confederacy was deeply affected by the death of each of his children, but he was not outwardly demonstrative. This stoicism did not enhance his physical health. The inner turmoil ate away at both his nerves and his constitution, slowly sapping his vitality as the years passed and his family tragedies increased.

Varina sent Winnie a letter right after Jeff's death informing her of the tragedy so she would not see it first in a newspaper account. Winnie had apparently asked for a photograph of her brother. But no letter from Winnie about this painful loss seems to have survived.[32]

Varina and Jefferson each mourned the loss of Jeff separately and questioned their ability to go on. The pervasive theme of each of their lives was loss: of family, of the war, of fortune. It was a bleak scenario against the backdrop of looming poverty that continued to haunt the couple. The significance also resonated with them and with their family and friends that there would be no male heirs to carry on the Davis legacy unless the next generation had children.

The future of the Davis family name was further thrown into question when Margaret lost her first child, a son named Jefferson Hayes Davis. Born in the fall of 1877, the baby died of cholera later that year at his parents' home in Memphis.[33] Like yellow fever, this disease also raged in Tennessee during the 1870s.

"King Cholera" is a deadly disease of the intestines, contracted through drinking or using unsanitary water tainted by human waste. The victim suffers from diarrhea, vomiting, excessive thirst, high fever, and unbearable pain in the limbs.[34] Like his uncle, baby Jefferson must have suffered an excruciating death. Margaret and Addison were shocked and devastated. The young wife was particularly despondent.

The oldest Davis girl understandably began to demonstrate evidence of depression after her first child's birth and subsequent death. After this tragedy Margaret often suffered from severe back pain and fainting fits. She excused herself to her mother for not writing more often, claiming, "Writing makes my spine and head ache so that even after writing a short note . . . I have to lie down."[35]

The young woman may have harbored a lingering resentment that her mother did not come to help her after her son's death from cholera. Why did Varina stay away from Margaret and Addison and let Sarah Dorsey once again become the family nurse? Varina may have hated Sarah, but she did allow her to take a central place in the family a number of times when she could have easily prevented it.

It is likely that the Davises' eldest daughter suffered from what we would now term "postpartum depression" caused first by the experience of being a new mother and later by the agonizing grief over losing her firstborn. Varina, who had experienced so many losses, would have certainly related to Margaret's situation—another reason why her lack of response to her daughter's crisis is so puzzling. There were legitimate reasons why Varina did not appear to aid her children in times of need: geographic distance, fear of infection, poor communication methods of the time, her continuing poor health, and pure bad luck. Even so, she missed a number of opportunities to watch over, encourage, or even bid final farewells to her offspring.

The first notable such occurrence was, of course, accidental. Little Joe's death after falling from the balcony of the White House of the Confederacy occurred when Varina was out of the Executive Mansion taking a meal to Jefferson. But when Winnie left London for German boarding school in 1877, Varina did not come to see her off, despite knowing how anxious and bewildered her youngest daughter was about being sent away. Winnie was shipped off to boarding school as a direct result of Varina's nervous state.

Varina did not go to her oldest son's, Jeff Jr.'s, side when she knew he was extremely ill from yellow fever in the fall of 1878. He was her last surviving boy. One imagines that after having already lost three sons, most mothers would be frantic to reach their child's bedside, despite the possible consequences. Her excuse about having to help her husband finish his memoirs, believing that her son's health was improving, is questionable in light of the generally terminal outlook for those infected with yellow fever in this era.

It is likely that Varina's own black depressions and the physical ills she manifested as a consequence were at times so crushing that she had to shut out any additional grief or stress just to survive. After years of tragedies and bitter disappointments, Varina had dealt with more grief than most people could have borne.

After her sister, Margaret, failed to write to her after her son Billy's death in 1874, Varina wrote a letter to Jefferson spelling out her feelings for Margaret and the Howell side of the family: "I have worked for them all, prayed, and denied myself the joys, the best of youth, and sacrificed the little vanities of life to them every one, and not one thinks of me, and I am done. I am done, I ceased to hope and then to care, and then to wish—how bitter this has been to me I can scarcely even say to you."[36] Perhaps Varina was also unconsciously talking about her own immediate family and her utter exhaustion due to the many trials she had faced in her life thus far.

While the former first lady of the Confederacy seemed to be distancing herself from family obligations, Addison was becoming more and more engaged in the Davis clan. Margaret's continuing depressions may have spurred him to take over the family correspondence to Winnie for a period of time. In a letter to Winnie on March 19, 1877, he made excuses for his own lack of communication: "I have been very busy during the day and your sister has been sick so much that I have been unable to write." He then continued in a sympathetic vein, "We are . . . very sorry dear Winnie should be left so far from home, but she will have to be a brave little girl."[37]

Addison closes his letter by cautioning Winnie not to become so attached to Europe that she thinks of her home as provincial. "You must not do like your sister though, fall so much in love with the country as to think we have nothing good ever here."[38] While Margaret's depression stemmed primarily from the loss of her infant son, she also may have missed the glamorous Paris she had known during her boarding school days.

Addison wrote to his young sister-in-law, perhaps more frequently than his wife did, repeating his desire to have Winnie back home in the United States. "I am very anxious to have our darling girl back among us once more, for we have continued to miss you, since the day you left."[39]

A few years later Margaret's physical and mental state seemed to have improved significantly. This was surely due in part to the birth in 1878 of another child, a healthy little girl she and Addison named Varina after her mother. In 1879 Margaret wrote to her sister about baby Varina, whom Winnie had yet to meet: "Darling how your old sis does long to see your dear face once more. It seems hard that my only little sister should never have seen my baby daughter. I know you would love her she is like you and so bright and good."[40] These sentiments eerily echo the comments Varina made to Mary Chesnut about Winnie as a baby in October 1864.

The next year Margaret wrote to Winnie at Karlsruhe, commenting on how much little Varina reminded her of her younger sister: "I wish you could see the little Daughter she is so like you when you were little in fact the pictures taken of you are excellent likenesses of Varina . . . She is very little but clever and bright as possible."[41]

Addison seemed lonely for family, as his wife often went on trips without him. The loss of his firstborn son had likely affected him deeply. He may have seen Winnie as a temporary replacement for his lost child, someone he could spoil and coddle through his letters because he had no daughter or son of his own to dote upon.

On August 4, 1880, Addison again wrote to Winnie: "Margaret is now at Blue Ridge Springs, Virginia, but has been sick since she has been there."[42] Illness seemed to follow Maggie often, just as it did her father and mother. Writing these letters to Winnie may have allowed Addison a place to vent his frustrations with his wife's poor health. Winnie was probably too young and too far removed from their marital situation to grasp the significance of these letters or the concerns that Addison may have had regarding his wife's physical and mental health.

Despite Margaret's fits of depression and Winnie's life isolated from family and southern culture in Europe, it would ultimately fall to the two Davis daughters alone to provide heirs. Having children was one way the two young women could participate in their family legacy. The cultivation and preservation of Confederate culture would prove to be another. Margaret would follow the first, more traditional path, while Winnie would soon become an iconic symbol of Confederate postwar dissent.

CHAPTER EIGHT

Portrait of a Lady

In the summer of 1882 Jefferson and Varina finally sailed to Europe to fetch Winnie home from Germany. Jefferson was apparently overjoyed at the prospect of seeing his daughter again. Theirs had been a long separation. Historian William C. Davis writes, "He had not seen his daughter in five years, and the reunion gladdened his heart."[1] Both he and Varina were thrilled to be able finally to bring Winnie home and introduce her to southern society.

The years of convent school had created a very erudite and accomplished young woman who was far more of an intellectual than most of her southern peers. Winnie had become fluent in German and French, knowledgeable about European history, and particularly well versed in German literature and history.[2] All this in addition to her notable skills in painting, writing, and music earned her a deserved reputation as "one of the most cultured women of her time."[3]

Winnie had been in Paris studying French for several months, and the family enjoyed a vacation there before returning to the States.[4] The Davis women strolled along fashionable streets shopping for clothes and visited Parisian art museums with abandon, Varina being more interested in the shopping and Winnie in seeing the museums. While Jefferson longed for home and was unimpressed with French culture, Varina and Winnie relished this idyll in the City of Light, a respite from the constant shadow the Confederacy had cast over their family in the United States. Varina particularly cherished her time in Paris and found it "a great wrench" to leave.[5] Winnie bid a fond adieu to her time in Germany and France, but this was not to be her last visit abroad.

Winnie had grown into a very attractive young woman of eighteen. She was described by her friend author Charles Clifton Ferrell as "tall, slender, fair-haired with grey eyes of peculiar beauty."[6] Although Winnie's beauty may have been a little less dramatic than most sources suggest, it became part of her legend. Grace, charm, and beauty were all crucial pieces of the southern lady mythology. The emphasis on Winnie's physical looks also enhanced her moral worth in the eyes of her admirers.

Yet Varina often bemoaned her daughter's lack of interest in the modes of the day. The former first lady of the Confederacy was savvy enough to realize that this "defect" could negatively affect the public perception of her child. "Winnie does not care enough for dress—and when I have been urging her to rearrange some half-worn dress, she leads off on the woes of the Irish, the labor question, or some system of philosophy which she has been studying with intense interest."[7] Newspapers of the era would echo her mother's sentiments, though they often attributed Winnie's lack of fashion savvy to the diminished financial state of her family after the war. This quality was typically presented as a virtue on her part: "She does not make the most of what she has to dress on, but dresses plainly but most elegantly, for the daughter of Jefferson Davis could not afford to get herself up in the gew-gaw style."[8]

Although the Davis's youngest girl was definitely attractive, as evidenced by her many photographs, she was perhaps not so much beautiful as striking. Winnie represented a certain archetype of female beauty that was fashionable in the late nineteenth century. She was a wistful, nervous heroine such as one might find described in the novels of Kate Chopin (*The Awakening*) or Charlotte Perkins Gilman (*The Yellow Wallpaper*).

Pictorially, portraits of women of Winnie's physical type abounded during her adult years: Thomas Eakins, Henry Ossawa Tanner, and Thomas Wilmer Dewing all produced works of women in white feminine frocks, with drooping countenances and pallid complexions. Winnie embodied this popular physical type, and her passive personality reinforced the image. Varina's biographer Ishbel Ross describes the Davises' youngest daughter: her "health was delicate, her manner pensive. All who knew her noted a certain melancholy about Winnie."[9] Melancholia and neurasthenia were prevalent Victorian era "diseases" that often seemed to be prerequisites for late-nineteenth-century heroines. In this sense Winnie fit the cultural mold of the times. Her sadness is quite evident in her photographs, in which she is rarely seen smiling. These pictures all capture a woman with a winsome expression and wan face.

Yet Winnie suffered from something more serious than occasional bouts of dark moods. She possessed a predisposition toward anxiety and depression likely inherited from her father. Ross writes that "Winnie had her father's overwrought temperament and suffered extremely from stress."[10] Her propensity to worry herself sick was a family legacy; her mother also had suffered from anxiety and depression. This genetic inheritance was likely the root cause of many of her later bouts with unspecified illnesses.

At eighteen, however, the world seemed mostly bright, and the young girl returned home from Paris with high hopes for the future. Winnie retreated to Beauvoir with her family, where she read, painted, and proved to be a reliable source of both entertainment and comfort for the aging Varina and Jefferson. She was arguably far more of an intellectual than either of her parents. She quickly became her father's confidante and best friend, acting somewhat as a replacement for Jeff Jr., who had acted as his father's secretary and companion before his untimely death.

Her parents and other observers often described Winnie as "a loving daughter . . . a tender and solicitous companion."[11] Jefferson particularly delighted in spending leisure time with his daughter. His biographer William Davis writes: "He walked with her along the beach . . . Each evening they played backgammon and euchre."[12]

There is some evidence that Winnie did not spend all her time alone with her parents at Beauvoir. She may have enjoyed her first romance shortly after her return from Europe when she met a handsome young artist named Verner White. The young man was also a southerner, born in Lunenburg County, Virginia, close to Richmond, in 1863. While he had little memory of the Civil War itself, its aftermath informed his childhood and his artistic aesthetic. James Graham Baker describes the young artist: "Although he grew up in the ruins of the Old South among people who clung to the memories of a culture that had been largely shattered, his was a privileged youth."[13]

Verner studied art at Southwestern Presbyterian University and then traveled throughout the South painting. From 1884 to 1886 he maintained a studio in Mobile, Alabama. At some point he supposedly met both Jefferson and Winnie and began work on their portraits.[14] Mertie Broughton White, later Verner's wife, claimed that her husband frequently visited Beauvoir during this period and soon fell in love with the Davises' accomplished youngest daughter. Verner's brother corroborated her story. He claimed the artist was commissioned to make a dual portrait of Winnie and Jefferson to be called "The Father and Daughter of the Confederacy," though the painting seems never to have been finished. Verner did complete a portrait of Jefferson Davis, however, that hung in the state capitol in Montgomery, Alabama.[15]

Winnie and Verner certainly would have had much in common: age, southern heritage, and geography. They both had one foot in the Old South and one in the New. It seemed to be their love of art, however, that attracted them to each other. Winnie was herself a talented artist, having studied drawing both at school in Germany and also in Paris. Her letters are full of her whimsical drawings in the margins, Beauvoir boasts a fireplace with her decorative touch, and the Museum of the Confederacy has several of her finely detailed drawings.

Verner's family members claimed that while Verner was working on portraits of the Confederate father and daughter, Winnie "recommended he go to Europe to study and improve his art before he finished her portrait."[16] Perhaps Verner departed in a huff at this suggestion, but he did take Winnie's advice, spending the next eight years abroad. This effectively put an end to the romance, if it indeed existed at all.

Things turned out well for the young artist. He was soon on his way to becoming a southern version of John Singer Sargent. According to James Baker: "Wealthy patrons liked this cultivated, cultured, well-traveled young man. His southern heritage stood him in good stead with Confederate veterans, who by 1900 were back in control of commerce and government across the states of the former Confederacy." Verner surely would have been an acceptable candidate for Winnie's hand. His "charm, good looks, connections, culture, and artistic skills made him one of the best-known and most respected artists in Texas between 1895 and 1904."[17]

No Davis family records or letters exist that mention a possible romance or Verner's visits to Beauvoir, so historians cannot know how Jefferson and Varina viewed their daughter's relationship with the young man, if indeed it existed at all. Docents at Beauvoir claim to have never heard this story.[18] The dual portrait of Jefferson and Winnie by Verner White has never been found. Verner's studio in Galveston, Texas, and much of his work was destroyed by a massive hurricane in September 1900.[19]

Perhaps the unfinished portraits of Winnie and Jefferson were among his artistic casualties?

If the romance did take place, it may have been just a passing flirtation. Winnie did not let her attraction to Verner tie her down socially, nor did he let the romance deter him from his extended artistic studies in Europe. In 1884 Winnie was asked to be a lady-in-waiting for General Lee's daughter Mildred, who was queen of Comus at the New Orleans Mardi Gras festivities. The occasion was Winnie's official launch into southern society. Jefferson and Winnie came in from "the country" at Beauvoir to attend the balls.[20]

Winnie's time in New Orleans was likely filled with glittering balls, tableaux, and parades. A reporter at the event described the scene as Rex, the king of Mardi Gras, appeared on Canal Street: the Mardi Gras monarch was "gorgeously throned, royally habited, glistening with jewels, and attended by Mamelukes soldiers, the woman of his harem, and nobles by the dozen."[21] New Orleans's over-the-top carnival spectacle likely did not impress Winnie. Indeed, the serious-minded young woman was probably overwhelmed by the mass of gaudy color, flash, and noise.

Southerners had selected Jefferson Davis to be president of the Confederacy in part because he seemed to represent the best of their society. In his study of race relations in the South, Joel Williamson writes that Davis "was a paragon of the gentlemanly ideal, the living representative of the potential high elegance of Southern culture."[22]

Although Davis was not as popular as other Confederate leaders, such as the much-loved J.E.B. Stuart, he possessed an air of unassailable confidence attractive to southerners looking for a rock during and after the chaos of the Civil War. Admittedly, this confidence stemmed in a large part from Jefferson's firm belief that he was always right. This trait did not always win him friends, created many enemies, and frequently troubled his marriage to Varina.

In June 1881 the first volume of Jefferson's memoirs, entitled *The Rise and Fall of the Confederate Government*, was published with little fanfare. It received a lukewarm reception, but Jefferson felt relief that he finally had a venue to tell his side of the story, the story he had not been able to express in a courtroom—that "secession was a constitutional right, not rebellion or treason." *Rise and Fall*, weighing in at a lengthy fifteen hundred pages, showed that the former president of the Confederacy had no doubts concerning his side of the argument.[23]

Although the massive tome was a modest success at best, the end result of its publication had far greater import. A slow trickle of visitors descended upon the Davises at Beauvoir. Even the eccentric writer Oscar Wilde arrived at the Davises' doorstep, much to Varina's delight.[24] Confederate monuments began to be dedicated across the South, and Jefferson's popularity as a speaker and standard-bearer of the Old South, along with that of his former military colleague Gen. Robert E. Lee, slowly began to escalate.

The fading of the war years seemed to create a halo of martyrdom around Jefferson and other former Confederate leaders. This nostalgia, together with defeated southerners' seething resentment toward their northern counterparts, proved to be a powerful social force in the postwar South. Jefferson became a living symbol of the growing "Lost Cause" movement. Although the Confederacy may have lost its fight, it still maintained the vision that the South was superior to the North in terms of culture, honor, and morals. Davis's 1886–87 speaking tour cemented his newfound prestige, and he began to ascend to new heights of glory.[25]

Beginning in the 1880s, Winnie gradually began to take her mother Varina's place as Jefferson's traveling companion, secretary, and literary assistant.[26] It was Winnie and not her mother who accompanied Jefferson on his many trips throughout the South to veterans' reunions and ceremonies and on speaking tours. In 1886, after fulfilling a series of obligations in Alabama, Jefferson and his youngest daughter decided to extend their journey to Atlanta and Savannah. This last-minute decision would change the course of young Winnie's life.

CHAPTER NINE

Daughter of the Confederacy

There are many daughters of the Confederacy, there is only one Daughter.

Mrs. Cornelia Branch Stone, United Daughters of the Confederacy

The South that Jefferson and Winnie traversed during the mid-1880s was falling deeper and deeper into economic depression. Jobs were scarce, and southerners who had been wealthy in antebellum times found themselves less and less able to provide for their families. Confederate veterans were particularly embittered by their wartime experiences, berating themselves for their sense of helplessness both during and after the war.

How could southern soldiers have let the Yankees steal their wealth, their land, and their homes? How could they have let their enemies terrorize their wives and children and in some cases rape and kill them? When these men returned home in total defeat to their ruined dwellings and "ruined" women, many felt that a sense of deep disappointment was all that remained for them. As historian Gaines Foster explains, "Defeat had indeed undermined Southern soldiers' confidence in their manhood."[1]

Partially in response to these unmanageable feelings, large numbers of these former soldiers began to organize into cohesive veterans' groups in the 1880s, forming "camps" and holding veterans' reunions each year. In June 1889 all these camps officially merged to become known as the "United Confederate Veterans," or UCV. The organization's primary focus was to honor veterans, especially important Confederate leaders, and to glorify the southern past.[2] Another one of its primary goals, explained an organizer, was to "preserve in the South the respectful devotion to its splendid womanhood that the Southern manhood inherited from their chivalric ancestors."[3]

In a kind of mass group therapy, veterans began to retreat into this quasi-medieval world of courtiers, knights, and their damsels in distress. Southern gentlemen had been preoccupied with the ideas of chivalry and courtly love even before the Civil War. Confederate veterans' reunions took this concept a step further and seized upon such ideals as an important underpinning of their organization.

These gatherings were filled with elaborate rituals, symbolic gestures, and strictly observed codes of conduct. Historian David Hardin notes, "In the shame of defeat and the squalor of Reconstruction, Southerners were again eager to fasten on to these cavalier notions." Hardin further comments that author and satirist Mark Twain, in *Life on the Mississippi* (1883), would sneer at the melodrama Sir Walter Scott had created in his novels, calling the writer out for his creation of a "'Middle Age sham civilization' and for culturally misleading southerners before the war."[4] Yet Scott's influence was long lasting; his portrayals developed how the antebellum South was romanticized in nineteenth-century literature.

Representative southern women were literally placed on pedestals during veterans' reunions, to be worshipped by their knights. This concept was not taken lightly; indeed, the idea of southern men being knights who would give their lives to protect their women was, according to historian Joel Williamson, "deadly serious."[5]

These courtly rituals concealed a darker fear that possessed and indeed obsessed many of the veterans. These men frequently expressed fears of rape of white women by "outsiders." The term *outsiders* referred to both northern white men and black men. Some southern males had an abiding horror that black men and Yankees were actively attempting to steal their women away from the South. Insecurity bred by wartime defeat and dramatically diminished economic status resulted in this preoccupation for many former Confederate soldiers.[6]

The concepts of chivalry ingrained in the type of southern aristocratic male who originally participated in the veterans' reunions dictated that a true gentleman must rescue ladies in distress. The fact that southern soldiers had often *not* been able to fulfill this dictate during the Civil War caused feelings of rage and inadequacy among many veterans that the rituals of reunion sought to alleviate.

When the Davis entourage pulled in to the train depot in West Point, Georgia, on April 30, 1886, its occupants were more than ready to disembark from their sooty quarters. A swelling crowd of Confederate veterans were waiting, eagerly anticipating their leader's arrival. Despite the South's crushing defeat in the Civil War, Jefferson still retained his stature, and his popularity that spring was rising.

Winnie was also on the train that day, accompanying her father as he helped unveil a series of new Confederate monuments. A band was playing as they arrived, and it is likely that Winnie and Jefferson heard welcoming brass bands playing "Dixie" or "The Bonnie Blue Flag," accompanied by Confederate veterans' savage-sounding rebel yells.[7] In contrast to the themes of courtliness and chivalry present at inaugural veterans' meetings, the former president and his daughter were now seeing wilder, more uncontrolled displays of enthusiasm from their supporters.

On this particular afternoon Jefferson had taken ill and was not able to speak. The host of the event, Georgia governor John B. Gordon, a shrewd former Confederate general with a flair for the dramatic, grabbed Winnie and propelled her to the platform to take her father's place. Gordon introduced Winnie as "the daughter of the Confederacy . . . the war baby of our old chieftain."[8] The huge crowd of world-weary, grizzled Confederate veterans roared their approval and delight when they saw the poised, attractive young girl.

Here, in burned-out, defeated West Point, Winnie was reborn and christened the "Daughter of the Confederacy."[9] The surprised but pleased young woman waved shyly to the crowd during the speeches that followed. Although she said nothing, her presence lent an air of authenticity to the veterans' rally. Her mother noted in her memoirs, "Governor Gordon, our heroic paladin of long ago presented Varina [Winnie] to the crowd as 'The Daughter of the Confederacy.'"[10] The very next day her new title was employed again in Atlanta at the unveiling of the monument to Benjamin H. Hill. Newspaperman Hon. Henry W. Grady introduced Winnie once again as the Daughter of the Confederacy.[11] This triumphal tour marked the beginning of Winnie's rise as the most powerful female symbol of the "Lost Cause."

Despite receiving her title in such an impromptu manner, Winnie quickly emerged as a southern superstar, eclipsing even her father in popularity. Her days of anonymity had disappeared forever, and she became a vessel for sentimental southern memories. These myths of an antebellum and Civil War era South were ones Winnie helped to propagate, even though they were visions that she did not herself possess.

As historian and Jefferson Davis biographer William C. Davis explains, it is the conquered, not the conquerors, who tend to indulge more in mythmaking: "Winners have little to explain to themselves. They won. For the losers, however, coping with defeat, dealing with it personally and explaining it to others, places enormous strains on the ego, self-respect, and sense of self-worth of the defeated."[12] Postwar Confederate veterans were continually trying to make sense of what had happened to them, to come to terms with their crushing defeat. They needed an icon to cling to, someone to guide them through the choppy and unknown waters of Reconstruction. Jefferson Davis's youngest child became this icon. She came to represent redemption to these defeated soldiers. Winnie's presence reassured them of their self-worth and manhood, while she also embodied the idea of the vestal virgin. Veterans and the adoring southern public deemed her "the unrivalled pearl of Beauvoir."[13]

Confederate veterans hailed Jefferson, their former president, for his suffering during and after the war. While her father's image signaled to veterans the need to preserve the past, Winnie symbolized their hopes for the future. As the female embodiment of the Lost Cause and the living representative of the principles for which the veterans had fought, Winnie afforded these men the sort of absolution they craved. She was quickly "adopted" by the veterans and became part of their tribe and tribal rituals.

It became more and more common at UCV reunions to introduce attractive representative women, usually the daughters of prominent Confederate leaders, to the veterans. Winnie quickly became the most sought-after candidate for this honor. She was always considered a cut above the other women presented at such gatherings.[14] These women were almost always young, pretty, and unmarried. They were always instructed to wear white to the presentation ceremony. Historian Gaines Foster calls this recurring tableau "a ritual presentation of virgins to veterans, it assured the soldiers that the women of the South loved them despite their defeat and thereby indirectly affirmed their manhood."[15] On the surface these spectacles resembled nothing so much as a modern-day beauty pageant, but beneath the surface bubbled a much more serious undertone.

Female sponsors at these reunions were intended to represent the ideal southern woman who had remained true to the Confederate men and the Confederate cause both during and after the war. Although the intent was to reward these women for their loyalty, the presentations also reaffirmed the antebellum stereotypes of ideal southern womanhood: piety, innocence, unwordliness, and complete deference to and unequivocal support of men—concepts Winnie's father Jefferson surely endorsed.

Winnie's married older sister, Margaret Hayes, also attended some of these reunions, but she never inspired the kind of furor and admiration that Winnie did. Some historians think that slender, beautiful, Paris-educated Margaret might have been a bit wounded by all the praise garnered by her sister. Joan Cashin writes that "Maggie Hayes sometimes felt excluded by all the attention lavished on her sister, but it was hard to duplicate Winnie's bond with the neo-Confederate public."[16] But Davis family letters between the sisters during this period show no evidence of the older sister's jealousy, only Margaret and Addison's longing to see Winnie more often.

Margaret wrote Winnie affectionately during this time but referred to childbirth injuries and a "nervousness" that disinclined her to write more often. "I cannot tell you what a relief and pleasure the charming letter you wrote me was . . . I would be always writing if I followed my inclinations but I find it increases my nervousness and produces so much pain I can't afford to do it."[17] Perhaps her inability to write as frequently as her mother and sister would have liked, coupled with her residency far from the South, in Colorado, kept her at a distance from both her blood family and their surrogate family of Confederate veterans. Margaret, Addison, and their brood had moved to Colorado Springs in the summer of 1885, due in part to Addison's debilitating asthma but also so the couple could seek their fortune out West, far from the ruined postwar South.[18]

General Lee's daughter Mildred also could not compete with Winnie's incandescent appeal. Winnie held a special place in Confederate veterans' hearts. The younger daughter of Jefferson Davis was enshrined in a way that no other daughter of a southern or northern general could rival.[19] The primary reason for Winnie's extreme popularity with vets was the fact that she had been born in the Confederate White House during the war, thus providing proof of Jefferson Davis's manhood and virility. Winnie's sweet and submissive nature and her unmarried status sealed the deal. She is almost always depicted in virginal white bridalesque dresses in her portraits. A married woman could not have represented the desires of the veterans as Winnie did.

Winnie was not simply a comforting goddess figure for the men of the South. She would also serve as a rallying figure for a growing number of southern women's Confederate memorial associations. Her first honorary title came when she was unanimously elected in March 1891 as the first president of the Missouri Daughters of the Confederacy.[20] This organization eventually became part of the United Daughters of the Confederacy (UDC), an important second-generation women's Confederate memorial association.

According to historians Caroline E. Janney and Karen Cox, the first-generation Ladies' Memorial Associations (LMAs) in the South were primarily populated with those who had experienced the war as adults (those born between 1830 and 1850).[21] LMAs paved the way for a newer, more modern women's memorial group: the United Daughters of the Confederacy, which was established on September 10, 1894, in Nashville, Tennessee.[22] UDC members considered the LMAs the "mother" association, but as the "daughters" of this group, Janney argues, the UDC "may have gained such widespread popularity because [it] appeared to be a more youthful association."[23]

Association with the young, beautiful, and well-educated Winnie lent credibility, an aristocratic tinge, and a sense of vibrancy and freshness to the UDC—exactly the image these young women wished to portray. Just as she had within the United Confederate Veterans Association, Winnie held a special status at the UDC that no other woman could touch. She was quite literally the patron saint who inspired the organization's name.[24] Winnie was a member of the Mary Custis Lee Chapter, No. 7, of the UDC in Alexandria, Virginia, which she had joined in October 1896. Her mother was also a member of this chapter.[25] Applications also exist for Varina and Winnie indicating they applied and were accepted for membership in the New York Chapter, No. 103, of the UDC in March 1897.[26]

The UDC continued its mission to preserve the traditions and historical memory of the Lost Cause even as veterans began to die off. Foster writes, "The preservation and the promulgation of the southern view of the war" was one of their stated goals.[27] The UDC also provided an important outlet for women of the era to channel their energies outside of the home. From the time of the organization's founding until World War I, the ladies of the UDC provided a legitimate place for southern women to work within the public sphere.[28] Even into the twenty-first century, Winnie retains a special status in the UDC. According to Jamie Likins, the current president general of the organization, Winnie remains an aspirational figure for the United Daughters: "It is no wonder that UDC members revere Winnie's memory because, during her short life, she demonstrated fulfillment of the Organization's objectives: Historical, Educational, Benevolent, Memorial, and Patriotic." Likins notes that the UDC sparingly awards "Winnie Davis" medals to members of exceptional achievement, those whose dedication "far exceeds the requirements of membership, just as Winnie went beyond the call of duty in her relationships and endeavors."[29]

Winnie Davis's image as the female icon of the Confederacy thus came to represent many of the goals and ideals of both the UCV and the UDC. According to historian Cita Cook, the young woman represented both a feminine Liberty figure and a damsel in distress that Confederate "knights" in their shining armor were bound to rescue and protect. Some took these personifications even a step further into religious deification, casting her as "the Virgin in a Confederate passion play."[30]

Despite Winnie's European education as a teenager, she did not rebel against her new role as Daughter of the Confederacy. She seems to have been groomed with the ideals of southern womanhood so early on that she could never fully reject them. From birth Varina and Jefferson had raised her to be a lady, though not a frivolous one. She accepted most of the traditional models for women without question at this stage in her young life.

Winnie was both by nature and by nurture the perfect tabula rasa on which to project Lost Cause nostalgia. She was the polar opposite of her strong-willed, opinionated mother, Varina, whose love for political conversation and wit had made her widely disliked in conservative Richmond. Winnie by contrast was quiet, shy, humble, and loved by almost everyone because she kept her opinions to herself in social discourse.

While Winnie was demonstratively an ardent advocate of the Confederate cause due to her familial roots and public persona, she would never take issue with those who opposed her on the subject.[31] She always set out to appease, never to offend. One can conjecture that Winnie observed her mother fight and lose almost all the battles with her father for control. She perhaps surmised that the way to win affection, particularly from men, was by showing complete and utter deference to their opinions.

Winnie was consequently apt to underestimate the worth of her personal opinions and often made self-deprecating comments to others about her own intelligence. In an 1887 letter to friend Gaston Robbins, Winnie proffered an opinion, only to negate its value by describing it "as just the opinion of such an unlearned person as I am."[32] Some of these comments were probably just forms of southern politesse, as social rules dictated that women observe a certain degree of modesty when conversing with men. But some of them can be attributed to Winnie's inherent shyness. She typically hung back from leading discussions of any nature. According to one source, "she was chary of expressing her opinions," and she was "too modest to lead a conversation."[33]

Winnie was unmarried and thus seen as pure and virginal, a quality much venerated by veterans. She was young and fresh, offering a striking contrast to the older, grizzled, and battle-scarred former Confederate soldiers. The Daughter of the Confederacy was a living representation of sweethearts on the home front who had stayed true to their southern soldier beaux even when the men came home paralyzed, with amputated limbs, and addled by what would now be termed post–traumatic stress disorder. This at least was the fantasy of Winnie Davis held by these veterans, who had lost practically everything in the war.

At first Winnie willingly accepted the adulation, honors, and pledges of brotherhood that the vets offered up to her. She was surely dazzled by all the attention and worshipful stance of the veterans who surrounded her, not yet realizing the binding consequences of such an association. When Winnie was given a badge of membership in the Robert E. Lee Camp, Governor Fitzhugh Lee of Virginia declared she was not only the Daughter of the Confederacy but also the sister of these men.[34] According to Keith Hardison, a former curator of Beauvoir: "Veterans saw Winnie as the female activist in the presidential family. Therefore, she belonged to them."[35] At twenty-one Winnie seemed to accept this role without question or hesitation.

Many former Confederates hoped fervently that Winnie would marry a son of one of the great Confederate generals, thereby preserving and even enhancing the Lost Cause legacy. Historian William C. Davis notes, "Well-meaning protectors of the Lost Cause even expressed a hope that through her a sort of Confederate royal bloodline might be preserved and passed on, suggesting to Davis that she marry some grandson of Lee or Jackson, Sidney Johnston or Breckenridge."[36] The former soldiers' affection for Winnie was further stoked by her frequent appearances at their meetings and her apparent willingness to play the part assigned to her by her father and his former colleagues. The veterans took a paternal, protective stance toward Winnie, one that eventually devolved into a fierce territorial jealousy.

Marriage itself was seen by many of these former Confederates as a degradation of women. Mary Chesnut, the Davises' friend and noted diarist, wrote, "There is no slave, after all, like a wife . . . You know how women sell themselves and are sold into marriage, from queens downward."[37] The idea of Winnie getting married and having children, thus losing her virginity and her special status, was anathema to many of the southern men who worshipped her.

What southern war veterans really wanted was a goddess or an angel, someone otherworldly who was above banal domestic occupations. The United Daughters of the Confederacy wanted a role model and an inspiration. Thus, Winnie Davis would become a revered part of the Confederate pantheon. But in exchange the chosen one would have to conform to an Old South code of conduct that would not fit easily into the ways of the New South.

CHAPTER TEN

Life in a Fishbowl

"Beauty is truth, truth beauty,—that is all / Ye know on earth, and all ye need to know." These lines from Keat's immortal poem "Ode on a Grecian Urn" had a tremendous impact on the literary public of the nineteenth-century South, reflecting the Romanticism inherent in its antebellum, upper-class way of life.[1] The medieval mind-set and the lost world of knights and their ladies remained very much on these southerners' minds. And for them Jefferson Davis's youngest daughter seemed like the perfect woman to carry this banner of Romanticism forward into the future.

Or was she?

The triumphant Confederate tour of spring 1886 had brought momentous change to Winnie's formerly calm, ordered lifestyle. After the twenty-one-year-old was crowned "Daughter of the Confederacy" in West Point, Georgia, with another engagement in Atlanta, the Davis entourage went on to Montgomery, Alabama. There Winnie stood next to her father at the state capitol in Montgomery on the exact spot where Jefferson had been inaugurated as the Confederate president twenty-five years earlier. Varina's biographer Ishbel Ross describes the event: "The band played 'The Bonnie Blue Flag.' The crowd cheered. Many of the women wept. For the first time, Winnie realized the full intensity of feeling that surrounded her father's history."[2]

Winnie was at this point a young woman who had been brought up with a European perspective. Her parents' well-meaning and deliberate isolation of her as a teenager in Germany made her unique among her southern peers. At twenty-one she was more German than American and saw life in the postwar South through a predominantly European lens. She had spent almost half of her short life away from the United States and the South. As a consequence, writes historian Joan Cashin,

Winnie was "fluent in German and French, and her accent when she spoke English was mittle-European."[3]

Winnie's "otherness" sprang from an education abroad that was partially designed by her parents to separate her both physically and psychologically from the bloody history of the Confederacy. She herself realized that she was different from other girls her age and often felt excluded and lonely. Years after she returned from her European schooling, she wrote firmly against this popular practice among the American elite. In 1892, in a piece written for the *Ladies' Home Journal*, Winnie recalled her own boarding school experience, living in drafty, unheated rooms with frozen pitchers of water, hard beds, and plain food, "conditions which in America would be considered hard usage for servants of the meanest class."[4] She revealed in an earlier piece what she called "the seamy side of a foreign schoolgirl's existence, some of the hardships endured patiently, some of the necessary things left unlearned, and the unimportant things laboriously acquired, only to prove unwieldy ballast when they enter the race for society favor."[5]

The newly minted Daughter of the Confederacy sometimes felt at odds with her native South and sometimes even with her family due to her European education. The niceties of English were a struggle for her, and she frequently felt misunderstood. She wrote in the *Ladies Home Journal*: "From the moment of her return to her native heath, the Europeanized American girl begins to find herself the victim of her misdirected education . . . All her little peculiarities are misunderstood, or unobserved, all her ideas regarded as odd, her mannerisms smiled over, she stands among her kindred an alien in her own family."[6]

Varina herself soon realized that her youngest daughter—so recently returned to her—was foreign, essentially German, and this made her entry into American society awkward. She noted that Winnie's intelligence and education also sometimes resulted in social difficulties. "My child is good and wonderfully clever—but not like the rest of the world. This mutual difference separates her from most girls, and she wonders why she feels lonely."[7]

Winnie also lamented her lack of education concerning American history, noting that American girls like herself who had been recently educated in Europe "stumble over the battle of New Orleans, and is not quite sure whether it was Washington or General Grant who commanded."[8] Her advice to upper-class Americans considering a European education for their daughters was clear. Although the academic experience might be superior, stay home: "Though her French or German may not be quite so fluent, in the dignity of her American womanhood she will proudly boast . . . 'I dwell among my own people.'"[9]

Winnie was essentially a European who had spent her formative years in countries governed by monarchs. She wrote that women like her had been "nurtured on the divine right of kings as an unanswerable hypothesis, and dazzled by glimpses of court splendor, she often learns to look upon a republican form of government as a crude expedient of people in the transition state between barbarism and monarchy."[10]

Although she clearly benefited from her studies abroad in terms of her academic and cultural development, Winnie also suffered from what a person from her time period would call an "over-education." In Europe she would have been welcomed into intellectual circles. In the United States, however, she was out of step with her peers and her family. Winnie clearly and correctly deemed herself a stranger in her own land.

How ironic it was, then, that this sheltered and thoroughly European convent girl was destined to become the most prominent living symbol of the southern Lost Cause. Her new role, while attractive to her, had been thrust upon her by an adoring but dispirited southern public. Winnie displayed all the qualities of the ideal southern woman. Yet she lacked the deep hatred of northerners that so many would have expected her to possess. She was a unique combination and a young woman who appealed to both her peers and those of her parents' generation.

After the tour ended and Winnie and her father returned to Beauvoir, she began to travel and act on her own. She slowly became part of a more national social scene, appearing not only in big southern cities, including New Orleans, where she was a Mardi Gras debutante, but also in northeastern cities such as New York. The young woman was invited to balls, parties, and teas by friends of Varina and Jefferson who had scattered all over the country after the war.

Although she still preferred art galleries and books to parties, she felt obliged to attend such events as a representative of her family. Her mother, Varina, also instinctively realized that this was the ideal time for her youngest daughter to find a husband. Winnie was at the peak of her attractiveness and charm and her popularity in the South continued its meteoric rise.

Winnie had looks, modesty, and an exotic lineage to her credit. She was soon also to receive a societal assist from powerful family allies. Before Winnie's return from boarding school in the early 1880s, Jefferson and Varina had become friendly with newspaper magnate Joseph Pulitzer through his wife, Kate, a distant Davis cousin. It was an interesting and ironic relationship because Pulitzer, a self-made man and also Jewish, had fought on the Union side in the Civil War. The newspaper owner's status had significantly improved since his early days as a poor, Hungarian immigrant who could barely speak English. Since he had taken over the *New York World* newspaper in 1883, according to his biographer James McGrath Morris, "the *World* had grown at meteoric speed, becoming at one point, the largest circulating newspaper on the globe."[11]

As a result of this success in the world of print, Joseph and Kate became fabulously wealthy. Joseph's newspaper voice often denounced the upper classes, even while he himself had joined their ranks financially. Although the press baron often ridiculed the elite in his papers, he had essentially become one of them himself. He was one of the fifty richest Americans by 1891, with three imposing mansions: one on New York's Upper East Side, one on Mount Desert Island in Maine, and a third estate on posh Jekyll Island, a millionaire boys' club retreat off the coast of Georgia.[12]

To an impressionable Winnie, Kate and Joseph must have seemed incredibly glamorous. They in turn must have been attracted both to the young woman's sweet nature and to her growing status as the Daughter of the Confederacy. The Pulitzers grew so attached to the young girl that they eventually asked her to be godmother to their middle son, Joe Jr. In May 1887 Varina wrote Joseph Sr. a somewhat fawning letter inquiring after his son and reassuring the Pulitzers about Winnie's commitment to her role: "How is Winnie's godchild? . . . Winnie says she means to be a 'fine enough Godmother' and intends to teach him his duty to his neighbor. She then added 'he would do well to follow his father's example.'"[13]

Later that fall Winnie wrote a warm letter to Joseph Sr., comparing his boy to her other high-spirited godson, her nephew, Jefferson Addison Hayes: "My two god-sons seem to be rather alike from all I can hear, as this little man is as bright, and as bad as he can be; and makes me very glad to think I have not to fulfill the sponsorial task of teaching him his catechism for some time to come."[14]

When Winnie made one of her first visits to New York after returning home from Europe, in 1885, Kate became her guide to the city's social scene.[15] The two women attended a December society ball together, but the *New York Times* society columnist did not remark upon Winnie at all. She was still relatively unknown to the northern public and did not particularly stand out.

Unlike her younger relative, the striking Kate did not escape notice, fashionably attired as she was in a satin gown trimmed with ostrich feathers and crystal pendants. A New York society columnist wrote: "Her manner is cordial and fascinating. She has large black eyes fringed with long lashes, a brilliant color, perfect teeth, lovely white sloping shoulders, a head well-poised and coils of dark brown hair."[16]

In the years to come, because of the Pulitzer connection as well as her status as the Daughter of the Confederacy, the New York press treated Winnie as if she were a southern princess and began to take more and more interest in her social movements. Historian Cita Cook observes that Kate acted as a "surrogate big sister for Winnie whenever she was in the Northeast."[17]

Kate and Winnie were opposites. Winnie was sweet, demure, not interested in fashion, gossip, or clothes, and without much in the way of financial resources. Kate was a firecracker: feisty, opinionated, fashionable, and worldly, with money to burn. Winnie played the role of *Gone with the Wind*'s Melanie Wilkes to Kate's Scarlett O'Hara.

Despite their vastly different temperaments, or perhaps because of them, the two women were destined to become fast friends and frequent traveling companions throughout Winnie's adult life. Joseph and Kate were both instrumental in launching Winnie into the broader, more diverse society of the Northeast, where she would begin to spend more and more of her time.

Perhaps Joseph Pulitzer also recognized a kindred spirit in Winnie. To the public both were American icons, he a newspaper baron and she a darling of the postwar South. But despite their elevated status, Joseph and Winnie often felt isolated from American society. Neither of them would ever quite fit in.

In 1886, once Winnie became known as the Daughter of the Confederacy, the anonymity she had experienced in New York with Kate Pulitzer just one year earlier was gone forever. Her every move was chronicled by the Victorian southern and northern presses, both perpetually hungry for scandal and gossip about the Davis family. Because of her new status as a Confederate goddess, the papers that had not remarked upon her presence at the 1885 ball in New York with Kate Pulitzer were now salivating over her. The press reported constantly on the young woman's socializing, making it difficult for Winnie to move about freely without judgment.

In late December 1886 Varina wrote about the issue to her old friends Connie and Burton Harrison, noting that Winnie "is so watched by reporters that I cannot telegraph and by the time I hear anything she has left the place where it happened . . . I have been so tormented by anxiety that but for my knowledge of her rare discretion and well-poised character I would summon her home at once."[18]

In the same letter Varina indicated her conflicted stance on Winnie's newfound celebrity. She seemed to want her daughter to get out and have a social life, despite her worries about the nineteenth-century paparazzi. Varina confided in Connie: "Mr. Davis, who is, as you know, very old, dwells on the past. The shadow of the Confederacy grows heavier over him as years weigh his heart down and my child is the coming woman, not the woman of my day still less of his."[19]

The young girl soon began to chafe against the chains placed upon her. As Confederate royalty, certain expectations were placed upon Winnie that would dramatically change the course of her life. The intense media scrutiny placed a heavy burden on Winnie, as she was held up to young women throughout the South as a role model. "Her every move would be watched paternally by millions," writes historian William Davis, "and in an era where a young woman could find herself idealized, Winnie bore special responsibilities to be the perfect daughter and, it was expected, the perfect wife."[20]

During the 1880s both Winnie and her mother began a warm correspondence with novelist and essayist Charles Dudley Warner. Charles was a good friend of Mark Twain, coauthoring a novel with him in 1873 entitled *The Gilded Age: A Tale of Today*. The letters between Warner, Winnie, and Varina reveal tantalizing glimpses of Winnie's personality as it

1. Jefferson and Varina early in their marriage. (Museum of the Confederacy, Richmond.)

2. William H. Mumler, *Mrs. Jeff Davis—"Don't provoke the President or he may hurt some of you."* This political propaganda image from 1865 of the former Confederate president trying to escape capture in petticoats was a northern fabrication. (International Center of Photography, gift of Charles Schwarz, 2012.)

3. (*right*) Carte de visite of Joseph Evan "Little Joe" Davis, who died tragically at age five (Valentine Richmond History Center, Richmond.)

4. (*below*) The balcony at the White House of the Confederacy where Joe Davis fell to his death. The balcony was fifteen to twenty feet above ground level when the house was built. Some sources say Jefferson Davis had the original balcony demolished after Joe's fall. (Photo by James Christopher Lee.)

5. (*left*) Winnie as a baby with her mother, Varina. Winnie would become Varina's favorite child. (Museum of the Confederacy, Richmond.)

6. (*below*) The Davis children in Montreal, circa 1866, when Jefferson was imprisoned at Fort Monroe. *Left to right*: Jeff Jr., Maggie, Billy, and Winnie. (Museum of the Confederacy, Richmond.)

7. Winnie as a little girl in fancy dress, already looking like the "Daughter of the Confederacy." (Museum of the Confederacy, Richmond.)

8. Margaret "Maggie" Davis on her wedding day, January 1, 1876, to Joel Addison Hayes. Despite the Davises' financial woes, Margaret still wore a couture gown from Paris as her wedding dress. (Beauvoir, Biloxi MS.)

9. (*above*) Winnie at sixteen, when she attended the Misses Friedlanders' School for Girls in Karlsruhe, Germany. (Museum of the Confederacy, Richmond.)

10. (*left*) Sarah Dorsey, "authoress," mistress of Beauvoir, and fervent admirer of Jefferson Davis. (Beauvoir, Biloxi MS.)

11. The photo, circa 1890, most often used to depict Winnie as the "Daughter of the Confederacy." (Museum of the Confederacy, Richmond.)

12. (*right*) Newspaper baron Joseph Pulitzer. He and his wife, Kate, were friends of the Davis family. He would become Winnie and Varina's financial savior in later years. (World Papers, Rare Book and Manuscript Library, Columbia University, New York.)

13. (*below*) Kate Pulitzer, wife of Joseph Pulitzer. Kate was Winnie's glamorous best friend and "chaperone" for many of her travels in the northeastern United States, Europe, and the Middle East. (World Papers, Rare Book and Manuscript Library, Columbia University, New York.)

14. A miniature of Winnie, 1880s. (Museum of the Confederacy, Richmond.)

15. Alfred "Fred" Wilkinson was a handsome, six-foot-tall Harvard graduate who became engaged to Winnie. He was also the northern grandson of famous abolitionist Samuel Joseph May. (Onondaga Historical Association, Syracuse NY.)

16. (*above*) Samuel Joseph May's home at 157 James Street in Syracuse NY, where Winnie and Fred courted. During the Civil War Fred's abolitionist grandfather hid runaway slaves under his back porch. (Onondaga Historical Association, Syracuse NY.)

17. (*opposite top*) Winnie as the 1892 Queen of Comus at the New Orleans Mardi Gras, surrounded by the ladies of her court. (Museum of the Confederacy, Richmond.)

18. (*opposite bottom*) A staged photo of the two Davis sisters, Margaret and Winnie, at tea, mid- to late-1880s. Margaret was the only child of Jefferson and Varina to marry and have children. (Museum of the Confederacy, Richmond.)

19. Photo of Winnie in New York 1890s. (Valentine Richmond History Center, Richmond.)

20. Photo, *left to right*: unidentified man with Winnie, Margaret, and Addison Hayes, taken June 19, 1894, at gold rush site Cripple Creek near Colorado Springs CO. Winnie was on a visit to Colorado Springs to see her sister and her family. Margaret and her husband, Addison, left the postwar South in 1885 and moved out West for the sake of Addison's health and to make their fortune. (Colorado Springs Pioneers Museum.)

21. The *Angel of Grief* statue on Winnie Davis's grave at Hollywood Cemetery in Richmond. (Photo by James Christopher Lee.)

related to her literary work. Winnie's letters to her newfound literary mentor are disingenuous and worshipful. On December 23, 1885, Winnie wrote Warner a Christmas card that she had illustrated herself with a beautiful sketch of a sailing ship: "[I] enclose a card of home manufacture, which having no great merit in itself, may yet perhaps bring with it some part of the gratitude all of your readers must feel for the lovely visions your pen conjures up before them."[21]

While Winnie was penning such charming notes to her mentor, the shrewd Varina was already networking on her beloved daughter's behalf. Varina wrote Warner from Beauvoir just after Christmas in 1886 that she hoped Winnie would go to Bar Harbor the next summer with her friends Connie and Burton Harrison but that Winnie would probably just as soon stay home: "Her father seems to think that she would rather see the reflection of the world in books, but I have found out that world is old, and hers is young and strangely different and she must study her own and make the most of it."[22] In the letter Varina pressed Warner to help Winnie with her writing career, should she eventually produce anything of value.[23] Warner did indeed help Winnie, and he would help her find publishing opportunities throughout her career. With his encouragement, Winnie began to pursue her literary career openly and with zest. Winnie's first work, an article about serpent myths, was published in the *North American Literary Review* in 1888.[24]

The Davis family had also become friends with Irish publisher John Lovell while in Canada in the late 1860s, and Winnie had remained friends with one of Lovell's daughters. Subsequently, Lovell agreed to publish Winnie's monograph of Irish revolutionary Robert Emmet, entitled *An Irish Knight of the 19th Century*, in 1888.[25] It is easy to see why the young author was drawn to Emmet, a young rebel of the Irish political cause. Winnie was interested in the subject partially because Varina's grandfather, Col. James Kempe, of Natchez, had acted as one of Emmet's men as a teenager, when he still lived in Ireland.[26] Perhaps Winnie was also inspired by Irish writer Oscar Wilde's 1882 visit to Beauvoir. There are also many obvious parallels in the book to the life of Jefferson Davis himself.

Like Jefferson, Emmet was jailed for his political activities and mistreated by his captors. In her book on the young revolutionary, Winnie wrote sympathetically as if she had known Emmet personally: "The prisoner's ankles were severely lacerated by the fetters; yet, though weakened by loss of blood, overcome by the fatigues of the previous day and the want of food, his uncomplaining fortitude seems to have touched even the heart of the prison official."[27]

Another part of Emmet's story illuminates Winnie's own views of romance, love, and duty. Emmet had loved a woman named Sarah Curran and longed to marry her. He denied himself this love, however, and devoted himself to the Irish cause. Like Jefferson Davis as well as Irene, the self-denying Confederate heroine of Augusta J. Evans's novel *Macaria; or, Altars of Sacrifice* (1864), Emmet felt it was best to yield up his personal life in service to a higher purpose. Winnie put these words into the Irish patriot's mouth: "Heaven forbid that an excusable passion should thwart the design of my life, or cause me for an instant to neglect my country's good for the purpose of promoting my own personal advantage."[28] She also created a verse at the very end of the book that can be read not only as a tribute to Emmet and his eventual martyrdom but also an homage to her own father's doomed leadership of the Confederacy: "Oh not for idle hatred, not for honor, future, nor self-applause, / But for the glory of the cause, You did what will not be forgot.[29]

Despite Winnie's clear literary talents, her well-known and widely praised intellect was not always seen as a plus. It was considered a defect by many men and was something Winnie often tried to conceal. Unlike either of her parents, Winnie had a sense of personal humility so strong that she was apt to underestimate herself. This behavior worked well in the marriage market, and she was often praised for her humble opinion of herself.

In order to attract the ultimate prize of a husband, Winnie would not only have to downplay her intellect, but she would also have to put her physical charms on display. Winnie did not go out of her way to show herself off—it was not her style. But she was constantly in the papers and subjected to much the same scrutiny that celebrities face today. Her looks were an endless source of debate for journalists of the era. The constant opining on her face and figure in newspapers and magazines of the day must have at the very least annoyed Winnie, if not completely upset her.

Despite her fishbowl existence among the nineteenth-century paparazzi, Winnie was finally allowed to make a trip up North on her own during the fall of 1886 to visit Bessie Martin Dew, her brother Jeff

Jr.'s old girlfriend, now married to a doctor and living in New York. Although her father apparently opposed the trip, Varina thought it would be healthy for Winnie to get away from Beauvoir, noting that the home was "as isolated as the island of Elba."[30]

On the visit Winnie's presence in New York City was duly noted and commented upon by numerous papers of the day. As she ate her first breakfast in the city at the New York Hotel, reporters freely commented on her looks and her demeanor: "She has a dark complexion and is a pure Southern type of brunette . . . She bore all glances with calmness and was not in the least disturbed. Miss Davis is distinguished-looking, tall and sylph-like, but not handsome. Her carriage and deportment though, are so refined and perfect, any one not knowing her would turn to look at her twice."[31] The Confederate "It Girl" was learning to deal with the press, and they in turn caught something of her luminosity in their reports.

After Winnie's trip to the city was over, Varina seemed to have had second thoughts about her daughter's solo excursion. She wrote Bessie in late December 1886, "I never desired Winnie to go to New York City, for I was in the extremest misery the whole time she was there lest the reporters talk to her." In her letter the former first lady of the Confederacy deemed New York a "babel" where both Winnie and Bessie—a resident of the city at the time—were "out of your depth . . . as much as I should be in Paris."[32]

Perhaps the mother felt like her youngest daughter might be slipping out from under her control. Winnie did not write her frequently enough, she complained. "When Winnie writes she sends a meager account," Varina told Bessie. "Night after night I lie awake fearing that the morning papers would bring me some wretched squib against her."[33] Winnie, for her part, seemed to be finally enjoying herself away from her mother's constant micromanagement. She neither courted nor shied away from the press; instead, she simply soaked up the atmosphere of this most cosmopolitan of American cities and enjoyed being independent.

The young woman thus began to spread her wings and fly from the confines of her sedate lifestyle in Mississippi. She was beginning to find her way on her own and to make friends outside of the South. As she began her foray into this more diverse northeastern society, however, Winnie's status as Daughter of the Confederacy was called into question. One man would stand as her champion, and he would be the most unlikely candidate imaginable.

CHAPTER ELEVEN

I Will Never Consent!

Winnie's love story begins, not unlike Shakespeare's *Romeo and Juliet*, with a party.[1] In the late fall of 1886, after Winnie and Bessie had enjoyed a visit together in New York City, Winnie moved on to Syracuse, New York, to visit her parents' friends Gen. and Mrs. William H. Emory and their son Dr. Thomas Emory and his wife. The northern town in the 1880s was at the peak of its prosperity, strategically located as it was on the Erie Canal.

Many locals were not too enthusiastic about the Daughter of the Confederacy visiting their town. Some northerners, according to a piece in the *New Orleans Times-Picayune* from mid-December 1886, "had hoped she would not come to Syracuse."[2] Many in this northern city still found the southern cause abhorrent, and Winnie was seen as part and parcel of this legacy.

Winnie was acutely aware of this ill feeling regarding her background, and as a consequence she had declined repeated invitations to visit the Emory family. Mrs. Thomas Emory had urged Winnie to visit for three years. Mrs. Emory's father-in-law, General Emory, was an old friend of Jefferson from his time as a senator in Washington in the 1850s. The time had come for the young woman to accept the Emorys' invitation. "[3]

Dr. Thomas Emory had served in the Confederate army and had later married the daughter of a prominent Syracusian family, the McCarthys. Dr. Emory became a partner in the dry goods store the family had owned since 1806. Over the years the Emory family came to be important leaders in the town's political and social circles.[4]

The Emory home, known to have the most elegant dining room in the city,[5] was located at fashionable 80 East Fayette Street. The neighborhood was replete with Greek Revival mansions bought with railroading fortunes. The dinner parties at the Emory mansion, according to the piece in the *Times-Picayune*, were well known in the community "for their excellence, and to be invited there is one of the tests of position in society here."[6]

This gracious home of the Emorys reportedly hosted both Winnie and Varina in the late fall of 1886. The famous mother and daughter were the Emorys' guests of honor at a fabulous ball one evening during their visit to Syracuse. It was a glamorous and festive event. A 1946 Syracuse radio dramatization described the scene: "Carriage after carriage drew up in front of the big house on Fayette Street and stylishly dressed couples descended to enter."[7]

Although all the northern press reports place Varina in the receiving line with Winnie that night at the Emorys' party, none of the southern reports mention her presence that night. Perhaps this is a deliberate omission? Varina was known to many to have northern friends and family. Many southerners still thought her loyalties during the war had been unpardonably divided.

The former Confederate first lady and her youngest girl did not have the money (or in Winnie's case, the interest) to dress at the height of fashion. Consequently, Winnie may have felt a bit diminished by the ladies she was meeting that evening dressed in their New York finery. At the time tiny-waisted bodices were de rigeur as well as starched lacy collars. Hair was either piled high on the head in a pompadour style or drawn up tightly in a topknot, perhaps anchored with a jeweled comb. Ensembles were finished off with billowing skirts and bustles of epic proportions.[8]

Although Winnie may not have been the most stylish guest, her personal magnetism was evident. Many reports noted that she entranced many of the Emorys' friends, skillfully avoiding contentious issues about her lineage and her views on the war. She insinuated herself into the Syracuse community, thanks to her unassuming and humble demeanor. A special dispatch to the *Washington Post*, on November 22, 1886, offered a description: "Miss Winnie Davis has quietly made her way into the good graces of the people of Syracuse. She has shown so much discretion in her conversation, and is so modest in her bearing, that those who have met her are already charmed."[9]

Winnie even tried to help the Syracuse hospital board by appealing to Joseph Pulitzer for financial support and advice.[10] Despite Winnie's charitable efforts on behalf of her northern host town, some resident socialites still refused to talk to her and continued to nurse their anti-southern sentiments. Consequently, it is not surprising to find mention of Winnie suddenly becoming ill and finding herself unable to attend a Tuesday evening dinner party shortly after her arrival in town.[11] Sickness was a socially acceptable way out of such obligations and became a coping pattern for the young woman that she often displayed in times of stress.

It was at the Emory home where Winnie first encountered Alfred "Fred" Wilkinson, an eligible young patent lawyer. She supposedly was introduced to Fred in the receiving line and was intrigued by the attractive and unattached Syracusian. The young man was described in one of Varina's letters to her friend and neighbor Maj. W. H. Morgan as "handsome and physically striking with an imposing height of six feet, dark eyes and even, regular features. He possessed a refined and cultured demeanor in addition to excellent manners."[12] Fred was regarded in the community as a confirmed bachelor at the ripe old age of twenty-eight but an individual whom young women of the town watched with interest. The eligible young man would have been considered quite a catch for any young woman in the Syracuse social set.[13]

The young barrister had attended Harvard, where he graduated in the same class (1880) as Theodore Roosevelt.[14] From a northern perspective Fred's lineage was illustrious. His paternal grandfather was a lawyer and one of the founding fathers of Syracuse, The young lawyer's maternal grandfather, the Reverend Samuel Joseph May, was a well-known abolitionist linked with Ralph Waldo Emerson, William Lloyd Garrison, Henry Wadsworth Longfellow, and Wendell Phillips. Samuel Joseph had wielded great influence both in the United States and in Great Britain as a spokesman for this cause and was known as "one of the bright gems in the Abolitionist sky."[15]

Samuel Joseph was best known for his role in the "Jerry Rescue" of 1851. "Jerry" was the nickname of William McHenry, a mulatto who had escaped slavery in Missouri and come to Syracuse, where he found work as a cooper. The 1850 Fugitive Slave Act compelled local police to arrest Jerry. In October 1850 Samuel Joseph, Gerrit Smith, and other local abolitionists arranged for dozens of men to break into the police station to free Jerry. He was then smuggled out of Syracuse to Kingston, Ontario.[16]

Each October thereafter, Samuel Joseph organized a public celebration of "Jerry Rescue Day," one reason that the city was known as a "laboratory of abolitionism, libel, and treason." From a southern perspective abolitionists were a dangerous lot and considered political extremists. Ironically, Gerrit Smith had been one of a group of prominent northerners who guaranteed a bond of $100,000 for Jefferson Davis's release from Fort Monroe in May 1867.[17]

When Winnie and Fred first began to spend time together during the late fall and winter seasons of 1886–87, the young woman had already suffered through some unpleasant encounters with Syracuse socialites who refused to be drawn in by her winning personality. According to the memoir of one of the town's native sons, travel writer E. Alexander Powell, Syracuse began as a clannish town that did not welcome outsiders, southern or otherwise: "Our local society was a close corporation, dominated by a few old families who were inclined to regard all outsiders with suspicion and distrust."[18]

Fred, despite his abolitionist heritage, did not view Winnie's background as a defect. Nor did she seem to give his grandfather's pivotal role in the abolitionist movement a second thought. As is typical of those young and in love, their forebears' political leanings made not a dent in their initial attraction for each other. "Really who cares about that now? It was so long ago," the couple might have said to each other, if they even acknowledged these facts at all.

Others remembered the past vividly, however, and could not forget it so soon. Fred gallantly championed Winnie, trying to protect her from the rudeness she encountered in the northern atmosphere. In Fred's eyes the young southern visitor, five years his junior, was beautiful, bright, cultured, and everything he could want in a potential mate. From all accounts Winnie regarded Fred in exactly the same manner. It was a classic case of love at first sight.

Because no love letters between Fred and Winnie have ever been found (women's personal correspondence was often burned in the nineteenth century to preserve their privacy), one must imagine the psychological and emotional factors that drew the young couple together. Physically, they were both young and attractive. Both were extremely well educated and well spoken. Both were kind, thoughtful people from close-knit families.

Their backgrounds, however, could not have been more opposite. Was this perhaps part of their initial attraction? Up North Winnie had the freedom to see whomever she chose, and there were few southern "friends" to keep her away from northern men, who would be seen as undesirable. She could breathe in the North, relax, and be herself in a way she could not at home. Her public persona in the South was too much in demand.

The new couple doubtless enjoyed the rounds of holiday parties. A description from Powell's first-person account of Syracuse in the 1880s describes the "Germans," or cotillions, of the upper-crust city as formal affairs with men in swallowtail coats with high collars and white kid gloves. The ladies, according to a later account by E. Alexander Powell, were stunning in "their wasp-waisted gowns of flowered satin that looked like human bouquets, though one wondered by what miracle of dressmaking the daring décolletages were kept from revealing more than was intended."[19] Because of Winnie's modesty and disinterest in clothes, it is likely that she was dressed demurely, without the slyly noted décolletage on display.

Winnie never ate much, like her father; she had anorexic tendencies and regarded food as a necessary evil. But these parties offered abundant and rich foods such as oyster patties, scalloped potatoes, sliced turkey, chicken salad, and ice cream. Cocktails had not yet been introduced, and generally only lemonade or punch was served for the liquid refreshment. Typically, however, someone would "spike" the punch by the end of the evening, thus adding to the festive atmosphere.[20]

During Winnie's extended visit to Syracuse, the couple was often seen riding in Fred's horse-drawn carriage or "strolling out of James Street towards the old home of [Fred's] grandfather, Samuel Joseph May."[21] Later generations speculated that the couple must have spent some of their time courting in the charming summerhouse outside of May's home—an ironic place for the northern Fred to romance the daughter of Jefferson Davis, considering that that his grandfather's back porch had been a known hiding place for slaves headed to Canada via the Underground Railroad.[22]

Although both Winnie and Fred were lovestruck, even in the midst of the heady holiday atmosphere of Syracuse in the 1880s, there were nevertheless rules and rituals that each party was bound to observe. These rituals transcended North-South boundaries and represented the mores of the social class to which both young people belonged. The pressure of wartime romances had ended, and social etiquette of the period now prescribed a more gradual courtship. Winnie was to be treated in much the same manner as her alter ego, the Daughter of the Confederacy. As was considered appropriate for southern young ladies of her social status, Winnie was to be placed "on a pedestal, enshrined like a holy object . . . and approached only through a set ritual."[23]

Fred for his part was probably not even considering the repercussions of pursuing a romance with the daughter of Jefferson Davis, former president of the Confederacy, at this point in the relationship. It is easy to imagine that he was not even thinking of family genealogy when he was first getting to know Winnie. He had just met an attractive, cultured, and lovely young girl in need of his protection and assistance. What could have been more appealing?

Winnie returned home to Beauvoir at the first of the year in 1887 in a glorious fog, probably envisioning her life to come with Fred up North, far away from her parents and what she may have seen as her temporary role as Daughter of the Confederacy. She had enough presence of mind, however, to keep the romance a secret from Varina, Jefferson, and her sister, Margaret.

The fact that she kept the romance hidden from her family for months may indicate that Winnie had indeed thought through the repercussions of her involvement with the grandson of an abolitionist. According to a former curator of Beauvoir, Jefferson Davis's final home, during this era, "Abolitionists were seen as the ultimate haters of the South, the lunatic fringe."[24] The young woman also knew that her father was the type who would not give his favorite daughter up to any man easily. Jefferson was in very poor health, and Winnie was most likely frightened of shocking him with her controversial news.

Winnie pined for Fred, corresponding regularly with him as she returned to her former life at Beauvoir. She was at this point completely infatuated by her tall, dark, and handsome beau and in the throes of her first mature romance. Her parents knew nothing of her feelings, and the pressure was on Winnie to entertain her father and continue to work with him as his secretary and companion for the Confederate cause. In February 1887 the *Washington Post* reported that the young woman was happily ensconced at Beauvoir, keeping "busy with her studies and literary work and helpful to her father in what historic research he may undertake." "Miss Davis's life is as different as possible from that of a 'society girl' of the period," the paper declared.[25]

Despite her seeming engagement in literary and historical pursuits, Winnie shared her father's predisposition for frailty in the face of major life events. The stress of keeping her romance under wraps while working hard to help preserve the family legacy made her physically ill, and she began to waste away, not eating or sleeping well. Her mother worried terribly about Winnie and hoped to build up her strength over the summer. Varina wrote that her daughter was "a shadow of her former self—thin to the point of attenuation and so weak a little drive tires her."[26]

Varina promised to send Winnie to Kate Pulitzer in Bar Harbor, Maine, for a restorative visit. She begged her distant cousin's pardon for the state of Winnie's wardrobe, which was always minimal due to the depleted state of the Davises' finances. "I hope you have considered in inviting Winnie that her wardrobe is increasingly very simple and made up your mind to take her as she is. This of course, you have done, but I hope your friends will too."[27]

Despite such distractions, Winnie and Fred continued to correspond surreptitiously. Things could not continue for long in this mode, so Fred began to prepare for his most important case to date: the request for the hand in marriage of Jefferson Davis's youngest, cherished daughter.

Although sickly, Winnie still made the social rounds that summer, first visiting with Kate Pulitzer and her children at their rented house on Mount Desert Island in Maine that June.[28] Later she accompanied her parents' friend and Confederate comrade Gen. Jubal Early and his family to a restorative spa in Virginia, where she spent the rest of the summer attempting to regain her health. The young woman returned home to Beauvoir feeling better in late August.[29]

Winnie had barely unpacked her bags from the spa when Fred arrived on Beauvoir's doorstep in September 1888 to ask for his beloved's hand in marriage.[30] Varina and Jefferson were completely unprepared for this encounter. Jefferson was not even at home at the time. Winnie had done such a good job of keeping her true feelings hidden from her parents that neither one of them had realized the depth of the attachment that had apparently formed between the couple.

Varina recalled that Fred was extremely agitated and nervous when he first arrived at Beauvoir and declared the purpose of his mission to her. Despite his apparent anxiety, Varina was immediately struck by Fred's dark good looks. In a letter to her good friend Major Morgan, she appraised Fred favorably, noting, "Not enough nose, but enough chin, lithe and energetic & had fine teeth & small feet and hands & as tender and boyish a heart as I ever saw & a very good mind as well as exquisite manners."[31] Varina continued: "He came having announced he could no longer be put off . . . I determined my consent never should be given to union with a Yankee—he urged the condition of health into which she [Winnie] had fallen, his great love—his patient waiting & forlorn hope."[32]

Shaking with emotion, Winnie fled to her room awaiting the no she felt almost certain would come from her parents. Varina noted that Winnie was "as white as death, after saying she could never love anyone else, but would give him up if I wished it."[33] Even in the throes of an epic love affair, Winnie was still deferential to her elders. The approval of her parents was crucial: she was not the type who would ever have married without their consent.

Jefferson, unlike his daughter, displayed no such qualms when he wed his first wife, Sarah Knox-Taylor, despite extreme disapproval from Sarah's father, Zachary, who forbade the match for several years. Even when Jefferson and Sarah finally did get married, neither of her parents attended the ceremony. Varina Davis herself was so deeply in love with Jefferson upon her own marriage to him that it is doubtful she would ever have given him up, even if her parents had objected. The adult Winnie was a people-pleaser, something neither of her parents could ever claim to be. This pronounced trait in Winnie would affect both her physical and mental health greatly in the months to come.

Varina claimed in her letter to Major Morgan that when she broke the news of Fred's plea to her husband, "he was cool and resolved—'Death would be preferable said he—I will never consent.'"[34] Later historians would claim Jefferson never said such a thing, but the initial sense of rebuff was there.[35] Despite Jefferson's immediate refusal of Fred's proposal, he seemed to like the young man. At least he did not send Fred away immediately or toss him violently out of the house.

How must the young couple have felt after this emotionally charged confrontation? It is doubtful they spent any time alone together. They may have dined together, however, perhaps in tense silence, with longing looks between them. Winnie would have been pale, thin, and exhausted, Fred agitated and upset. Varina and Jefferson were undoubtedly shocked and perhaps angry with both Winnie and Fred for having been taken so off guard by the proposal.

Yet something magical happened the night that Fred arrived at Beauvoir. The grandson of a northern abolitionist somehow engaged Jefferson Davis, past president of the Confederacy. Some kind of alchemy was forced into existence by the old man's love for his youngest daughter and his concern for her well-being. Fred's lawyerly ability to negotiate a deal may have also come into play. In any case everyone involved in this drama must have retired feeling emotionally spent that evening.

The next morning Varina related to Major Morgan, "To our profound astonishment the next day Mr. Davis invited him to go up to Brierfield in Oct. next—and then the next day Mr. Davis invited him to go down to the bath house to watch the flounders, a liberty never accorded to any other young man."[36] Very quickly, "Fred had won Jefferson Davis's attention, if not his total approval."[37]

It is interesting to note that Varina took on a traditionally male role during Alfred's visit and in subsequent other meetings with him. It was she and not Jefferson who talked to him about Winnie's lack of dowry or practical skills. Varina was also the one who asked for a frank estimate of his financial situation.[38]

Fred assured Varina he had taken care of his mother and sisters after his father had lost his fortune. He also confided to her that a recent favorable lawsuit had resulted in eighty thousand dollars for his mother; these monies would also help fund the marriage with his new bride. The young lawyer also claimed "his law practice was thriving and that money was no problem . . . He has already achieved some renown through his successful litigation against the General Electric Company over patents for sockets for incandescent lamps. His clients included many of the large businesses in central New York."[39]

There were, however, some skeletons lurking in the Wilkinson family's proverbial closet. Although it is highly possible that Winnie had heard a bit about Fred's family during her visits to Syracuse, Varina and Jefferson were not aware at this point about the local gossip regarding Fred's father. Details of the "Wilkinson affair" were well known among the upper-crust Syracuse set, and it is almost certain that the Emorys were aware of the scandal as well.

Fred's father, Alfred Sr., had inherited a fortune from his father, John Wilkinson, the first postmaster general of Syracuse and the former president of the Syracuse and Utica Railroad. Alfred Sr. himself had enjoyed an illustrious banking career, even earning a seat on the New York Stock Exchange. He was also an influential player in Democratic political circles of the time.[40] Fred and his siblings had grown up wealthy, with every comfort, as a result.

But the substantial Wilkinson family fortune was lost, and the family's reputation was tarnished following the failure of Fred's father's banking and investment firm, Wilkinson Brothers, in 1884. Alfred Sr. and his brother Forman were charged with grand larceny. According to Louisa May Alcott's biographer Eve LaPlante, "The Wilkinsons had swindled more than half a million dollars, creating a 'sensation in the city, as it had been supposed their high social standing would protect them' from prosecution."[41]

Fred, along with his mother, Charlotte, his brother, and his four sisters, spent the next decade trying to recover both their former lifestyle and the family's good name. Charlotte was forced to open a boarding school for girls in her home to support the family, while her husband descended into an alcoholic haze. Mrs. Wilkinson had to lock up the family silver to prevent Alfred Sr. from selling it for drink.[42]

Alfred Sr. never went to prison, probably because of his political connections. When he finally died, on July 28, 1886, Charlotte's famous cousin, the writer Louisa May Alcott, wrote in her diary: "A. Wilkinson dead. Relief to all."[43] His father's death and the scandal surrounding him must have greatly impacted Fred. Fortunately, according to Joan Cashin, Varina's biographer, "no one accused Alfred Jr. of misconduct, and he does not seem to have known what his elders were doing."[44] Fred was able to attend Harvard University thanks to the help of his cousin Louisa May. The author also generously paid for Fred's sisters, Charlotte and Katherine, to attend Smith College.[45] After graduation Fred returned home to Syracuse to study law.

When the young man arrived at Beauvoir to ask for Winnie's hand, the banking scandal was unknown to the Davis family. Jefferson and Varina's main objection to Fred was simply a matter of his having been born in the wrong geographic region. In Varina's letter to Major Morgan she notes Alfred's insistence that, as he put it, "I am a States' rights democrat and had nothing to do with the war & he must see that, I could not help being born a Yankee."[46] Varina took the precaution of telling Major Morgan to burn the letter upon reading it (which he clearly did not do) and not to tell a soul about the engagement: "Winnie's affair is to be a dead secret, no one knows but you, not even Maggie."[47]

Jefferson acquiesced to the engagement relatively quickly. To everyone's great surprise, within a few months a wedding date was set for the next winter.[48] Winnie was thrilled, as was Fred, and all seemed to be moving along splendidly. In Syracuse the event was optimistically heralded as the solution for sectional issues caused by the war. "This union will obliterate the last vestige of animosity between North and South," declared the *Syracuse Standard* on April 17, 1890.[49]

Fred and Winnie's romance was perfectly in tune with the times. In the 1880s and 1890s a "culture of reconciliation" began to blossom between North and South. Plays, tableaux, novels, and songs heralded the rejoining of hands between the two regions. Popular playwright Augustus Thomas offered audiences dramatic interpretations emphasizing the sentimental story of love between a southern girl and a northern man, at first separated by war but eventually brought back together, much to the audience's delight.[50] The surface atmosphere and popular culture at the end of the nineteenth century seemed ready to embrace such a union.

Yet resentment and rebellion still seethed under the facade of southern politesse. The theater crowd might weep empathetically at scenarios of romantic reconciliation between North and South. But in reality many circumstances and events beyond Winnie and Fred's control were conspiring against them: Fred's northern birth, his abolitionist heritage, and his family's financial scandal and ruin. Winnie's family lineage was completely at odds with that of her fiancé and sure to turn heads both North and South when the news was announced.

The Daughter of the Confederacy desperately wanted her parents' approval for the match; her physical and mental health depended on it. The couple was most certainly deeply in love and well matched both intellectually and socioeconomically. But serious obstacles lay in their path, many of them still unforeseen.

CHAPTER TWELVE

Engagement Issues

One would expect much rejoicing in both the Davis and Wilkinson households after Jefferson Davis, former president of the Confederacy, gave his consent for his adored youngest daughter to wed her gallant northern beau sometime in the winter of 1889. In the weeks after the private betrothal, the happy news was announced only to close friends and family of the couple.

Winnie was radiantly happy—at first. She soon realized, however, the distaste with which many of her southern friends viewed the match.[1] Winnie had managed to wear down the resistance of her parents by appealing to their fears for her mental health and well-being. "Friends" of the family, including Gen. Jubal Early, were not so sympathetic.

Many members of the Davises' southern coterie were more concerned that Winnie's image as the Daughter of the Confederacy remain untarnished than that she obtain personal happiness and domestic bliss. If Winnie married a northerner, especially one with such an abolitionist heritage, many felt that the union would negate the sacrifices made by so many southern women and men both during and after the war. The Davis family began receiving threatening letters regarding the engagement.[2] Upset by the negative response of family, friends, and the southern community, Winnie, following a familiar pattern, again commenced a spiral of emotional and physical decline.

Although the outcry concerning Fred and Winnie's romance may seem melodramatic to some, the situation brought barely suppressed southern hostility toward the North to a head. The significance of the controversy lies in the fierce state of emotions the young couple unwittingly revealed. Even in 1889, more than two decades after the war had ended, the scars of battle were yet to heal in the South. Southern feelings of resentment simmered under a facade of southern gentility.

Southern men in particular objected to the proposed union. What would Winnie's marriage to a northerner, after all her presentations and representations as the perfect southern woman at Confederate veterans' reunions, say about their manhood? Her engagement was seen as an outright rejection of all the men of the South had to offer her. Indeed, it was seen as a denial of southern culture and Confederate heritage.

Moreover, if the Daughter of the Confederacy chose a northerner whose forebears were Abolitionists as her groom, what was to stop other women from following her lead? Southern men felt threatened and humiliated by the idea that southern females might choose their northern conquerors for husbands instead of men from their own communities.[3] In the eyes of many southerners, Winnie's marriage to a New Yorker would be tantamount to treason.

Why the Davises' youngest daughter would stray from the ranks of eligible southern bluebloods when choosing a husband was unimaginable to many southerners of the era. Even Varina herself indicated that a marital alliance with an aristocratic young man from New Orleans would be most desirable for her youngest child.[4] Winnie's choice was most unexpected for the girl known publicly as the Daughter of the Confederacy. But considering the interests and background of the private Winnie, Fred was not a surprising choice at all. He was perfect for her and she for him.

Despite the couple's clear compatibility, they faced serious opposition to the match. Fred for his part was totally bewildered by southern reactions to their proposed union. He had followed Victorian engagement protocol to the letter. He had proposed to Winnie, and she had accepted. He had then approached her father for his approval. All the courting rituals of the day had been followed, and Fred was deeply in love with his fiancée.

Although Fred had waited longer than most men of his generation to marry, once he proposed, his commitment to Winnie never wavered. He was a solid, kind, and thoughtful man whose common sense and calm demeanor could help stabilize Winnie's nervous tendencies. But all accepted traditions and practices for an 1890s engagement quickly flew out the window. Typically, at this juncture, affianced American couples would each send out formal marriage announcements. The young fiancée would then retire from public life until her wedding day.[5] This expected scenario did not occur.

The realization that the engagement was eliciting not jubilation but consternation was slowly dawning on Varina, Jefferson, and Winnie. For some reason neither Varina nor Winnie, nor even Jefferson, seemed to have anticipated the negative reactions they began to receive. Their lack of concern was odd considering the vehement hatred of the North that still consumed so many of their southern friends.

Winnie's health, always delicate, had been declining for months, if not years. The *New York Times* claimed on October 20, 1889, that "for the past year, or in fact, since she made her tour of the Northern States, Miss Davis has not been in good health. Her eyesight troubles her seriously, and she suffers from constant pain in her side."[6] Winnie's ocular problems, which also seemed to develop in early adulthood, were often blamed on her secretarial work for her father.

Gastrointestinal problems also plagued Winnie from her twenties onward; there are numerous mentions of her stomach ailments beginning in 1883. In a letter to family friend Jubal Early in May of that year, Varina declined a trip to Virginia on Winnie's behalf due to her daughter's "New Orleans gastritis."[7] Varina remarked in the letter that Winnie "is not a robust girl and sorely needs rest."[8] Any kind of stress seemed to exacerbate the young woman's underlying health problems.

Varina also attributed her youngest daughter's health issues partially to the hot, humid climate so prevalent at Beauvoir. Varina wrote to her good friend Constance Cary Harrison that "Winnie is at Beauvoir in bad health, poor child she hardly gets her boxes unpacked on the Gulf Shore before the climate makes her ill."[9] Conversely, Varina blamed Winnie's "respiratory ills on the poor heating from the porcelain stoves in Germany."[10]

No recorded documentation has been found with Winnie's firm medical diagnosis. It seems evident, however, that the young woman's symptoms, which manifested as physical ailments, often had their root cause in mental strain and her approval-oriented personality. Winnie likely had, according to the primitive psychiatric terms of the day, a vague and all-encompassing condition labeled "neurasthenia," a state of exhaustion of the nervous system.[11] Known as a "period disease," the term *neurasthenia* had been introduced by New York neurologist Dr. George Beard in 1869.[12]

This popular physician and his followers claimed that nervous disorders were becoming more and more common due to the industrialization and urbanization of post–Civil War America.[13] Well-educated, upper-class white women such as Winnie were particularly susceptible. During this time women began to flock to urban centers for work. They consequently began to spend more and more time in public, unchaperoned.[14] Young women like Winnie were becoming more involved in paid work such as secretarial jobs, writing, or artistic projects.

Winnie's real-life neurasthenic drama just slightly prefigured the plight of the heroines of both Charlotte Perkins Gilman's short story *The Yellow Wallpaper* (1892) and Kate Chopin's novella *The Awakening* (1899). In both stories the female protagonists are driven mad by enforced rest cures for their supposed mental illnesses. In both tales paternalistic marriages keep them from pursuing artistic fulfillment.[15]

The Daughter of the Confederacy's underlying tendency toward neurasthenia might have also been coupled with another nineteenth-century "illness" brought on by her romance with Fred. *Excess of passion* was a melodramatic term coined by an 1883 doctor, who, according to Melinda Beck in the *Wall Street Journal*, described the condition as such: "The passions are like burning coals tossed into the dwelling of life, or serpents that spit poison into the vessels."[16] Winnie's intense romance plus her strenuous literary work for her father were apparently sucking the life out of her fragile frame.

What was the cure for such dire diagnoses? Enforced rest for the victim, preferably abroad in luxurious European resorts. As a result of Winnie's continuing poor health and the alarmed reaction of their southern friends to her Yankee romance, the Davises shipped their fragile daughter off to Europe with her good friends Kate and Joseph Pulitzer.[17] Her January 1889 trip to Europe was completely paid for by the Pulitzers, and it was their generous attempt to shield Winnie from the mounting engagement controversy.

The stricken young woman certainly had a sympathetic audience. Both the Pulitzers were urging Winnie to marry Fred "in spite of Confederate sentiments."[18] They had a progressive view of such things bred from Joseph's background as a self-made man and their frequent travels around the globe. Winnie set sail first to Paris, where she was to spend some time shopping for her wedding trousseau. Fred was to meet her in Italy in early 1890. Varina hoped Fred would press his suit with Winnie and return home with a firm date for the marriage.

This was a particularly stressful time for both halves of this young, attractive couple. Both Winnie and Fred were under enormous pressure to restore their families' broken reputations, Fred with his father's scandalous financial problems and Winnie with her own father's failed bid for southern independence. The two young people may have felt they had to be perfect, make the "right" choices, and play their cards correctly in order to redeem their family fortunes and reputations.

Each dealt with these pressures in an entirely different manner. Fred was optimistic about his future. Things were going well for him financially, and he was prepared to risk southern disapproval and make Winnie his bride. He was confident and sure of himself—his litigation background had prepared him for such challenges. Unlike her fiancé, however, Winnie's faith in true love was beginning to waver. Even as a child, she tended to be crushed by any disapproval from authority figures. Despite the support of her northern friends such as the Pulitzers, the southern reaction to her engagement was slowly beginning to poison her feelings about the match.

Had she made a terrible mistake? Was Fred really the one for her? Winnie's resolve about marrying her northern beau began to weaken as she realized how disappointed fellow southerners, particularly her parents' set, were in her controversial choice. After all, many of them (including her own mother) had suggested there were plenty of eligible bachelors in the South for her to pick from—why was she looking up North for a husband?

Many of her Confederate veteran friends were beside themselves with rage. Winnie regularly questioned her own judgment and undoubtedly did so at this juncture. As she set sail for Europe that fall, she must have hoped that the brisk sea air would clear her head and help her to make up her mind.

CHAPTER THIRTEEN

Italian Idyll

When Winnie and the Pulitzers arrived in Paris in October 1889, she and her host Joseph were both semi-invalids. The atmosphere was that of a convalescent ward. Winnie and Joseph both suffered from eye and stomach problems.[1] In both individuals stress and anxiety seemed to exacerbate, if not cause, their physical symptoms.

Despite her illness, Winnie was willing to participate in the cultural delights that Paris had to offer. Socialite Kate enjoyed coordinating their activities and shepherding Winnie and the children to glittering events such as an evening performance at the Paris Opera. Winnie wrote her father on December 5, 1889, from the Pulitzers' rented home on the Rue Courcelles in Paris about taking Kate's eldest son Ralph Pulitzer to the show: "The other night Kate and I took Ralph to the opera, and you should have seen the grandeur of that little fellow with his miniature beaver and dress suit! He opened the box with an air, and altogether behaved like the fine little gentleman he is."[2]

In her letter Winnie told her father of her concerns for his health. She had learned recently that he had fallen ill on a November visit from New Orleans to his plantation Brierfield in Mississippi. The young woman adored him, and she had departed for Europe nearly oblivious to his increasing frailty. Jefferson and Varina deliberately led Winnie to believe that her father's health was continually improving. Jefferson did not want to alarm his daughter, given her own fragile physical and mental state, and he wished for her to go ahead with her European trip.

Winnie continued her letter on a more serious note. "I am broken-hearted to think that you could have had bronchitis and I have been away off here. Had I known, or had any idea of what was the matter, I should have come home immediately, but from the telegrams I concluded it was one of those exaggerated reports so often in the newspapers about prominent men."[3] Jefferson Davis died on December 6, 1889, in New Orleans, just a few hours after this letter was written, and never saw his daughter's last words to him.

Upon reading the awful news, in the papers and probably by telegram, Winnie was, according to the *Middleton Daily Press* back in the States, "beside herself with grief. But she bore up bravely."[4] The same newspaper article noted that the Daughter of the Confederacy, still in Paris, had widespread support from those in the French community: "During the afternoon and evening, a great number of people called to leave cards and condolence in evidence of their sympathy with her under the great bereavement."[5]

All the sources agree that Winnie's doctors in Paris urged her not to make the trip home for the funeral due to her feeble physical state. Her mother agreed and would not allow her to make the long sea voyage home for the funeral. Even before his death, Jefferson forbade Varina from urging either Margaret or Winnie to come to his sickbed in New Orleans.[6] Racked with grief and guilt over her father's death and her failure to be by his side during his last illness, Winnie began an even more precipitous physical and mental decline.

A few months after her father's death, Winnie was still struggling to control her emotions. She became uncharacteristically angry with her mother for insisting that Fred come over to visit her in Europe. Varina told her friend Maj. W. H. Morgan on March 9, 1890: "There is no news of Fred and Winnie except a sharp letter from her which I do not think she knew was sharp reproving me for letting or advising Fred to go abroad and jeopardize his prospects."[7] Winnie did have a valid point, as her mother was constantly worrying about Fred's financial situation yet had urged him to take several months off to vacation with her daughter abroad.

Varina had asked Fred to go to Europe in the late winter of 1890 to check on Winnie's fragile emotional and physical state. The letters Varina received from Winnie seemed to indicate that her youngest daughter was deeply depressed and in the midst of a nervous breakdown. Varina had another motive for sending Fred to see Winnie. After months of keeping the engagement mostly a secret, and temporarily on hold, she wanted Winnie to set a firm date for the marriage and hoped that Fred could persuade her. By the time Fred arrived in Naples, Italy, in late

February 1890, Winnie was unsure she wished to continue the engagement, although her mother was urging her to move ahead with wedding plans.[8] The emotional trauma of her father's unexpected death, coupled with the experience of being away from Fred for long periods, had created a chilly distance between the young woman and her fiancé. For Winnie absence seemed to have made her heart grow colder and more fearful of commitment.

The letters contained in the *Jefferson Davis Papers*, housed in the Library of Congress, give historians significant insights into the minds of the three principle players in this drama: Winnie, Fred, and Varina. The letters from Fred and Varina in particular help decipher the situation somewhat. Very few of Winnie's letters from the time of her courtship and 1889–90 stay in Europe survive. It is very likely that Varina destroyed most of the couple's correspondence—a typical practice of this era, as women's personal letters were seen as private family documents, too personal to be kept for posterity. Much of what Winnie thought about Fred and the engagement therefore remains a mystery.

From the letters that do survive, it seems that the possible husband and mother-in-law were locked in a power struggle over the reluctant bride-to-be. Fred, for his role, acted in a paternal manner toward the now fatherless young woman. He tended to cosset and indulge her. Varina displayed the behavior of a meddling mother-in-law, even though no marriage had yet taken place.

Despite all the bickering back and forth across the Atlantic, Winnie did seem genuinely glad to see Fred when he arrived in Naples. She reported to her mother soon after her fiancé arrived that "Fred is here and as dear an old goose as ever."[9] The couple and the Pulitzers all stayed at the famous Grand Hotel in Naples, described by travelers of the era as "a luxurious five-story building on the bay whose shuttered windows looked out on Mount Vesuvius, the Castel dell'Ovo, and the bustling city that smelled of the sea."[10] Still, Winnie would not or could not commit herself to a firm wedding date, which greatly troubled Varina. Fred took a much more cautious and long-term approach in dealing with his troubled paramour.

Was Winnie's anxious state simply due to stress, or were there more serious issues at play? Certain letters that passed between Fred, Varina, and Major Morgan have been used to support the idea that Winnie was pregnant when she sailed for Europe. Before Fred journeyed to Italy to see Winnie, for instance, Varina wrote her friend Major Morgan an urgent letter asking him to meet with her. She claimed Winnie was in some sort of "trouble."[11]

More intimations of a possible pregnancy may be read into Fred's letter of March 4, 1890, to Varina, written after he arrived in Italy. He confided in her that "the more that I think about it the more impossible it seems to me to live without seeing her often, particularly now that I know about her physical condition and how more than ever she *turns to me in everything*."[12] The urgent tone of the letter certainly might suggest that Winnie and Fred had a secret that bound them tightly together. It also shows Fred attempting to assert his authority over Varina and perhaps to draw a line between them and her attempted meddling in the couple's romance.

It is curious that the Davises would let their daughter travel abroad with her fiancé under only the loose supervision of friends. Such a trip would not have reflected well on Winnie's image as a virginal, Confederate icon. The Victorian period, lasting from the mid-1830s to the beginning of the twentieth century, is famed for its excessive attention to rules and regulations concerning courting couples. European customs in particular mandated chaperones for all unmarried women when dating young men.

Winnie and Fred's trip violated all the rules of Victorian courting etiquette. They were often alone on the trip, particularly when they went on excursions to distant ruins in the Italian countryside. In this era etiquette experts insisted that "no young lady should consider driving alone with her fiancé or attending the theater alone with him. A chaperone must be present at all times."[13]

The 1890s did mark the beginning of women's rebellions against such formalities as chaperones, but it is noteworthy that Winnie, Daughter of the Confederacy and daughter of one of the most conservative men in the South when it came to women's roles, was allowed to flout established rules of conduct on her own, largely unsupervised trip abroad.

Illegitimate pregnancies were not without precedent in the Howell and Davis families. Margaret Howell, Varina's flirtatious sister, had a son, Philip, out of wedlock, and Jefferson Davis's brother Joseph had several illegitimate children.[14] Such occurrences were shocking but certainly not unheard of even in upper-class Victorian families.

Joseph Pulitzer, one of Winnie's hosts, was practically blind at this point and completely absent at various points on the trip. Because of his many both real and imaginary ailments, writes biographer James McGrath Morris, "Joseph wandered the globe in the company of secretaries, doctors and valets, while Kate led a busy social life in Paris, London, and New York."[15] Thus, Kate and Winnie were destined to spend great amounts of time together in the 1880s and 1890s due to Joseph's peripatetic lifestyle. The eccentric newspaper baron spent most of his time on his various yachts, tending to business with his secretaries while searching for health cures. Kate was a sophisticated and worldly woman who would later conduct an extramarital affair.[16] She was more of a companion and confidante to Winnie than a chaperone.

Winnie and Fred's largely unsupervised Italian holiday was without a doubt highly unusual for this era. With so much mistrust of Fred and his background bubbling at home, the situation seems all the more remarkable. What must Varina have been thinking by allowing her beloved daughter to vacation in Europe with her controversial fiancé? Perhaps Jefferson's ill health and subsequent death had distracted them from their usual worries about how things might look to the southern public, which they all, willingly or unwillingly, represented.

Varina trusted Winnie implicitly, and she must have convinced herself that her youngest daughter had the judgment and maturity to handle herself in the correct manner. Europe was also far enough away from the southern United States that she would have a measure of privacy there that she did not have at home. There were no instant communication networks to report on her activities, illicit or otherwise.

Still, the question remains. Despite every opportunity to be alone with her beau, in an exotic setting far from her parents and the American press, did Winnie and Fred give in to temptation? The young couple certainly had more than one opportunity to sleep with each other. Despite suggestions that Winnie had become pregnant, it seems doubtful that a physical consummation of their relationship ever occurred.

Evidence suggests that Jefferson and Varina's youngest daughter was far too approval oriented, rule conscious, and nervous around men to have risked having premarital sex with Fred. The idea that she was pregnant and had to go away to have her baby does not fit her customary, and well-documented, behavior. She was no wild child like her aunt

Margaret, whose nonconformist behavior had been a great source of worry for Varina for many years before Margaret indeed became pregnant out of wedlock. Nor was she lord and master of a large plantation like her uncle Joseph, who was in a position to do as he pleased, producing several illegitimate offspring.

A Davis family friend noted cryptically years later that Winnie's "soul brought a secret into the world; it carried it out. None ever guessed it."[17] While this quote has been used in the past as support for Winnie's supposed secret pregnancy, it is far more likely that the family "secret" was a marked tendency toward anxiety and depression, the pattern of which Winnie inherited from her father. Varina's bouts of depression seemed to be more reactive, while Jefferson's depressive states, like Winnie's (and her sister Margaret's melancholy), seemed endemic. Winnie's neurasthenic complaints were most likely a type of "masked depression," a depressed state that manifests itself first as a physical ailment.[18]

Winnie was not a slavish follower of fashion, gossip, or trends. She was a sweet but serious personality unconcerned with the vagaries of style. Yet in one respect she was in lockstep with the prevailing winds of the "nervous century," as the nineteenth century later came to be known. Stomachaches, headaches, sore throats, eye troubles—they all seemed to prevent her at times from attending social events and enjoying her life as a young, attractive, and popular young woman. This so-called neurasthenia, like depression and anxiety-related illnesses in our contemporary society, created major relationship problems for Winnie and prevented her from forming any real long-term commitments or intimacies with the opposite sex.

A letter from Winnie, written to her family friend Major Morgan in March 1890, reflects her deep and persistent gloom. "As for myself," she said, regarding her time in Italy, "I have very little joy in anything."[19] Fred was now able to observe his fiancée's behavior up close. Was Winnie just recovering from a reactive bout of the blues following her beloved father's untimely death, or was there something more sinister affecting her moods and her health?

The young Syracusian may also have had his doubts about the situation. Although he steadfastly clung to the notion that the two would be married, hopefully sooner rather than later—he had already courted Winnie for almost four years—he must have seen Winnie's confusion, her hesitation, and her anxiety over the match. She often seemed to doubt his love and was beginning to mistrust him. He needed to convince her to leave both her anxiety and depression and her persona as the Daughter of the Confederacy behind in Europe. Otherwise, their chance for mutual happiness might be doomed.

CHAPTER FOURTEEN

Dear Diary

To my beloved Mother, with the hope that the love, by the light of which these pages were inscribed, may blind her a little to their numerous imperfections.

Varina Anne Davis to Varina Howell Davis, January 29, 1890

Winnie's European travel journal from January 29 to April 3, 1890, resurfaced in 2010. The Museum of the Confederacy in Richmond, Virginia, was able to obtain the diary at auction through a third party. The item had long been in the possession of a distant branch of the Davis family living in New England.[1] This 8" x 5½" leather-bound volume has a locking clasp and is 242 pages long, full of the young woman's insights and comments.

The volume is dedicated to Winnie's mother, Varina, who her daughter felt would probably never be able to venture abroad again due to her advancing age and poor health. There is, surprisingly, not a single reference to Jefferson Davis in the diary.[2] Perhaps Winnie was so traumatized by his recent death that she could not bear to even mention her father's name. Or perhaps she felt guilty about her unchaperoned time with Fred in Italy and wanted to keep it entirely separate from thoughts of her father. This image conflicts with the role of the dutiful daughter she played so often at home.

Winnie's diary entries vividly describe the high life she experienced as part of a wealthy American traveling group. At the beginning of the tour Winnie admired her traveling companion Kate Pulitzer's glamorous ensemble: "Kate is in pink tonight with all her diamonds on."[3] Famous personalities of the day appear throughout the journal, including Buffalo Bill and his entourage,[4] and the infamous society portraitist and playboy Carolus-Duran. One of Winnie's very first entries describes an encounter between Carolus-Duran and Kate Pulitzer, who had engaged Carolus-Duran to paint her portrait: "Carolus Duran came to see Kate this morning and whisked her off to have a dress made according to his taste at Worth's shop. [Worth was one of the premier Parisian couture houses of the era.] He is a handsome man, but always in his own French type."[5]

Winnie's writing gives the modern reader a rare window into upper-class Victorian society and tourism of the day. The volume was ostensibly written for the purpose of keeping her mother up to date about her experiences, so we do not gain access to Winnie's innermost feelings. Yet glimpses of a conflicted and at times distraught young woman who could not make up her mind between love and duty still peek through the heavy Victorian prose. Despite the unusual circumstances of the trip and the angst that Winnie was so clearly experiencing, she seemed thrilled when her fiancé finally arrived in Naples in late February 1890. The stage seemed set for a romantic and picturesque idyll in the Italian countryside à la E. M. Forster's famous English novel *Room with a View* (1908).

Museum of the Confederacy historian John Coski observed that the travel journal commentary shows that Winnie and Fred quibbled and quarreled with each other affectionately, "just like an old married couple. They talk about health issues, going out to tour versus staying in."[6] Winnie noted that Fred often brought her flowers, such as violets and forget-me-nots, during their outings.[7] They attended the ballet and the opera, visited art museums, shopped, and enjoyed long carriage rides together. Winnie's enthusiastic journal descriptions seem to indicate her pleasure in such excursions.

On March 4 Winnie openly describes her unchaperoned excursions with Fred to her mother. Unbelievably, she mentions an outing in which they specifically go out driving together in a "closed carriage" alone.[8] It is as if they were a married couple and not a courting one. Winnie knew her mother was desperate for her to marry Fred. Perhaps she was testing the limits of her freedom by telling her mother this detail?

Once the couple settled into a regular routine, however, Fred quickly began to notice Winnie's profound melancholy. In a letter to Varina from February 1890, he noted with concern, "Physically, she is decidedly better, but mentally she has some depressed days, almost anyone else I should call morbid."[9] Fred's diagnosis seems to ring true when compared to one of Winnie's journal entries from that time. The couple visited Naples and saw Vesuvius in the background under a full moon. This sight enthralled Winnie with its savage beauty. Yet her reaction was mixed: "I had another look at all this beauty which I pray I may never forget if I live to—well, if I live a long life which I can't say I desire as I used to . . . I hope I shall not be left like some frightful survivor to linger here when my generation has passed away; it would be far better to go out like that moon than to burn forever like Vesuvius."[10]

One imagines that a woman of any era would have been delighted to have the freedom to tour Italy unrestricted on an all-expense trip with her handsome Harvard-educated fiancé. Fred was completely devoted to Winnie; she was insulated from the American South and its gossip both by distance and by the Pulitzers' wealth. Varina had urged Fred to join Winnie in Italy—both to help seal the marriage deal and to uplift her spirits. But she still seemed unable fully to enjoy the pleasures that lay in front of her. Melancholy hung on Winnie like a shroud. This can be attributed in part to her neurasthenic tendencies and also as a normal response to Jefferson's recent death.

By early March, Fred was writing to Maj. W. H. Morgan, a Davis family friend who was sympathetic to the young couple and their engagement. Fred confided many of his fears regarding Winnie's melancholy to Morgan and expressed concern about pushing the engagement too hard upon her, as Varina had been urging him to do. "I shall let her wait as long as she wishes," declared Fred in a March 1 letter from Naples to Morgan. He wrote also that he understood how much the disapproval of her friends upset her. "You know that she longs all the time to have her friends love her."[11]

Fred was coming to terms with the desperate need for approval that was so deeply ingrained in Winnie's character. This was a legacy both from her parents and from her time under the roof of the strict Misses Friedlanders' school in Karlsruhe, Germany. In a March 4 letter to Varina, Fred acknowledged the depth and breadth of Winnie's despair: "I must tell you, that while I am not much discouraged about her, I am just beginning to wake to the fact of the care that must given to her the next year."[12] The reality of the situation was setting in for Fred as well. He surely must have wondered if he could take care of Winnie, a semi-invalid at this point, adequately.

In his letter to Varina, Fred noted that Winnie was becoming worried that he was not fully disclosing his business affairs to her—a worry Varina had surely planted in her mind. "The least little thing starts her off," wrote Fred. "For instance yesterday she asked me a question about my business because I hesitated a few seconds before answering, she thought I was trying to deceive her and of course it took an hour to quiet her."[13]

As their Italian vacation neared its conclusion, however, Winnie's spirits seemed to improve. She, Fred, and the Pulitzers had an exciting, though somewhat dangerous, visit to Mount Vesuvius. Fred once again proved to be Winnie's valiant champion. Winnie wrote about their adventure: "By this time I had so much been touched by the volcano fever, that nothing else would do but I most go to the top of the new crater . . . We waited until the smoke flag showed that the wind was blowing from our side . . . the breeze suddenly turned the whole volume of shifting fumes and the rain of red hot stones in our direction."[14]

The young woman continued her tale, noting the sartorial loss by her fashionable female companion: "One fell on my neck burning my veil in two before Fred could knock it off . . . with my hat over one eye, my dress torn and my boots destroyed . . . noticing the strong smell of burnt feathers, looked around to see [Kate] contemplating the ruin of her fine feather boa . . . It had been such an exciting day that none of us wanted to go home."[15]

For a young woman who had just avoided a potentially fatal accident, Winnie's report of the incident shows no fear or regret. She seems to shrug it off and view it in an almost romantic sense. Her sense of adventure and enjoyment of foreign travel and unique experiences seem evident. Fred had once again demonstrated his devotion to her at Vesuvius. He had given up months of income from his law practice to come see her and take care of her; he dutifully reported her condition to her mother and to Major Morgan. Despite Winnie's clear melancholy, he did not run away; he still wanted to marry her. He had seen her at her worst, but he still did not falter in his affections. He had convinced himself that "a few quiet happy years will make her as well as she ever was."[16]

When it was time for Fred to sail home, in early April 1890, he insisted Winnie remain in Europe due to the frayed state of her nerves. He told Varina frankly before he left, "I will never consent to her staying in Beauvoir all summer."[17] There were certain "things" at the Davis home that would upset Winnie. Did he mean memories of her father or possibly her meddling mother herself?

Varina had pushed both her daughter and Fred to seal the marriage deal, but she simultaneously seemed to be poisoning Winnie against Fred by planting worries in her mind about his finances. The micromanaging mother further diminished Fred's ability to produce income by insisting he take weeks off to make the long voyage to Europe to see his fiancée. None of this behavior on Varina's part made sense, nor did it smooth the way for Fred's marital suit with the Davises' youngest daughter, who was in such a precarious mental state.

Varina and Winnie were discussing the idea of going to Colorado Springs for the summer of 1890, both for the climate and to visit Winnie's older sister, Margaret Hayes. While he was in Italy with Winnie, Fred suggested some modifications to their travel plans. "If you carry out your plan of going to Colorado, she [Winnie] might come somewhere a few hundred miles nearer Syracuse, perhaps to Asheville. Once home from Europe, never again shall I let her stay so far from me that I can't get to her often, even if we can't be together all the time."[18] The young man was asserting his claim to his bride-to-be, something Varina did not like, despite the engagement and marriage she was pushing so hard. She still wanted to retain control of Winnie somehow. This push-pull between the mother and the fiancé is clear in the correspondence that survives.

Although he wanted Winnie to be close by him after her return from Europe, Fred told Varina of his decision not to press for a wedding date right away. "Feeling as she does right now," he wrote on March 4, 1890, "it would be cruel to talk to her of marriage before next winter. I don't agree with her but understand how she feels so."[19] The decision to stay apart after their European tour allowed Winnie time and space to think about the romance—perhaps too much. Fred's kindness and decision not to force her into marriage would also have a profound effect on their future together.

Winnie's travel journal ends April 3, 1890, when she was in Paris. All too soon, the Daughter of the Confederacy and her northern beau would return to the more restrictive, disapproving environment of the American South. Romantic and glamorous interludes such as the couple's trip to Italy would prove few and far between. Continued rumors of Fred's financial troubles—dug up by "friends" of Varina—and a tragic fire in Syracuse would profoundly affect the couple's future. The Mediterranean respite the couple had known would soon seem truly a world away.

CHAPTER FIFTEEN

A World on Fire

Fred returned home to Syracuse in April 1890, leaving his adored but uncertain fiancée abroad with the Pulitzers. The young couple was at a critical juncture in their relationship. Fred was deeply concerned about Winnie, but he needed to get back to work at his law practice. Since his father's banking scandal, the Wilkinson wealth and reputation had dissipated, and the young man's goal was to rebuild the family coffers. Fred had a mother and sisters who relied on him financially, and he could not afford to extend his European idyll any longer. Winnie was sure of nothing at this point and was fast losing her enthusiasm for the romance.

Varina, forceful as always, decided to take the couple's love life into her own hands. In April, shortly after Fred returned to the States, she publicly announced their engagement. National newspapers such as the *New York Times* quickly picked up the story.[1]

The engagement announcement was a huge tactical error, both from the standpoint of Winnie's faltering mental and physical health and from a public relations perspective. Winnie's meddling mother also went straight to the wrong person for support. Former Confederate general Jubal Early was a Davis family friend but was shortly to become Fred's most implacable enemy. Early became known after the war as the "Watchdog of the Confederacy," a guardian of Lost Cause ideals and mythology. The unmarried lawyer was also known to be proprietary with widows and daughters of Confederate generals. In his view they belonged to the South, and woe to any northerner who tried to spirit them away.[2]

Varina wrote a placating letter to Jubal on April 20, saying, "I have thought several times of telling you that Winnie was engaged to be married, and only been deterred by the doubt it might never take place."[3] Early's replies have not survived, but his attitude and later actions confirm that this news only further enraged the venomous general, who with like-minded cronies such as former Confederate general Lunsford Lomax, promptly set out to undo the engagement by any means possible.[4]

Then, too, there was the omnipresent press. Some northern papers seemed merely surprised by the announcement and mildly curious, treating the proposed match as if it were an amusing circus sideshow. A piece in the *Rochester Herald* in April 1890 declared, "Love perpetrates many freaks, but few are more curious than would be manifested in such a union."[5] But most papers outside the South thought the pairing a positive step toward reconciliation between old foes, with the South submitting willingly to the victorious North. The *Troy Times* proclaimed, "The proud 'daughter of the confederacy' has capitulated to the scion of abolitionism, and all the bitter memories of the past will fade before the sweet promises of the future."[6]

Not quite. The southern reaction to the news was devastating and swift. The announcement exploded in the press like a bomb.[7] Letters disparaging the engagement rapidly arrived at the Davis household with some regularity. Southerners were not just upset; they were completely outraged. Winnie's initial apprehensions began to seem justified in light of the furor that now erupted at home.

Alfred Wilkinson, who had nothing to do with the Civil War, became the scapegoat for all of the South's suffering. Confederate Veterans in particular channeled their rage against the bewildered young man. He represented their worst nightmare: that the women of the South would desert them for the victors of the North.

Although the Davis family received letters with threatening overtones concerning the engagement, Fred received direct threats against his life. One infamous letter from a veteran of the Robert E. Lee regiment read:

> I write you at the request of my comrades in arms '61 to '65 to say that the choice of the "Daughter of the Confederacy" is by no means approved by us. No, Sir, and should she bow our heads and crush our hearts in humiliation most damnable by marrying the offspring of an Abominable Abolitionist, she will have to go to some northern city of burg to do so. The very sleeping dead Southern soldiers would rise from their graves, and hustle you back to Yankeedom ere they would see the daughter of Jefferson Davis ruined, and shame-

> covered forever by marrying one whose only desire in marrying her is to get a Southern woman—preferring such and one with warm feelings to the Salamander-like girl of Yankeedom.
>
> No, Sir, a thousand balls would be shot into your Negro-loving heart ere we would permit such an humiliating outrage consummated in our own Southland—and even should Miss Winnie, whom we so deeply love as infinitely purer than any Yankee woman on earth, consent to go North, then we will bind ourselves together to lay you in the dust.[8]

Under such circumstances it is surprising that Fred wished to continue their relationship at all. Many suitors would have fled in the face of such heated sentiments.

The letter's reference to Fred's "Negro-loving heart" is telling. Although Fred had never expressed any strong political opinions at all, his lineage was damning evidence. He could not escape the well-known views and actions of his grandfather Samuel Joseph May, one of America's first and best-known abolitionists.

As a northerner, Fred was already classed by many southerners of the era in the same category as a black man when it came to marriage with a southern woman. He was an outsider, and southerners violently opposed the idea of such a union with Winnie, who was considered not only Jefferson Davis's daughter but also the symbolic daughter of the entire defeated South.

The engagement situation deteriorated still further in July. Winnie returned from Europe in the middle of the summer, terribly upset by all the menacing letters being sent to Fred and her family. Aside from facing southern death threats, Fred was also soon to be dealing with another serious matter on the home front in Syracuse.

Fred's mother's home in Syracuse was named Harperly Hall after the Wilkinson ancestral home in Yorkshire, England.[9] This stately mansion was located at fashionable 809 James Street. Before his death Alfred's father, Alfred Sr., surrounded the house with lush and extensive gardens much admired by those in the exclusive neighborhood.[10]

In a family memoir written by Fred's sister, Katharine May Wilkinson, she describes the summer of 1890 as one full of promise and expectation.

Fred had recently returned from his Italian adventure with Winnie and the Pulitzers, and their engagement had been announced in April. "They would be married perhaps in the fall, and Mama had bought in Philadelphia for the house they would have a handsome eighteenth century sofa, and also a mahogany desk and great sets of bedroom furniture."[11]

Fred's mother, Charlotte, and his sister Marion (known to the family as "Mal") had just left for a highly anticipated European tour, where they would attend the 1890 performance of the famous German Passion Play in Oberammergau. The other four sisters—Charlotte, Katharine, Josephine, and Louisa—had gone to Blue Mountain Lake in the Adirondacks to escape sweltering Syracuse for the humid months of July and August.[12]

Fred remained in town with his legal practice. Henry, or "Harry," Fred's younger brother, had just graduated from architecture school at Cornell. Life seemed finally to be in perfect order for the Wilkinson clan. Sadly, events were soon to take a tragic turn. Katharine noted in her memoirs, "The season that began with every prospect pleasing came to a violent end."[13]

Horror disrupted the James Street neighborhood on the hot, humid morning of July 22, 1890. Around ten thirty that morning, according to a newspaper account a month later, "a noise like the discharge of a cannon startled neighborhood residents, and those who were near enough witnessed a sight they will never forget."[14] The roof of the Wilkinson mansion on the rear west wing was suddenly and violently blown off of the house. At the same time, a man was seen flying out of the west side window. The house was soon completely ablaze.

The victim of the house fire was the Wilkinson family's longtime gardener, Cyprian Couvrette. Couvrette had apparently been directed to use the chemical benzene to rid the house of bugs and fleas that had infested the stately residence during Mrs. Wilkinson's extended visit to Europe. In her memoir Katharine claimed her dog had fleas, which had gotten into the carpet of her mother's bedroom.[15] The vents had been sealed off when the benzene powder was laid on the rugs, though no one could later provide a suitable explanation for how the explosion had occurred. Perhaps Couvrette or his helper had lit a cigarette while they were working.

Couvrette was soon found covered in flames on the Wilkinson lawn, writhing in pain. Doctors arrived right away, but it was too late. As his clothes were being taken from him, his "flesh clung to his underwear." He died mercifully quickly, by 4:30 that afternoon, in the hospital, leaving behind a wife and five children, all of them under fifteen years old.[16]

James Street at this point in time did not have a neighborhood water supply, so water had to be brought up the hill to the house by hand. This lack of water proved devastating for the home and for those involved in the accident.[17] Fred was at his law office when the explosion occurred, while his brother Harry was at home with the maids in another part of the house.

The house, valued at about thirty thousand dollars, was considered a total loss, though much of the furniture and valuable paintings were carried out to safety by neighbors, Harry, and the servants. Everything on the first floor, including the billiard table, survived. These household treasures were then stored in the barn on the property and next door at the neighbors', the Moore's, house.[18]

By that evening eyewitnesses to the fire observed "the darkened mansion looked like a long-deserted ruin. Some of the walls were still standing, but the entire roof is gone and the interior gutted."[19] The sisters who had been in the Adirondacks enjoying a respite from the summer heat returned to Syracuse immediately to help, staying at their Aunt Louisa's on McBride Street until new quarters could be located. Harry set sail for Queenstown, Great Britain, where he would meet his mother and sister on their way home from Europe to prepare them for the state of affairs.[20]

Fred was devastated, not for the loss of his mother's house, which, he pointed out, could be replaced. But Couvrette, the family's faithful servant, could not. He had stood by the Wilkinsons in tough times, during the family's financial scandal. Fred said: "I do not care so much about the loss of the homestead as I do about poor Couvrette . . . We always considered him one of the family. He was a trusty, faithful man and I can't express my grief for his wife and children."[21]

It now fell to Fred, as the eldest son and acting head of the family, to make arrangements for a new home for his shaken mother and sisters. His father's scandalous past had created in Fred a strong sense of moral duty and a desire to do right by his family and by Winnie. Even under intense scrutiny in his hometown and nationally over his family, the house fire, and his romance with the Daughter of the Confederacy, the young lawyer from Syracuse always remained a gentleman. But the strain that these events etched upon Fred would remain with him in the years to come.

After the tragic fire, Fred quickly leased two houses farther down James Street, moved in all the remaining family possessions, and bought new furniture and bedding to replace items lost in the blaze. Friends of the family worked diligently to make the new living space attractive. Other friends, including Wilkinson neighbor Mrs. Land, even offered money for daughter Charlotte's tuition that upcoming fall at Smith, though it was declined as not necessary.[22]

In light of this tragedy, as well as Winnie's nervous agitation after she returned from Europe, Varina and Winnie decided to delay the marriage. In August 1890 Varina announced to the press that the young couple's marriage had been postponed until June 25, 1891. According to historian Ishbel Ross, the reason proffered in Varina's formal announcement was that "Miss Davis [is] not desiring to be married until after a year of the date of her father's death."[23] It is almost certain, however, that the postponement was a play for time on the Davis women's part. With the fire at Fred's mother's home, Varina may have been worried about whether he could support her daughter any longer. The actions that followed created a firestorm of another sort.

Shortly after the tragic events in Syracuse and the announcement of the engagement delay, Fred learned that a "prominent Mississippian" has arrived in his hometown to do a background check on his finances, his family situation, and his career prospects.[24] This unknown Mississippian also carefully investigated Fred's father's banking scandal, attempting to find out exactly how much of the debt had been paid and how the family had supported itself since the incident. It is quite possible that this person was an emissary of Jubal Early or of some other former Confederate keen on ending the engagement.[25]

Fred was furious. He had been transparent with the Davis family about his finances. But Varina continued to plant doubts in Winnie's mind about Fred's ability to support her. Varina and her other southern "friends" had decided that the house fire in Syracuse would put a huge dent in Fred's bank account.

In October a New York newspaper, the *Utica Globe*, sprang to its native son Fred's defense: "It does not appear just how young Wilkinson sustained any loss [from the fire] except prospectively. The great property of the Wilkinson estate was sold a couple of years ago and more than half a million dollars was realized."[26] The house belonged to Fred's mother outright: no debt remained.

Varina's miscalculations were especially ironic given that she and Winnie were living in genteel poverty at Beauvoir. Fred was incensed. He angrily wrote his mother-in-law-to-be that he had been open with her about his family and his financial circumstances and did not approve of or understand her actions.[27] Fred's letter has since been lost or, more likely, was destroyed by Varina.

In hindsight these accusations of Fred's shaky finances were baseless. Varina may have fallen under the sway of those such as Jubal Early and Lunsford Lomax who could not bear the thought of the Daughter of the Confederacy marrying a northerner. But Varina had many northern friends and relatives. She herself much preferred the cosmopolitan atmosphere of New York to the humid backwaters of Mississippi. So, she may have been at war with herself on this issue.

More than likely, what finally turned Varina against Fred was that he could not be counted on to carry out her wishes regarding Winnie. Fred's kind refusal not to push Winnie for their engagement to be announced infuriated his potential mother-in-law. Varina could see clearly that he was not going to do her bidding just as she wished. In her own marriage Varina had experienced a total lack of control. Jefferson was always in charge, and he constantly reminded her of that fact. With her husband gone, Varina may have thought she finally had a chance for control over her family and their destinies.

Fred was the interloper, and though he was a kind person, he was firm in his beliefs regarding his fiancée. When Varina saw she was not going to be able to control Fred, nor Winnie once they married, she turned on Fred. The idea that she might lose control and influence over her youngest daughter might have been too much for her to bear.

As the wedding date approached, Varina must have also known she would be utterly alone once her daughter walked down the aisle. With her own husband dead and her oldest daughter, Margaret, living far away from her in Colorado, Winnie had become her life, and all of Varina's energy and focus was placed on her. This almost obsessive level of attention operated to the detriment of both Winnie and her fiancé.

Varina was a smart, strong, capable, and resilient woman, but the tragic losses she had suffered over the years had traumatized her. The aging widow loved, as Shakespeare wrote in *Othello*, "not wisely but too well." She was simply unable to allow Winnie, her central focus, to live her own life, which by necessity would not always include her.

Margaret was long married with children and living far away in Colorado Springs. But more than distance separated mother and daughter: Varina had created a rift in her relationship with her oldest daughter by failing to return from Europe to comfort her after the death of Margaret's firstborn son, thus driving her eldest daughter into the maternal arms of the widow Dorsey at Beauvoir and in the process damaging her own marriage to Jefferson still further. If Winnie married Fred, Varina would no longer have a child and companion who belonged to her alone.

The serious doubts Varina whispered into Winnie's ear, which had come up in discussions between Winnie and Fred during their time in Italy, had poisoned the couple's relationship. Winnie now did not trust Fred, though she still seemed to be in love with him. Fred for his part did not understand Winnie's inability to break free from her mother. He remembered only that they had been madly in love and could not understand Winnie's hesitation.[28]

After Fred's angry response to Varina about the financial inquiries going on in Syracuse that summer, she imperiously summoned him to Beauvoir for an interview. He made the long journey from New York to Mississippi just after his mother and sister returned to Syracuse from their European trip. His younger sister Katharine recalled, "The responsibilities of all decisions had naturally fallen on Fred, and after Mamma and Mal had returned and before school opened, he went South for the comfort that a visit to Winnie Davis would give him."[29] Katharine, her mother, and sisters probably did not yet know the true reason for Fred's visit to Beauvoir. It is doubtful Fred would have burdened them while they were away with the unpleasant details regarding southern inquiries into his reputation.

As Fred sat through the nearly fourteen hundred–mile train ride to Biloxi from Syracuse, he had ample time to become both anxious and angry at the summer's turn of events. The young lawyer would have had several days on the train to cogitate on his unhappy state. He may have been incensed by the casual cruelty inflicted on him by Varina and her friends as they threatened his reputation in the midst of the personal tragedy he had just been through. Even more important, he must have known that a permanent separation from his beloved Winnie was the possible outcome of this unpleasant journey.

Fred arrived at the Davises' Mississippi home "looking like a criminal and sat expecting sentence evidently," wrote Varina.[30] The young man, so used to courtroom drama through his own legal practice, now found himself on trial. Varina accused him of concealing not only his financial state from her but also the scandal surrounding his father's bank. He was utterly taken aback by her accusations, as he had been quite frank with Varina about all of these issues. But Varina, so often compared to imposing French empress Eugénie, had convinced herself that Fred had deceived them all.

She later wrote her friend Major Morgan, describing the last interaction between her and the young man who was so deeply in love with her daughter: "He said then that he had told me all about his Father . . . I said, my poor boy, frankness is the only policy in life that succeeds if it is to be a family connection. I then told him that I loved him and grieved over the sorrow to him."[31]

Winnie, who tended to quit eating when under stress, was surely emaciated at this point, pale and listless. Her resistance had been worn down by the months and years of her mother's chipping away at her romance and her trust in her fiancé. She nevertheless did see Fred off after this devastating final conference between her mother and her now former suitor.

Varina's letter to Major Morgan noted that Fred did not want to see Winnie but that she had come down to see him off anyway. "After they had a long and affecting conversation," she wrote, "he went off on the 4 o'clock train looking about the same as he did when he came. She suffered dreadfully for a while but is now cheery and eats more. He has written her since a farewell letter in which he said he would never give her up. The correspondence has stopped however, and thank God it is over."[32]

One can only imagine what this young couple, still so deeply in love, said to each other in this last, tragic conversation. Surely Fred pleaded with Winnie to come away with him up North, away from all the southern madness; she had the perfect excuse to hang up her laurels as the Daughter of the Confederacy and start over in Syracuse with Fred.

Despite what Varina said, the young lawyer did have money, prospects, and excellent social connections in Syracuse. If Winnie married him, she could break free of the chains of duty to her family legacy and the long-dead Confederacy and start a new unfettered life in the North, breathing an air of freedom there far from the ruined South.

Winnie, however, was not a rule breaker nor one to depart from everything she had been taught to value since birth. Duty, honor, family ties—they all bound her up more tightly than true love ever could. Ties of blood and symbolism kept her away from Fred. The young woman's nervous temperament, which might have benefited greatly from leaving all this emotional baggage behind, simply could not break free from the familiar, even if it made her miserable. She lived in a gilded cage of sentimental memories crafted by her family, Confederate veterans, and southern Lost Cause supporters that was ultimately impossible to leave.

Poignantly, when Fred returned home to Syracuse, his sister Katharine was the first to notice his downcast demeanor: "I shall never forget his return," she wrote in her memoir. "I ran up to his room to greet my adored brother. Standing by the window, he hardly turned to me but said he must see Mamma at once and I ran down to get her. Long afterward in her [Fred's mother's] diary from 1890, I found the only entry for that day was 'One can doth tread upon another's heels so fast they follow,' for at the command of her mother, Winnie had broken the engagement to Fred."[33]

CHAPTER SIXTEEN

Queen of a Mystic Court

The dreams of sweet young womanhood
Were sacrificed at last;
She gave the utmost that she could—
A martyr to the Past!

Mary Craig Kimbrough, *Queen of a Mystic Court*, bk. 1

One can suppose that Winnie wandered around Beauvoir wraithlike in the days after her final rupture with Fred. Perhaps she and one of her father's old hunting dogs roamed the Mississippi beach together, looking for sea glass, shells, anything to distract her from her failed romance. Rumors of the breakup had been rampant in both southern and northern papers in the early weeks of October 1890.

A New York paper reported on October 16, 1890, that the engagement was definitely broken, as confirmed by Miss Davis herself. This particular account claimed that Winnie gave an interview to a reporter at "family friend" Mrs. George A. "Libbie" Custer's apartment at the Fifth Avenue Hotel. Libbie was the wife of the famous general George A. Custer. During this conversation Winnie supposedly quashed rumors that she had severed her relationship with Fred over financial matters: "Suffice it to say that no mercenary motive prompted me in the course I decided to take. Mr. Wilkinson and I severed our relation by mutual agreement."[1]

Winnie was portrayed in the article as a young, self-centered woman exasperated by the attention given to her broken engagement who denied emphatically that her friends and family had influenced her in ending her relationship with Fred. "'The decision was left entirely to myself. Many of my relatives in the South were particularly fond of Mr. Wilkinson, but,' said Miss Davis, checking herself and biting her lip just perceptibly, 'I don't think such matters are for the public. I prefer to keep personal affairs to myself.'" As for her immediate family, Winnie noted, "they are perfectly satisfied with my conduct."[2]

Winnie and Varina left the scene at this point, and their "friend" Libbie supposedly gave her opinion on the matter, much of it unflattering and not at all in alignment with what we know about Winnie and her personality: "Miss Davis is very self-willed and likes to have her own way. She has been the idol of every aristocratic southern family since her birth, and has formulated some very decided notions concerning the late war, which she never hesitates to express."[3]

This newspaper report was completely false, one of a number of false press reports and rampant speculations about the Davis-Wilkinson romance post-breakup. First and foremost, Winnie was not in New York City on the date mentioned in the article. Varina was in the city for business reasons, but her daughter had remained in Mississippi at Beauvoir. There is also no evidence that Libbie Custer was friendly with Varina and Winnie and thus absolutely no reason she would have lent the pair her apartment or grounds for having made such disparaging comments about the Daughter of the Confederacy's character.[4]

Furthermore, it is unlikely that Winnie would have granted an interview to anyone about the engagement breakup. She was a very private person and would have cringed at the thought of her romance being analyzed in the newspapers. The view put forth in many northern papers such as this one was, of course, anti-Confederate and deliberately portrayed Winnie in an unflattering light. The northern media was still tremendously biased toward the South and its leaders or anyone related to them for that matter.

It is true, however, that both Winnie and Fred made separate brief announcements concerning the dissolution of their romance and engagement. On October 14 Fred was quoted in the *New York Times*, stating, "A few weeks ago, [Winnie] expressed the wish of both herself and her estimable mother that the engagement cease." Winnie reportedly responded, rather brusquely but kindly: "Mr. Wilkinson is an estimable young man. I think a great deal of him and his family. That's all there is to it."[5]

Even after these announcements regarding the dissolution of the engagement were reported, other melodramatic and sordid rumors continued to circulate about the real cause of the breakup. Although many southerners as well as their northern counterparts were relieved that the marriage would not take place, embellishments continued to be embroidered upon the bare-bones information released to the press by Varina, Winnie, and Fred.

The first myth that gained wide credence, especially in the South, was that Winnie had refused to give up the Davis name. A Richmond scrapbook with articles from the time claimed, "Because of her anxiety and determination to preserve and perpetuate the hallowed name of her father, she persistently refused to enter into any matrimonial alliance that would have resulted in the change of her own name."[6] No written record exists, however, of Winnie expressing this sentiment. These words were almost certainly not Winnie's but those of Confederate veterans who were loath to part with their beloved "daughter." Varina encouraged these thoughts in her press releases regarding the engagement.

The second more fantastical rumor that spread across the South was a complete falsehood and slandered Fred's character. The shocking story claimed that Winnie had rejected her northern beau because "the young man is said to have imbibed too freely of . . . 'Kentucky Elixir.'" In a drunken state, so the tale goes, Fred told Varina his generally negative opinion concerning mothers-in-law, undressed in front of both Winnie and her mother, and followed Mrs. Davis into her bedroom, whereupon Varina ordered him to leave the household.[7] While many southerners, such as Fred's old enemy Jubal Early, probably delighted in this story, it was patently untrue. Nevertheless, the wild tale gained acceptance in some southern circles. The rumor illustrates the extent of the lies that some were willing to believe in order to rationalize their harassment of Winnie, her family, and Fred.

Die-hard Confederates were willing to put such rumors out there in order to protect the honor of their cause. In the words of Eron Rowland, Varina's biographer, "Winnie's story of loyalty to the Confederacy in her love affair was just as they wanted it to appear in history, and none dared to put any other construction upon the circumstance."[8]

One might imagine that after the highly stressful experience of a broken engagement, feelings of relief and release might have displaced Winnie's feeling of loss for a while. Finding peace after all the controversy that swirled around her doomed engagement might have provided some balm. Yet a sense of tragedy seemed to haunt Winnie from this point forward. Old friends and acquaintances often remarked upon the change evident in Winnie after she parted ways with Fred. She had lost even more of the enthusiasm for life that she had pondered while viewing Mount Vesuvius with her fiancé during her trip abroad with the Pulitzers.

The strain of the breakup and the furor surrounding the match had left its mark on Winnie, and her natural lack of resilience seemed to make her wary of forming any new romantic attachments. She had other admirers after Fred, but she remained indifferent to all of them. Winnie's friend the writer Harry Stillwell Edwards wrote, "Life's conflict was telling upon her, some labor was never to be finished; some aspiration never ceased to allure."[9] Perhaps that aspiration had included marriage, children, and an idyllic domestic life with Fred in Syracuse.

While Winnie may have privately despaired at times about her choice to part from Fred, she was publicly praised throughout the South for having made this difficult decision. After a few years had passed, accounts of the breakup paint the picture of a woman whose supreme goal was intentional sacrifice for the Lost Cause. The press tended to portray Winnie as a woman who willingly denied her personal needs for the good of the South, just as her father had done during the Civil War. Many years later the *Richmond Times* referred to Winnie's sacrifice in glowing terms: "No matter what had been her feelings, she recognized that, like the heroic daughter of Jephthah, she was vowed to the Cause for which people had fought, suffered, and died. It was grander to be the 'Daughter of the Confederacy' than a wife, and to that land which had christened her and anointed her . . . she was faithful."[10]

Winnie's perceived conduct in ending her ill-fated engagement manifests some striking parallels to the life of the Confederate heroine Irene in *Macaria; or, Altars of Sacrifice* (1864). This popular Civil War novel by Augusta Jane Evans examines the psychology of women's wartime sacrifices. In Greek mythology the character of Macaria saved Athens from war by sacrificing herself to the gods.[11] Sacrifice rapidly became a vocation for right-thinking Confederate women. In the novel Irene tries to submerge her personal identity in the war effort, forgoing previously coveted items such as stylish clothes. Individual wants were secondary to the glory of the cause.[12]

During the war this hope for self-obliteration upon the Confederate altar seemed to reflect the fear of spinsterhood prevalent among women of this period. Potential husbands were dying by the thousands, creating a frightening "man shortage." Evans's novel spoke to these women's legitimate fears of a life lived without a husband or children. Yet Confederate heroines such as Irene who chose to remain unmarried were able to play significant roles that set them apart from their married peers. Married women might be happier, notes Irene, but a single woman could be more *useful* to the Confederacy because a women who "dares to live alone is certainly braver and nobler and better" than one who consents to a "loveless marriage."[13] Thus, single women were able to create a career out of this forced sacrifice.

As historian and Harvard president Drew Gilpin Faust points out: "Evans heroine is ambitious of martyrdom. The novel is structured as her pilgrimage toward 'Womanly Usefulness,' which she ultimately realizes in the Confederate war effort."[14] Irene and those who imitated her were praised and accepted as single women because of their devotion to the cause. This occupation exempted them from their traditional roles as wives and mothers.

Although Winnie's sacrifice of her northern beau was not acted out within the context of the Civil War, her engagement was certainly crushed by the memory of that event. Her motivations and actions reflect the Confederate mind-set that had been deeply implanted in her by both her parents and the southern community. The Daughter of the Confederacy was a postbellum public figure inculcated with a wartime mentality that she could not deny. Like Irene, she was allowed to remain single after she demonstrated her devotion to the cause through the denial of personal desire. She had exchanged her freedom for a pedestal in 1886, though she did not realize it at the time.

Winnie was also similar to the fictional Irene in that she had a significant symbolic job that took precedence over long-established feminine roles. As Daughter of the Confederacy, she already had a "family" in the form of Confederate veterans and later also through her relationship with the United Daughters of the Confederacy. As a single woman with no husband and children to tie her down, she was much more "useful" to the Lost Cause legacy.

The young, now unattached Winnie did not disassociate herself from the cause that had denied her true love. She did not turn upon its principles and become bitter over this loss. Instead, she simply resumed her duties in her allotted role. She again attended veterans' reunions and appeared before huge crowds, representing the virtues of her father. She attended balls and parties in his honor, both with and without her aging mother.[15]

Winnie seemed to accept this fate with resignation and no complaints, just as her father would have advised her to do. Outwardly, she even seemed to enjoy her required duties as Confederate mascot and head cheerleader. But beneath the surface there was always a sense of sadness, of longing and loss. In 1889 Fred had prophesied that his life and Winnie's would be lost if the marriage did not take place.[16] Winnie's sacrificial choice required them to continue on alone, along their separate paths, each toward a different kind of existence.

Winnie's popularity climbed steadily in the 1890s. Following her break with Fred, she became highly sought after for society functions. She was given a variety of honorary posts, such as "World Manager" at the World's Columbian Exhibition in Chicago in 1890.[17] The post was purely figural, but it recognized her special status. New Orleans society in particular had admired Winnie's grace and poise since she had served in the first "Court" of Comus under Queen Mildred Lee in 1884.

Eight years later the New Orleans community tried to show its admiration for Winnie once again by awarding her the title of Queen of Comus in the New Orleans Mardi Gras celebrations of 1892. The invitation seemed a sort of a consolation prize for having given up her northern beau. This was a historic choice of a queen for the Mistick Krewe of Comus, as Jefferson Davis's youngest daughter was the first nonnative of New Orleans to be tapped for the role.

Although Winnie never knew it, the original young woman who had been chosen for this honor, Miss Emma Sinnott, daughter of former Confederate colonel James Butterfield Sinnott, had relinquished the throne at her father's request, as he insisted that Miss Davis not walk behind his daughter at the ceremony.[18] The queen's robe, which had already been ordered from Japan to fit seventeen-year-old Emma was secretly altered to fit twenty-eight-year-old Winnie. Emma considered it a huge honor to have relinquished her throne to the Daughter of the Confederacy. Until her death in 1941, she deftly turned aside all questions about her relinquished crown.[19]

Winnie's reign as Comus queen was significant as a firm acknowledgment of the legitimacy of the Lost Cause. The New Orleans press rhapsodized: "It was a gallant and touching tribute to that dead cause from the ashes of which sprang, Phoenix-like, such blessings of amity and peace, that the Daughter of the Confederacy, Miss Winnie Davis, should have been chosen from all the beautiful women of the Southland to be queen of the godly Comus."[20]

The Mistick Krewe of Comus, founded in 1857, was the oldest of the New Orleans parade organizations. Its all-male members favored representative women endowed with both beauty and good taste who also had an aristocratic and politically acceptable pedigree. Winnie distinctly fit the bill. Historian Reid Mitchell says of the choice: "In 1892, Comus picked the ubiquitous 'Daughter of the Confederacy' as Queen of the ball. Nothing could have made clearer that the honors of the Carnival Court were often meant more for the fathers of the chosen than for the women themselves."[21] Winnie was again tasked with carrying on the legacy of both her father and of the Confederacy.

The 1890s marked a period of growing interest in all things Asian. The theme of the 1892 Mardi Gras, "Nippon, Land of the Rising Sun," reflected this trend. Winnie and her entire court were outfitted in ball gowns made out of Japanese silk and "decorated with lavish embellishments and Japanese-style sleeves."[22] One of Winnie's portraits as Queen of Comus that now resides in a Confederate Memorial Hall in New Orleans shows a half-smiling Winnie in this resplendent gown embroidered with golden chrysanthemums and an obi sash. She is covered in Mardi Gras jewels—including a colorful red sunburst brooch, necklace, panel, and scepter—which she wore to the Comus celebrations.[23]

Winnie's glamorous time in New Orleans inspired a "biography" entitled *Queen of a Mystic Court*. Mary Craig Kimbrough, Winnie's young Mississippi neighbor, wrote this fanciful, romanticized version of Winnie's life. The Kimbrough family's summer home, Ashton Hall, was about a half-mile down the road from Beauvoir. Mary Craig's mother, Mary Hunter Southworth Kimbrough, became a good friend of Varina over her years spent at Beauvoir and fought tirelessly for the home's preservation after Varina's death.[24]

Mary Craig's book provides vivid descriptions of New Orleans of the 1890s, its social whirl and intoxicating carnival atmosphere. Most girls would have been giddy with excitement to rule socially over it all. But for Winnie outfitting herself in fashionable clothes and attending parties were simply duties to be fulfilled rather than pleasures to be enjoyed.

Mary Craig noted that many in the New Orleans community were well aware of the Davis family's lack of funds. Apparently, the Krewe of Comus benevolently decided to provide both Winnie and her maids of honor with their gowns. According to Mary Craig, this gift had never before been bestowed on a Queen of Comus and her court and was a distinct honor. "Winnie Davis must be spared the expense of her coronation robes, without offending her sensitive pride."[25]

New Orleans Mardi Gras revelries of the 1890s were much the same as those of the present day. Mary Craig described the atmosphere: "Everywhere throughout the town, there was bustle and pleasant excitement. Everywhere from roof to cellar, festooned from window to door-way, were the royal colors, purple, green and gold . . . The city was full to overflowing with a great holiday crowd." Luncheons, dinners, teas, pageants, and parades filled Winnie's days and nights.[26]

In the midst of all this color and light, Mary Craig observed that Winnie appeared to many as a gray dove, spiritual and solemn. Melancholy seemed to surround her like a halo. Ioranthe Semmes, a childhood friend of Winnie who appears as a fictionalized version of herself in *Queen of a Mystic Court*, comments about Winnie's penchant for simple gray dresses with their overtones of mourning: "I have often wondered if the color of the prison walls that Winnie Davis shared with her father impressed its somber grey upon her infant mind?—or probably, she is partial to the color because the Confederate soldiers wore it."[27]

The highlight of the season came on March 1, 1892, as Winnie opened the grandest ball of Carnival with her Comus court. She was the center of a triumphant living tableaux with her maids of honor at the city's French Opera House. Mary Craig described her as "a beautiful girl robed in white satin, heavy with gold embroideries with a glittering crown upon her head . . . attended by her ladies in waiting." Mary Craig continued dramatically: "For a moment, she paused and stood pale and composed while the tremendous applause from the audience that greeted her resounded through the vast building."[28]

A gorgeous canopy composed of hundreds of colored Japanese lanterns hung over the reviewing stand of the Pickwick Club, sheltering Winnie and her court during the parade as floats rolled by. Accompanying the Queen of Comus were other Carnival queens, Governor Francis T. Nicholls and Gen. P.G.T. Beauregard. Winnie's maids were Miss Josie McGinnis, Miss Nettie Miller, and Miss Emma Sinnot.[29]

Although Winnie's heart was surely elsewhere, she seemed to participate enthusiastically in the event to the delight of her southern audience. The performance bolstered and even cemented her place in the hearts of the Lost Cause faithful. Writer Martha M. Boltz notes this reaction: "Winnie's participation as Queen of the Mistick Krew of Comus further endeared her to Southerners as well as to the Confederate Veterans, who had so loved and respected her father."[30]

An elaborate ball followed the presentation at the Old French Opera House. Mardi Gras Queen Winnie reigned sad but supreme, dressed in her gorgeous embroidered silk kimono. The Daughter of the Confederacy was publicly feted and worshipped by the crème de la crème of New Orleans society. Privately, however, the acclaim meant little. The one man she would ever truly love was gone, sacrificed to the memories of another generation.

Mary Craig herself had suffered a broken engagement, which, her mother decided, uniquely qualified her to tell Winnie's tale. According to her daughter, Mrs. Kimbrough had declared dramatically: "You must become a writer. You are the only person who can tell the true story of the love affair of Winnie Davis. You have suffered exactly as she did." Yet Mary Craig was ultimately advised to keep Winnie's tragic love affair under wraps. It would reflect badly on Confederate veterans, she was told. Best keep the embarrassing scandal out of the public eye. "Almost everywhere I had gone for opinions of Winnie," she wrote, "I got only opinions of the inadvisability of publishing the facts."[31]

Mary Craig interviewed many of Winnie's friends as well as some of the ladies of her 1892 Mardi Gras court.[32] She gained the official approval of both the United Confederate Veterans and Varina Davis for the book, though it was never published.[33] A combination of fact, fiction, and Mary Craig's own social aspirations, *Queen of a Mystic Court* nonetheless presents some intriguing details of the time period, in addition to the New Orleans tableaux.

The great influence Jefferson Davis had over Winnie was duly noted by Mary Craig: "He adjured her always to uphold the 'Right' no matter what the cost to herself, and to pray to God for the strength with which to do it." The author also described an interesting point of view held by Winnie's childhood friends from Memphis. The Davises' youngest child came across to many as haughty and reserved. Unlike her siblings, she often did not play with the other children in the neighborhood. Mary Craig again used the voice of Winnie's old friend Ioranthe Semmes to note: "The truth was, as Ioranthe realized now as she thought the matter over, nothing more than a little girl's insatiable taste for study and her parents' constant encouragement of it, had kept her apart from other children in their play."[34] Winnie's parents, it seemed, had kept her apart from her peers deliberately and contributed perhaps as much to her outsider status as her later schooling in Germany did.

After her return from Europe, Mary Craig noted, Winnie seemed even more aloof to her contemporaries. "This cultivated girl, so accomplished, so foreign in her manners, was head and shoulders above . . . provincial tastes. Though really demure and shy, she frightened the young men who realized that she was educated beyond them."[35] Her comment rings true and matches up with many other descriptions of Winnie from this period.

Ultimately, however, *Queen of a Mystic Court* is not a biography of Winnie. The work is a fanciful portrait of a woman who never existed. The author described the Daughter of the Confederacy as a flirtatious coquette whose constant intrigues got her into serious trouble: "The young woman who resembled royalty in the eyes of her friends was dispensing with royal lavishness her charms upon courtiers in her train. But, poor little princess, she seemed constantly in a maze of intrigue and adventure, continually striving to straighten out the tangles she made of her affairs, maneuvering to keep peace in a jealous court."[36]

Mary Craig may have been projecting her own personality—that of a true southern belle—onto the far more serious and intellectual persona of Winnie Davis. No one who knew Winnie would ever have called her a flirt or a coquette. She certainly had no taste for the social intrigue that Mary Craig imagined.

Fred Wilkinson morphed into "Frederick Van Vleet" in Mary Craig's account. Instead of being from Syracuse, New York, he lived in "On-the-Hudson, N.Y."[37] The author imagines Fred's visit to Beauvoir to ask for Winnie's hand, the trip to Italy the couple shared, and the subsequent broken engagement. Fred's story follows the correct timeline, but many details are fabricated, such as love letters between Winnie and Fred. The correspondence between the young couple that Mary Craig presents in *Queen* is a figment of her own imagination. The words in these fictional missives sound nothing like what the real Fred and Winnie might have ever penned.

But Mary Craig clearly had access to some of the letters and documents of the Davis family. Fred's letters to Varina from Naples, Italy, are here, as along with some of the letters Varina wrote to friends such as Major Morgan. Winnie's letters to her mother from Italy also are transcribed word for word.[38]

Mary Craig's father, Judge Kimbrough, was a trusted friend of the Davis family who later would help Varina with legal issues. Mary Craig mentioned that he kept some of the threatening letters that Confederate veterans sent to the Davises during Winnie's engagement.[39] Mary Craig clearly obtained these documents from her father, and it seems likely that Varina gave her permission to use them in her biography of Winnie.

Queen of a Mystic Court reveals Mary Craig's philosophy that southerners possessed "racial traits" that made them more moral than northerners. In it she theorized, "These were the things that blood and breeding meant to them—not a groundless pride or snobbishness, but the preservation of racial traits of honor and nobility."[40] In her mind, and in the mind of many southerners of the time, "Yankees" did not possess such finer qualities. The war had shown southerners the ugly side of human nature, and many of them blamed their wartime experiences on the entire northern population. Mary Craig wrote: "The Southern people had seen little evidence of these traits and qualities—which they believed to be noble—in the people of the North. On the contrary, they had seen decided evidence of the lack of them" within the context of their wartime experiences.[41] Mary Craig then proceeded to put these very words into Winnie's mouth, as she imagined the breakup between Winnie and Fred: "Fred, I have found out only recently that we really are two different races—we of the South, and you of the North."[42]

This idea of racial purity, of white southerners being noble, superior beings, appears often in the literature of the period. Marrying a northerner was akin to marrying a black man in the minds of many, particularly Confederate veterans. Mary Craig noted this sentiment of superiority specifically in *Queen*: "It would be a shame for Winnie Davis, who represented the womanhood of the Confederacy, to unite herself with one of those who has conquered her country by brute force."[43] The theme of rape by an outsider surfaces again here. *Queen of a Mystic Court* was definitely a representative product of a southerner inculcated with the specific values of her class and community.

Mary Craig was later to become the second wife of famous writer and social reformer Upton Sinclair, author of *The Jungle* (1906). After reading her "biography" of Winnie, he declared: "Your book is terrible! You can't write, I can't honestly encourage you." Perhaps Upton was correct in his assessment of his wife's literary abilities. Even Mary Craig admitted she later "lost interest in the prim, sentimental story I had written about Winnie Davis."[44]

Nevertheless, *Queen of a Mystic Court* provides a valuable document for historians. Mary Craig gave us a window into the minds of the upper-class South at the turn of the century. Winnie's romance and subsequent broken engagement were viewed as a genuine sacrifice on her part, and she was rewarded in the minds of many with honors such as the Queen of Comus title. Yet this sacrifice was expected and demanded by Confederate veterans and others with little thought about how it would affect Winnie personally. It was her duty, they thought, to both her father's memory and to the South.

Mary Craig duly noted the Faustian deal made by Winnie with these Confederate veterans when she was named Daughter of the Confederacy in 1886: "How she had thrilled at the tribute! And she had vowed that she would return it with everlasting loyalty to them, striving always to be worthy of such a patriotic, great-hearted people. It was her coronation and she accepted her mystic crown with grace and dignity, and gratitude for its bestowing—little dreaming that it was but a shadowy symbol, freighted with real and crushing responsibility."[45] *Shadowy* is the key word here—the tribute given to Winnie was that of a lost shadow civilization, one that no longer existed and had perhaps never truly existed at all.

CHAPTER SEVENTEEN

New York, New Woman

> We felt, at times, our bird had flown
> Into the North too far from home.
>
> Rev. R. M. Tuttle, a fragment of his poem
> "Miss Winnie Davis, a Tribute," 1905

Winnie certainly could have had her pick of southern men. Her parents and many a Confederate veteran hoped that if she did deign to marry, it would be to a young man of prominent Confederate heritage. In this manner she could help carry on the Davis name and legacy—as her sister, Margaret, had done through her marriage to former Confederate officer Joel Addison Hayes of Memphis, Tennessee. Fervent supporters of the Lost Cause dreamed, as historian David Hardin describes it, that through Margaret and Winnie "tiny Rebels would be spawned, not only to replace the dead but to preserve certain forms—good manners, for instance—that would segregate the South from Yankee vulgarity."[1]

Winnie's path in life was to prove far different, however, than the traditional one followed by her older sister. Her existence post-engagement to Fred would be unconventional and geographically distant from her past. Although the young woman could have pursued the role of a glittering socialite in New Orleans or anywhere in the South, she had no interest in this kind of vapid existence. Winnie was far too serious-minded to enjoy such frivolities. Lack of funds also curtailed her social life; the money to buy gowns and jewels and to support a life of leisure were beyond her grasp without a husband or family wealth to support her.

Many people both North and South had the mistaken idea that Varina and her youngest daughter led a pleasant life after Jefferson died, one full of amusing trips and entertainments. Even the Davises' young Mississippi neighbor Mary Craig Kimbrough bought into this myth. "Did I not know," she wrote, "that Winnie and her mother had left Beauvoir and gone to live like royalty in New York and Narragansett Pier [a fashionable Rhode Island resort of the era]?"[2]

To the contrary, Winnie had a small income from Beauvoir, willed to her upon her father's death by Sarah Dorsey. She and her sister, Margaret, also had a modest income from Tunisberg in Louisiana, the Howell residence that had been confiscated during the war and finally returned to them.[3] But these funds were simply not enough to support Winnie and her mother. Both women tried to get work with southern newspapers but to no avail.

At this point Varina again asked her author friend Charles Dudley Warner to help her and Winnie find work up North.[4] Warner and other southern writers such as Thomas Nelson Page had realized almost immediately after the war that their careers were dependent upon the northern literary market. Page wrote, "The great monthly magazines were not only open as never before to Southern contributors, but welcomed them eagerly as a new and valuable acquisition."[5]

Both Winnie and Varina were forced to make a choice. They could stay at Beauvoir, moldering away in genteel poverty, or make a new life for themselves elsewhere. They could have gone any number of places—Varina had always loved London and Paris. They had also lived in Memphis and Montreal. Winnie had spent most of her girlhood in Germany. They were citizens of the world and at this point had many doors open to them. They were unfettered by husbands or young children and could start over in a place entirely of their own choosing. They chose New York.

Even in 1890, twenty-five years after the war had ended, the choice seemed shocking and inappropriate. New York was Winnie's former fiancé Fred's home state, a former hotbed of abolitionist sentiment. New York City seemed like the last place on earth the women should have chosen if they were worried about how they might appear to their southern friends.

The pair did not escape the southern soil unscathed. A Birmingham paper accused Varina and Winnie of "abandoning" the South. The *New York Times* quickly reacted, defending their right to live where they pleased. Varina and Winnie were not alone in choosing New York as their postwar place of residence. Numerous other former Confederates lived in New York City: Burton and Constance Cary Harrison, James

Longstreet, and John Singleton Mosby,[6] as well as Davis friends Roger and Sara Pryor.[7]

Winnie and Varina's close friends knew the decision to live in the North was partially to the result of financial exigency. Varina wrote her friend and neighbor at Beauvoir Mary Hunter Kimbrough (Mary Craig's mother) declaring she had little choice in the matter: "I got literary work here and do get it now. Winnie gets it also, and thus we manage to eke out an anxious existence."[8]

Aside from her financial worries, Varina had never loved Beauvoir like Jefferson had. It was not her home, and she was never really its mistress. Sarah Dorsey, the former owner of Beauvoir and Varina's literary and perhaps romantic rival for Jefferson, had stipulated that after Jefferson's death, the house belonged to Winnie and not to Varina. Adding to Varina's personal distaste for Beauvoir was the fact that the Gulf Coast home was becoming expensive to maintain.

The women's financial knight in shining armor ended up being family friend and press baron Joseph Pulitzer. Both Varina and Winnie enjoyed writing and preferred literary pursuits to other work. Pulitzer knew this and presented an honorable way out of their financial dire straits for the impoverished pair. He proposed the women go to work for his paper the *Sunday World* for a stipend of fifteen hundred dollars each per year. Winnie, the more creative writer of the two, would write short fiction, sketches, verse, and book reviews. Varina, ever the more practical one, would write nonfiction that often recalled her days as the first lady of the Confederacy.[9]

The two women also worked for other magazines, such as the *Ladies' Home Journal*. Varina showed herself to be a classic stage mother, still trying to drum up contacts that Winnie may have been too shy to cultivate on her own. A letter from a private collection documents Varina writing a fawning letter to a Miss Alice Graham Lanigan, an editor at the *Ladies' Home Journal*. In it Varina urges Alice not to cut a word from Winnie's article, asking: "Now, can you arrange this? If so, it would be a great satisfaction to us both. I do not feel the least concern about your notice of her for I am quite willing to trust in your strong but gentle hands."[10]

Varina told her friends that she and Winnie much preferred New York City due to the lower cost of living, the healthier climate, and the much more cosmopolitan lifestyle there. Beauvoir was isolated from both city culture and friends, and she and Winnie claimed they sometimes felt unsafe there.[11] Varina's serious heart condition was aggravated by the hot southern climate, while Winnie's literary future was also stagnating at Beauvoir.[12] Privately, Winnie also found life in the Northeast to be far more culturally stimulating than that of the Gulf coast community she deemed "sleepy."[13]

So, the two women left behind the humid, Spanish moss–draped estate of Sarah Dorsey for the artistic, literary culture of New York City. Here they would work for their livings, but they hoped finally to have found a place that would appreciate their artistic talents more than their connection to the Lost Cause and the Confederacy.

New York in the Gay Nineties was a lively, busy place. The city was the country's nexus of the literary and publishing world, the perfect place for aspiring writers like Winnie and her mother to congregate. Manhattan in the Gilded Age was also full of contrasts—with rich and poor living cheek by jowl in the crowded city.

Photographer and activist Jacob August Riis shocked the country with his 1890 documentary book, *How the Other Half Lives*, which gave readers a glimpse of New York ghetto life, with its shabby shanties, sweatshops, and saloons—places Winnie and her mother would probably never have seen.[14] The book produced its intended result in helping expose the plight of the urban poor, though Riis's methods were not necessarily welcome; he had no compunction about bursting in on his unwitting subjects in the middle of the night for a surprise photograph.

But Manhattan was also a location bursting with more laudable superlatives. New York boasted Wall Street, the country's financial hub; the nation's leading commercial port; and its chief manufacturing center. The city was also the arts and philanthropic capital of the United States, filled with world-class museums, theaters, and charitable organizations.[15]

Far from the heat and isolation of Beauvoir, Winnie and Varina found a cultured island where boredom was almost impossible. The pair first lived at the Hotel Marlborough, where Varina hosted Sunday literary salons that included artists, actors, writers, and playwrights. According to historian Carol Berkin, "She charmed and dazzled the young men and women who visited her, just as once, long ago, she had charmed senators and presidents" in 1850s Washington DC.[16] Winnie was often present at these gatherings, and she probably enjoyed watching her vivacious mother entertain while she herself quietly absorbed the literary and artistic talk of which she was so fond.

The Old Guard from the South also came to call, among them Jefferson's former secretary Burton Harrison and his enchanting wife, Connie. Despite her chameleonlike ability to fit into New York's Gilded Age society parlors, Connie missed the South and its genteel ways. Her sharp eye noted the greed and shallowness around her in northern society, though she moved through it expertly.[17]

By 1893 mother and daughter had moved to less expensive quarters—the Hotel Gerard at 123 West Forty-Fourth Street, in what is now the Theater District.[18] Winnie and Varina were now part of the city's social fabric, attracting some surprising friends, among them Julia Dent Grant, wife of former Union general and later president Ulysses S. Grant. Varina met Julia by chance in June 1893 at Cranston's Hotel on the Hudson River. The two women met several more times over the next few days and then again later in 1893 and 1894 at Narragansett Pier, a Rhode Island resort. Winnie and her mother also developed a fond acquaintance with Julia's daughter, Nellie Sartoris. The Davis women lived all of twenty blocks away from Julia, and the two former first ladies became good friends and correspondents for the rest of their lives.[19]

The year 1893 also marked the time when Jefferson Davis's remains were transferred from their temporary resting place at Metarie Cemetery in New Orleans, where he had died in 1889, to Hollywood Cemetery in Richmond, Virginia. Hollywood was home to numerous Confederate generals and officers but also, more important, to Jefferson's beloved sons: Samuel Emory, Joe Jr., Billy, and Jefferson Jr. Varina clearly dreaded going to the ceremony and all the painful memories it would evoke for her and her girls. On May 26 she wrote her friend Ann Grant, noting the unusual and tragic nature of her circumstances: "It does not devolve upon many women to twice bury a husband and four children, and I am overcome by memories of the past."[20]

The Jefferson Davis funeral train left New Orleans on May 28, 1893, and arrived in Richmond on the morning of May 31, after traveling over twelve hundred miles for fifty-five hours.[21] Winnie and Margaret accompanied the coffin from New Orleans to Richmond. During the long and arduous journey Winnie made her way to the funeral car to visit her father's coffin, which at that point was heaped with flowers. The *Richmond Dispatch* of May 30, 1893, reported that she "moved slowly to the head of the coffin, stopped and looked at the silent men before her and started to speak, but broke down and then hurriedly turned away and left the car."[22] The event may have renewed Winnie's original feelings of guilt and distress over her inability to return home for her father's original funeral in 1889.

Varina met Winnie and Margaret at the station in Richmond early the next morning. At three in the afternoon on May 31, the funeral procession wound its way to Hollywood Cemetery, six white horses drawing the funeral carriage. The *Richmond Dispatch* account of the event noted that "at least 75,000 people were along the streets and at the cemetery, and not since the war had so many Confederate soldiers been seen in Richmond."[23]

Winnie, Margaret, and their mother were surely exhausted after the emotionally draining event. Everyone wanted to see "the Davis Girls" and the "Widow of the Confederacy." But after years of negotiation about the location of Jefferson's final resting place, it must have been a relief to have the matter resolved. Varina's biographer Joan Cashin writes, "When her husband's body was reinterred in Richmond in 1893, she [Varina] negotiated the complex business of who should be invited to the event, and then endured the long elaborate ceremony, feeling overcome by memories, she left town as rapidly as possible."[24]

Aside from burying Jefferson, seeing the tombs of all four of the Davis boys could not have been easy for Varina or her daughters. More than half the family was dead. Those who survived were left with melancholy memories. Winnie and Varina soon left for New York, and Margaret headed west to Colorado Springs. Perhaps distance from the South made tragedy easier to bear for all the Davis women.

In August 1894 Winnie traveled on her own to see her older sister in Colorado. A photograph now in the collection of the Colorado Springs Pioneer Museum confirms Winnie's visit. In the photo Winnie, Margaret, Addison Hayes, and a friend are pictured at famous Cripple Creek—where gold was discovered in abundance in 1891.[25] The Colorado papers made mention of Winnie's visit, calling her "The Daughter of the Rebellion."[26]

This Western visit, far away from haunting memories of Richmond, was presumably a refreshing respite for Winnie. The sunny climate and blue skies of Colorado Springs were undoubtedly alluring and cleansing for her. All was new, and here the Civil War and its bitter aftermath were only distant, sepia-toned memories. Even so, the Daughter of the Rebellion was soon back in her beloved Manhattan.

Although Winnie participated enthusiastically in the cultural and social life of the city, she had little interest in the opposite sex. Was this due to her unrequited love for Fred? Winnie apparently called herself a "bachelor" and declared no man would have her. Many acquaintances, including a neighbor in New York, claimed she never got over her romance with Fred.[27] There is one story, probably apocryphal, that Winnie and Fred met once after their broken engagement at a dinner party given by the Pulitzers, where they completely avoided each other.[28]

Perhaps, even if Winnie did secretly pine for Fred, she ultimately preferred a literary life with her mother, with no other domestic obligations. Marriage and children might have proved too much of a strain for Winnie, given her physical and mental ailments. Perhaps Winnie and Varina realized this on a subconscious level?

When the Davis women moved to New York City in 1890, Winnie's writing did not remain a genteel pastime; it became a necessity. Fortunately, both the quality and quantity of her work flourished in this new and inspiring atmosphere. The old rules about women working simply did not apply to Winnie. In her unmarried state she was free to experiment with both her writing and her opinions about relationships between men and women.

Although most of her time was spent writing and participating in Manhattan's literary and cultural scene, Winnie still made time to represent her father at Confederate veterans' Reunions. Her mother always urged her to keep up appearances in this arena. In 1895 Winnie attended one such reunion in Houston, Texas, quickly discovering that she was the focus of the event. Her retiring nature and dislike of the spotlight must have been psychologically difficult for her to overcome. At reunions such as this one, the much-admired Daughter of the Confederacy was mobbed. Thousands thronged one reception for her until she was forced to come out onto a balcony to wave to them like a foreign princess might do.[29]

Varina described Winnie returning to New York after the event in Houston with "her hands sore and swollen with greetings to 'all sorts and conditions of men.'"[30] Winnie was not going to disappoint what we would term today as her "fan club," even if it meant suffering physical discomfort. In this respect she was very much like her father, for whom the sacrifice of personal well-being was a guiding principle.

Within the same year Winnie published her first novel, *The Veiled Doctor*. The story reveals much about the young woman's attitudes toward marriage and perhaps illuminates some of her long-term anxieties about the institution. The story is fairly traditional, with a husband and wife, Isabel and Gordon Wickford, playing the central roles. Early in the tale, however, Isabel questions her existence, sadly noting the status of many a Victorian wife. "I am only a 'subject' to him after all," she says.[31] Isabel, as her author notes, is literally her husband's property.

The heroine of *The Veiled Doctor* chafes under the constraints her spouse places upon her, but she is ultimately punished for her rebellion. Her husband dies, and she apparently becomes a better woman through her suffering and consequent remorse. The moral of the tale reflected Winnie's own experience of failed romance.

Winnie's second novel, *A Romance of Summer Seas*, was published in 1898. This tale is distinctly more cynical than its predecessor. Through her characters the author begins to express sentiments contrary to the prevailing beliefs of her era. A sense of independence shines through this literary work. One of her characters ridicules the institution of marriage, declaring: "Abstractly, I do not approve of dueling. Like marriage, divorce and many other institutions, it leaves a great deal to be desired."[32]

Winnie had been compelled to give up her great love for a higher cause and consequently found both her career and her independence outside the traditional wifely sphere. This arrangement fulfilled her on personal and intellectual levels in a way that being a wife and mother probably never could.

In *Romance* Winnie's characters question the accepted definition of a husband as well: "Obedience is a dead letter and why should not the old conception of a husband's position as protector and avenger die with it?"[33] The author's fictional characters allow her to express opinions and thoughts that she would likely not voice in her personal life. She empowers these women to speak their minds and vent some of her own frustrations with and perspectives on the domesticity-mad society in which she lived.

In the rigid Victorian family structure, women were forced into a role that rarely allowed for outside ambitions or opinions. Once safely married, women were expected to be the moral guardians of society.[34] The heroines of both *The Veiled Doctor* and *A Romance of Summer Seas* began to reject Victorian social constructs and gender roles. Winnie's novels reflected society's fascination in the late 1880s and 1890s with a new concept: that of the "New Woman." Winnie was surely aware of this definition, coined by writer and public speaker Sarah Grand in 1894. The term was a buzzword in the last few years of the nineteenth century.[35]

This bicycle-riding, cigarette-smoking female was pictured brilliantly by Massachusetts-born Charles Dana Gibson, the premier pen-and-ink artist of the era, who created his "Gibson Girl" in 1890. She was a flirtatious femme fatale who was often riding a bicycle, playing golf or croquet, while simultaneously breaking hearts. Australian art critic Robert Hughes once depicted the Gibson Girl as the American version of "La Belle Dame sans Merci," Unlike her European seductress counterpart, the Gibson Girl was a fresh, less-worldly spin on this female archetype.[36]

This caricature was inspired by Gibson's close association with the famed Langhorne sisters, wealthy Virginians whose family fortune was swept away by the destruction of the Civil War. When Charles married Irene, their wedding in Richmond in November 1895 was not only the social event of the year; it was seen by many southerners as the symbolic end of the War between the States.[37]

A whole genre of New Woman literature sprung up to accompany such visual depictions. This vision of American loveliness, with her bloomers and bicycle rides, became a focal point for discussions of female liberation.[38] The heroines of Winnie's novels, and indeed Winnie herself, were evolving toward the Gibson girl model, though they were not fully there yet. Winnie and her heroines still sat on the fence between Victorian repression and fin-de-siècle rebellion against traditional women's roles.

The bicycling craze of the late 1890s was inextricably linked with the image of the New Woman. This was an activity in which Winnie fully participated, gleefully whizzing around her Narragansett Pier resort on holiday. The freedom offered by this new mode of transport dovetailed nicely with New Woman sentiments of the time.[39]

In 1896 Susan B. Anthony, the leader of the women's suffrage movement, told the *New York World*'s reporter Nellie Bly that bicycling had "done more to emancipate women than anything else in the world."[40] Winnie was evolving more and more into the type of heroine she described in her novels—a role that was much closer to her true nature than that of the Daughter of the Confederacy.

The sentiments manifested on the pages of Winnie's two novels point clearly to the author's burgeoning spirit of independence. Although Winnie was clearly devastated by her decision to end her relationship with Fred, there were definite upsides to the situation. Once she was freed from the all-absorbing Victorian tasks of finding and pleasing a husband and then creating a bubble of domestic bliss, complete with children, she was able to sort through her own literary needs and ambitions.

As one can see through her writings in the mid- to late 1890s, the Daughter of the Confederacy ironically seemed to be among the few women of the time who realized that many of the demands placed upon the wives and mothers of Victorian society were antiquated and unreasonable. Although she submitted to the will of southern society by rejecting marriage to Fred, she rebelled against the social dictates of the era in the context of her novels, in her literary life in New York, and within her leisure pursuits such as bicycling.

Winnie also still delighted in traveling abroad with her glamorous cousin Kate Pulitzer. In 1898 she, Kate, and Kate's son Ralph, who was on leave from Harvard, decided to make a sightseeing tour of Egypt.[41] On February 11, 1898, before she sailed for Egypt, Winnie made out her will. In this document she bequeathed Beauvoir, the family home her father had left to her, and everything else she had to her mother, leaving remembrances of her jewelry to her cousin Anna Smith and to her old nurse, Mary Ahern. She instructed Varina to select a few items of remembrance for her sister Margaret and her children.[42] How intriguing that Winnie would have chosen this time to make out her will. Was this a prescient notion? Or was it perhaps just a precaution due to the exotic locale of her trip?

Winnie, Kate, and Ralph all seemed thoroughly to enjoy their exotic adventure in the Middle East. While on the trip, Winnie also visited

Rome, Venice, Florence, and Paris.[43] She must have at least had a passing thought or two about Fred and the time they had spent together on her last trip to Italy in 1890. Despite the exhilaration of the trip, Winnie was still not feeling her best. The strain of nineteenth-century travel could not have helped the precarious state of her health. She returned to the States in May feeling worn-out.

While her physical health was diminished, her literary reputation was on the upswing. Her new novel, *A Romance of Summer Seas*, had received critical praise. She remained beloved by Confederate veterans, and the women of the United Daughters continued to hold her up as their distinguished role model.[44] At last Winnie had blossomed into the New Woman she wrote about in her novels. Like the famed journalist (and reporter for Joseph Pulitzer's *New York World*) Nellie Bly, she was an intrepid explorer of mysterious lands. She was independent, earning her own money from her literary work. As a single career woman, she was also a nonconformist. Things were indeed looking up, but Winnie's mother and her Confederate ties would soon unwittingly place the young woman on a dangerous and life-threatening path.

CHAPTER EIGHTEEN

The Last Casualty of the Lost Cause

In July 1898 Varina decided that Winnie should take her place at a large camp gathering of Confederate veterans in Atlanta. Winnie did not wish to go and was feeling poorly, but her mother strongly urged her to attend the event on her behalf. Varina expressed her rationale for this decision in a September 7, 1898, letter to her friend Connie Harrison, saying that it was best for Winnie to go to Atlanta so as not to lose touch with her father's friends.[1] Varina was later to regard this choice as tantamount to signing Winnie's "death warrant."[2]

With her trip to Egypt and her fame as a writer, Winnie was evolving further and further from her Confederate roots. She was developing her own life and personality. She was an adventurer, a writer, and a novelist. She was a "New Woman" with a career, a social life, and no husband or children to keep her from her literary ambitions. She could have been free. What held her back, then, from taking advantage of such freedom, a state unknown to most women of her era? Her mother and her Confederate past still held her captive. Winnie's desire to please authority figures—her father before his death, her mother, and the southern war veterans who idolized her—was still strong.

At Varina's insistence Winnie unwillingly made the journey to the Atlanta veterans' reunion. By this time Winnie was a practiced hand at such symbolic events. She knew her job was to consecrate the gathering with her presence. The Daughter of the Confederacy's role was to look pretty, wave, and meet with all those who supported the Cause, no matter what their level in society. Winnie had to deal with the southern hoi polloi as well as its aristocrats.

As part of the Atlanta celebrations, Winnie rode in an elaborately decorated carriage with Mrs. "Stonewall" Jackson. The top was left up, and a sudden downpour drenched Winnie, who was forced to keep her clammy clothes on for hours. Winnie did not have the opportunity to change her outfit because of the large crowd pressing around her carriage. When she finally did get back to her lodgings, she immediately headed back out to a glamorous evening ball at Kimball House, a fashionable Atlanta hotel and hot spot for southern politicians of the era.[3]

Surrounded by a swirl of silks and satins, Winnie should have enjoyed an amusing and glamorous evening. The extreme corseting required by gowns of the period surely, however, did not help her physical state. Even more damaging was the chill caught during the day's open carriage ride. After the party Winnie's health, already precarious, rapidly declined. The next morning, still suffering the effects of the previous day's events, the exhausted young woman returned by train to Narragansett Pier to meet her mother.[4] Sick and worn-out, Winnie had to endure a bumpy ride back to Rhode Island.

Normally, Winnie was overjoyed to reach Rhode Island for her holidays. Narragansett Pier was a summer playground for the wealthy and prominent. By the late 1800s the community was thriving and rivaling its neighbor Newport, across Narragansett Bay, in terms of social prestige. Narragansett had a more relaxed, familial atmosphere than Newport, where guests tended to display their wealth more conspicuously. Winnie and Varina's chosen resort had more conservative tastes.[5] Summer visitors could enjoy sunbathing or play golf, tennis, and polo at Point Judith Country Club if they had the right connections.[6]

Perhaps the best spot to see and be seen was the impressive Narragansett Pier Casino, built by the famous New York architectural firm of the Gilded Age McKim, Mead & White. The casino stood directly across the street from the Rockingham Hotel, where Winnie and her mother spent their summer vacations.

The hotel Winnie and her mother had chosen was among the most lovely and elegant in Narragansett. Built in 1883, the Rockingham had broad piazzas overlooking a bathing beach, electric lights, hot and cold running water, and 150 rooms for its patrons to choose from. Its glamorous ballroom was raptly described in the hotel brochure as "one of the most charming of the public rooms, being decorated in white and gold." An orchestra installed in the ballroom provided daily concerts for guests.[7]

Winnie and Varina must have enjoyed observing the social cavalcade that took place right outside their windows on a daily basis. The country's elite appeared there regularly. Famous actor Edwin Booth (brother of Lincoln's assassin, John Wilkes Booth), Gen. (and later president) Ulysses S. Grant, abolitionist Henry Ward Beecher, publisher Horace Greeley, and Lincoln's secretary of the Treasury Salmon P. Chase all visited Narragansett Pier. Decades later Jacqueline Bouvier, the future Mrs. John F. Kennedy, would summer in the still-chic resort.[8]

Instead of plunging into her usual round of summer parties, promenading on Ocean Road alongside the rich and famous, playing croquet or lawn tennis, and indulging in her beloved hobby of bicycling, Winnie found herself in bed with a dangerous fever. She could not eat or sleep for days. Varina wrote to her old friend Major Morgan on the first of August that her daughter was "dreadfully reduced and very patient in her pain."[9]

By early September Varina was deeply worried about Winnie, but she still refused to believe that her youngest daughter was mortally ill. In a letter to Constance Cary Harrison, she said: "My Winnie is the most suffering person not to be dying that I ever saw . . . She cannot retain any nourishment except the occasional teaspoonful of cracked ice and raw white of egg, and even this she cannot assimilate."[10] The summer season typically ended the first or second week of September, and the weather typically soon turned chilly.[11]

On September 8 Varina wrote a heartbreaking letter to her grandson, Jefferson Hayes-Davis on Rockingham Hotel stationery. In the letter she thanked Jefferson for his letter to Winnie—or "Nannie," as Margaret's children called her. She described his aunt as "patient as an angel and [one who] never says a word of complaint." The doctor was visiting her twice a day, and the two women had the help of a trained nurse. The note of desperation is clear, however, in Varina's parting words to her grandson: "You must get down on your knees and pray God to help her and ease her pain and send her angels to guard and comfort her."[12]

Even in her frantic state, Varina noticed the striking similarity in the manner with which both her husband and daughter bore their mortal trials. "She has wasted away dreadfully," she wrote to Constance Cary Harrison, "but she bears everything with fortitude and patience I have never seen equaled except by her father."[13] During this illness Winnie again mirrored her father's stoicism. Forbearance, lack of complaint, and gracious acquiescence to suffering and pain were the hallmarks of her behavior during this trying period. These qualities were also perfectly in line with those of the idealized "southern womanhood" variety.

As the disease progressed, according to biographer Joan Cashin, Varina felt "increasingly guilty as she nursed her daughter, crying that never again would she send her child on such a 'useless errand.'"[14] Varina also admitted to her friend Constance that Winnie had not wanted to go to the reunion. Varina told Connie the doctors still expected Winnie to recover fully within a month.[15]

As she grew weaker and weaker, Winnie worried about her mother and their precarious financial state. Her second novel, *A Romance of Summer Seas*, was due to be published by Harper's in the fall. "'We shall have our carriage when my book sells," she reassured her mother.[16] As ill as she was, Winnie remained concerned both about her potential income and her literary reputation. Charles Dudley Warner wrote her during this time, and Varina made sure to read Winnie his letter full of praise for her literary career. Warner would ultimately write Winnie's obituary.[17]

During the last week of Winnie's life, she had frequent rallies that led her mother and her doctors to believe she would recover. Because of her illness, she and Varina were allowed to stay in the hotel even after the establishment had closed for the season. The atmosphere must have been lonely and desolate. The summer socialites had left and taken their gaiety and glamour with them. On Saturday evening, September 17, Winnie had a terrible relapse. By Sunday morning death was imminent, and she died in the Rockingham Hotel at noon that day.[18]

Varina must have been completely traumatized by this turn of events. It may have felt a bit like her son Joe's death back in 1864. In that instance she had blamed herself for not having been at the Executive Mansion when her little boy fell off the balcony. In Winnie's case the distraught mother had already proclaimed her regret to Connie Harrison over having sent Winnie to the veterans' reunion in July. In neither death was Varina directly to blame, but such thoughts may have preyed heavily on her conscience. The Widow of the Confederacy's youngest daughter was the child she had bonded with most completely of all her brood. Winnie was her companion, her caretaker, and her confidante.

Winnie's death remains mysterious and is still not sufficiently accounted for. Nineteenth-century medicine was still a crude science, so historians will probably never know the exact cause of her strange affliction. It is unlikely, however, that one would die from being drenched in a rainstorm. There must have been underlying physical and perhaps mental factors at play. Perhaps the young woman caught a stomach bug or other infection on her trip to Egypt. She was exhausted from that trip abroad and the journey that followed soon afterward to Atlanta. Winnie was physically frail to begin with and had always suffered from stomach ailments.

The young author never ate much, sometimes not at all. It is possible she suffered from an underlying eating disorder that had damaged her stomach. Or perhaps the stress of many years of living under the public microscope had strained her physical limits. Her death register notes that she died from "acute gastritis and gastroenteritis."[19]

Her father's medical history was very similar to Winnie's. He was constantly ill, with a "never-ending series of symptoms and complaints."[20] Like Winnie, Jefferson had suffered from frequent eye and stomach troubles. Any kind of stress took a physical toll on him. When Jefferson was serving as president of the Confederacy, the extreme stress he was under often forced him to withdraw for days. Bad news would often precipitate his nervous attacks.[21] Unfortunately, Winnie seemed to have inherited a similar pattern of her father's physical tendencies as well as his predisposition toward stress and anxiety.

After the young woman's death, telegrams and condolence letters poured in from friends all over the country as well as from United Confederate Veterans' groups and United Daughters of the Confederacy chapters but not, apparently, from Winnie's former fiancé.[22] Elaborate floral arrangements were sent from all quarters, filling the hotel parlors. The townspeople of Narragansett Pier were allowed to come pay their respects once the body had been dressed and laid out.[23]

A small wake was held for close friends and family at the Majestic Hotel, located at 125 West 44th Street in New York City, where the Davis women had moved from the Hotel Gerard.[24] Accounts mention the presence of Winnie's dear friend Kate Pulitzer as well as that of Mary Custis Lee, the daughter of Gen. Robert E. Lee.[25] Winnie's young friends could simply not believe she was gone. No longer would she be part of New York's vibrant literary and artistic scene, nor would she be seen again in her role as princess of the Confederate veterans' events.

Kate must have felt Winnie's loss keenly, as the two women had been constant companions and best friends for years. Perhaps she also wondered if their recent trip to Egypt had somehow resulted in her dear friend's early demise. We have no record of her thoughts, just of Kate's constant soothing presence while mourning her friend and relative both in New York and in Richmond.

It was Kate in fact, and not Varina, who signed Winnie's death certificate in Narragansett. Under "informant" is Kate's signature: Kate Davis Pulitzer. Varina was presumably too upset to attend to this clerical detail. Kate was also a distant Davis cousin; perhaps it was because of this relationship, as well as her calm personality, that she was allowed to take care of this unpleasant duty for Winnie's distraught mother.[26]

It was quickly decided that the funeral would take place in Richmond, the former capital of the Confederacy. Indeed, on September 19, 1898, the *Richmond Dispatch* newspaper proudly underlined the significance of this choice: "In no city was the announcement of her death received with more genuine sorrow than in Richmond. Though Miss Davis had not visited this city frequently, she was born here, and the people of the capital of the Confederacy felt that she was peculiarly near to them, for Richmond people cherish more dearly than those of any other city, probably, the memories and traditions of the Lost Cause."[27]

The public mourning surrounding Winnie's unexpected demise came equally from her friends North and South. No one could believe it. The Daughter of the Confederacy was just thirty-four. As southern writer and poet Robert Penn Warren famously observed, the South that had adored Winnie with a consuming passion ultimately rendered her "the last casualty of the Lost Cause."[28]

CHAPTER NINETEEN

Death and the Maiden

Varina was surely stunned that in a matter of weeks her youngest daughter could have been taken from her. Like Samuel, little Joe, Billy, and Jeff Jr. before her, Winnie had died tragically and far too young. How could a mother bear it? Many parents would have been crushed by so much tragedy. But Varina had already been through hell and back several times. And she still had one last shoulder to lean upon.

Margaret Hayes, Winnie's older married sister, quickly responded to the crisis with a telegram, making her travel plans to join Varina as soon as possible: "Darling Mother am broken hearted no train till tonight."[1] She made her way directly from Colorado Springs to Narragansett Pier to meet the funeral train. From there Varina, Margaret, and several other close family friends, including Burton Harrison and Kate Pulitzer, prepared to set off on the grueling overnight trip to Richmond on September 22.[2]

Seven Union veterans, members of the Sedgewick Post No. 7, Grand Army of the Republic, Wakefield, Rhode Island, escorted Winnie's body from the Rockingham Hotel to the railroad station.[3] Winnie's body was loaded onto the train at Narragansett, and the funeral train began its long journey south.

The young author's northern friends were just as shocked and aggrieved as their southern counterparts. Winnie had died so unexpectedly. It was said that "the entire city, and even state, of New York turned out to pay tribute to the Daughter of the Confederacy . . . joining the funeral march to the railroad station."[4]

Many agreed with the symbolism of burying the Daughter of the Confederacy in the former capital of the Confederacy. Although Winnie had spent most of her adult life abroad or in New York, Richmond was eager to claim her as one of its own. She had been born there, and memories of the Lost Cause and all those associated with it were still strong.[5] Winnie was granted a full military funeral, a rare honor for any woman and one her mother would insist on for herself (Varina died in 1906).[6]

The funeral train finally arrived at 8:40 a.m. at Union Depot in Richmond on Friday morning, September 23, 1898. The day was gloomy and cheerless. The sun would not shine until much later in the afternoon. A large crowd met the weary and bereaved travelers at the station. The throng included many members of Richmond's Lee and Pickett camps of Confederate veterans, important members of the United Daughters of the Confederacy (UDC), and family friends and prominent Richmonders such as Col. and Mrs. Archer Anderson, Hon. and Mrs. J. Taylor Ellyson, Col. and Mrs. E. L. Hobson, and Dr. and Mrs. George Ross.[7]

The Victorian obsession with death is clearly evident in the many morbid descriptions of the mourners' grief, the funeral proceedings, and "death dreams." A Richmond newspaper related a prescient vision Varina had supposedly had earlier that summer. Winnie reportedly told a family friend that she had had a dream about her own death. The friend related Winnie's nightmare to Varina, who then had her own dream about Winnie's demise. A few days before Varina left New York for her annual Narragansett Pier vacation, the newspaper claimed: "Mrs. Davis said she dreamed one night that she was in some place which she did not recognize. There seemed to be a great commotion among the people around her, the cause of which she could not understand . . . Suddenly, someone passed her hurriedly, and she asked of him the cause of the excitement . . . 'Winnie is dead!' was the reply."[8]

Varina, never a favorite with the press, was among the first to be scrutinized as she left the cocoon of the funeral train into the blazing glare of publicity at Richmond's Union Depot. "Bent with the weight of years," reported the *Richmond Dispatch* on September 24, "she leaned heavily upon the arm of Colonel Archer Anderson, and upon her stick, as she walked slowly and painfully to the carriage awaiting her. There was a look of intense anguish on her face, but she bore up bravely."[9] Varina, though slim as a young woman, had grown stout with age. She greatly resembled Queen Victoria in her later years and was dressed in much the same fashion for mourning that the queen had worn since the death of Prince Albert in 1861.

Traditional mourning dress of the period required women to wear heavy black crepe dresses, bombazine (a combination of silk and wool) cloaks, crepe bonnets with veils, and a full complement of mourning accessories, such as black gloves, belts, fans, and handbags. The fashion for mourning jewelry reached its height during the Civil War period because of the constant heavy casualties. Jet, which was made of fossilized coal, was used frequently in earrings, bracelets, brooches, and necklaces.

An entire art form sprung up during this era around ornaments made from the hair of the deceased. This morbid but wildly popular practice involved twisting the hair of the departed into intricate knots to be used in mourning brooches in particular. The women of Richmond and the honored guests who attended the funeral—including Varina, Margaret, and Winnie's close friend Kate Pulitzer—would have been dressed according to such mourning fashion dictates.[10]

The description of Winnie's corpse found in the *Richmond Dispatch* is particularly gruesome in its invasiveness, feeding a Victorian public and press ravenous for details of the deceased: "The appearance of the corpse was perfectly natural, the face being serene and smiling, showing no evidence of the illness through which she [Winnie] had passed." Winnie's casket was also described in detail in the Richmond *Dispatch* newspaper account: "The casket was an exceedingly handsome one of walnut wood, copper-lined and satin finishings covered with black velvet. The handles were of silver and a plate of the same metal bore the inscription:

VARINA ANNE DAVIS
Died September 18, 1898
Aged 33 Years."[11]

Close friends of the Davis family and members of the Confederate veterans' camps escorted the body to St. Paul's Church in downtown Richmond. A guard of honor led the procession in a single line, followed by the casket borne by pallbearers and Confederate veterans. The casket was placed on a hearse and drawn by four white horses, arriving at St. Paul's by way of Seventh and Grace Streets.

Upon arrival at the church, Winnie's coffin was placed on a catafalque, where she would remain under the charge of a guard of honor until the service began at 3:30 p.m. Twice during the morning the casket was opened, once for Winnie's sister, Margaret, and once for cousin and friend Kate Pulitzer.[12]

Many noted the "great outpouring of patriotic feeling throughout the South for the popular Daughter of the Confederacy."[13] According to historian Cita Cook, the event may have been "the largest funeral held for an American female in the nineteenth century."[14] As early as one o'clock on the day of the event, a huge throng filled the streets from the church railings near the St. Clair Hotel on one end to the railings near Capitol Square on the other.[15]

For the United Daughters of the Confederacy, Winnie's death was a terrible blow. A general order from the organization on September 20, 1898, declared the UDC's grief at losing its inspiration and chief role model: "The love and devotion bestowed on her, by the entire Southland, was but a just tribute to her glorious womanhood. As daughter, sister, friend, she was true to every duty, and we can proudly take her as a fitting model for all to imitate and revere."[16]

UDC members would wear a badge of mourning for thirty days, each chapter would hold its own memorial service for Winnie, and a special page in the book of records was set aside for the organization's fallen icon. Her early death would immortalize the Daughter of the Confederacy more definitively than any UDC event she had attended or blessed during her lifetime.

Most written portraits of Winnie from this time did not acknowledge the melancholy that haunted her. She was portrayed as a one-dimensional icon without the complexities that lay just under the surface. A Richmond newspaper article from September 23, 1898, fancifully stated: "There was a sunshine in her heart that illumined the lives of those about her. A thousand men had said today that she was the cheerfullest woman that had ever lived; and surely there can be no better epitaph."[17]

The church of choice for Winnie's funeral could have been none other than St. Paul's Episcopal Church in downtown Richmond. The enormous Greek Revival structure had dominated the downtown landscape since the church's consecration in 1845. St. Paul's is the city church most identified with the Confederacy and its prominent leaders. Still one of the largest Episcopal churches in Virginia, the church seats up to eight hundred congregants. Gen. Robert E. Lee and his wife had their own pew at St. Paul's for the duration of the Civil War, as did Jefferson and Varina. In 1862 Davis was confirmed as a member of the parish. Four of the church's most striking stained glass windows are dedicated to Jefferson Davis and General Lee.[18]

When downtown Richmond burned at the end of the Civil War, St. Paul's was miraculously spared. It has always retained its status as a church of choice for prominent Richmonders as well as visiting delegates, church officials, and even British royalty. In 1860 the Prince of Wales (later King Edward VII) attended services at the church. Despite St. Paul's strong association with the Confederate cause, the parish also performed baptisms, marriages, and funerals for both free and enslaved blacks.[19]

This particular house of worship provided the perfect theater for Winnie's tragedy. At the time the interior of the church was devoid of much religious symbolism—an interest in reviving medieval imagery within St. Paul's decor had only just begun in the 1890s.[20] The lack of decoration in the church allowed space for the Lost Cause imagery to take hold, with Winnie playing the part in the minds of the Lost Cause faithful of a young vestal virgin who had willingly sacrificed herself for the ideals of the Confederacy. Winnie's death at such a young age—and the fact that she was unmarried and unfettered by children, marriage, or a household—allowed her image to be fixed and frozen, awarding her perpetual celebrity status within the community of former Confederates.

At 3:30 p.m., as the service began, the First Regiment Band played Bottman's funeral dirge as the bells of all the city churches tolled mournfully. As the procession entered the church, the organist appropriately played the "Jefferson Davis Funeral March." At the request of Mrs. Davis, "a huge wreath of orchids with yellow roses, sent by family friends Joseph and Kate Pulitzer, was placed at the head of the coffin. The Confederate battle-flag lay upon the lower half and covered the black fur rug which lay beneath the catafalque."[21]

Hundreds of other floral arrangements crowded both the church and, later that day, the burial site at Hollywood Cemetery. Funeral wreaths were sent from Confederate veterans' chapters throughout the country, United Daughters of the Confederacy chapters, and personal friends of the Davis family. The profusion of gorgeous botanical displays included roses, palmettos, carnations, lilies of the valley, geraniums, American Beauty roses, ivy, heliotrope, magnolia branches in bloom, and a red lyre-shaped wreath of dahlias.[22] All these flowers' scents mingled together may have provoked a slightly nauseated feeling, combined with the heat of so many guests in the pews.

Within this gorgeously decorated Grecian temple, the Daughter of the Confederacy was worshipped publicly one last time. The Reverend Dr. H. Carmichael, rector of St. Paul's Church, conducted the service, with the Reverend Dr. Moses D. Hoge assisting. Dr. Hoge, a ruddy-faced man with muttonchop whiskers and a serious manner,[23] led an antiphonal reading of the Psalms, and Dr. Carmichael read the lesson and delivered the sermon. The hymns sung for the service were some of Winnie's favorites: "Nearer My God to Thee," "Art Thou Weary," and the final hymn, "Peace, Perfect Peace." Before the final hymn began, Dr. Hoge intoned, "Blessed are the pure at heart, for they shall see God."[24] Once again, the notion of Winnie as pure and unspoiled was reinforced for the audience of Confederate veterans, family, and friends.

Many oral histories and accounts of the funeral claim that Winnie's former fiancé, Fred Wilkinson, figured into the last scene of this dark Victorian drama. According to these reports, he attended Winnie's funeral at St. Paul's and was described as being greatly distressed, sitting in a pew far back in the church, and gazing sorrowfully across the crowded room.[25]

Like Winnie, Fred would never marry, having lost his heart, his youth, and his reputation to the Lost Cause. He died on May 18, 1918, at the age of fifty-seven, in Atlantic City, where he was recovering from a severe nervous breakdown.[26] It is certainly possible that the public furor caused by the northern lawyer's engagement to Winnie and the resulting intense scrutiny of his personal life were factors in his breakdown. Ultimately, even practical, matter-of-fact Fred suffered from feelings of angst so prevalent in the "nervous century."

Varina was practically prostrate for the entire service, leaning heavily on her one remaining child, Margaret, for comfort. She was clearly devastated and bereft. When the service ended, Varina had a difficult time standing up to leave the church. As the cortege finally was ready to depart, the *Richmond Dispatch* reported: "Mrs. Davis's emotion almost overcame her, and three of her old friends stepped forward and kissed her, uttering words of love. She regained her self control in a few moments, however, and took her place in line."[27]

The melancholy funeral procession next wended its way from Grace Street to Cherry Street, where Hollywood Cemetery lies. Many of the Confederate dead were already buried there. Winnie was put to rest in the Davis family plot, to the left of her father, just as the sun was setting that evening. This serene spot commanded a view of half of Richmond and the whole panorama of the James River.

At the head of the young woman's grave stood a giant palmetto tree, planted there by the South Carolina delegation from Isle of Palms. Varina and Margaret gave Winnie one last kiss, and the casket was sealed and lowered into the ground. Varina, Margaret, and their companions did not return to the Jefferson Hotel until well after dark.[28] The light had been extinguished not just from their long and arduous day but from the one they called the "Daughter of the Confederacy" forever.

Winnie's death signaled the end of an era. The most significant link between the Old South and the Lost Cause was now broken. In its tribute the Walter Barker Chapter of the United Daughters of the Confederacy described Winnie as if she were an antique object, not a person: "The last and only souvenir of the 'Lost Cause' has passed from earth to heaven."[29]

Winnie was a signifier, a face on the veterans' badges worn at Confederate reunions; she was in essence a "souvenir." *Souvenir*, if used in French as a noun, translates as "memory, recollection, and remembrance": a fitting motto for the deceased Daughter of the Confederacy. The young woman was not described by this UDC chapter in human terms—she was too special for that and clearly could not be replaced.

The Daughter of the Confederacy had functioned as the true representative of Jefferson Davis's legacy since his death in 1889. Although the mourners at St. Paul's that day and the Confederate veterans' groups thought they knew who Winnie was, she remained an enigma even for those closest to her, including her mother, her former fiancé, and her sister. Because she had remained with Varina and had stayed loyal to the memory of her father and the Confederacy, she could never truly leave the all-consuming sadness of the Civil War behind. Although Winnie had moved to New York and become a workingwoman, she lived there on borrowed time. Her existence was ruled by the past, despite her brave attempts to move her life into the present.[30]

To understand the circumstances of Winnie's death, one must first understand the dynamics of the Davis family. Passion, death, politics, and southern culture all combined to produce an atmosphere in which the Old South and the New collided. Although Winnie had a foot in both eras, she ultimately became trapped by the past, unable to reconcile her private personality with her public persona. As the daughter of Jefferson Davis, she could never shake the family legacy that ultimately consumed her, despite having grown up abroad, having been engaged to a Yankee grandson of an abolitionist, and having experienced a most unconventional life.

Four years later Varina summed up her thoughts on her beloved Winnie's existence and her deep despair at losing her youngest daughter: "She was born in the blackest storm of war which overwhelmed us, she suffered all the penalties without much of the glory, but accepted them gladly and triumphantly bore aloft her distinguished father's name in her own personality before contending parties North and South and no woman descended from a great man of our day has done so much."[31]

Varina would die of pneumonia in New York on October 16, 1906, the anniversary of her sons Jeff Jr. and Billy's deaths. She was eighty years old. Both her oldest daughter, Margaret Hayes, and Davis cousin Kate Pulitzer were at her bedside that day. She had outlived everyone in her family but her younger sister Margaret Howell Stoess and her daughter Margaret.[32]

Margaret Hayes did not outlive Varina for long. She died a scant three years after her mother, on July 18, 1909, of breast cancer. She was in Colorado Springs at the end, with her children and grandchildren around her.[33] Although Margaret was the last of the Davis children to pass away, the Davis legacy would not die with her. Varina Davis had already prevented that. In 1890 Varina marched Margaret and Addison's eight-year-old son, Jefferson Addison Hayes, down to the Mississippi legislature. That very day the boy's legal name was changed. His new name was Jefferson Addison Hayes-Davis.[34] This change ensured that the Davis name, at least, would be preserved.

But it was the Daughter of the Confederacy's early and untimely death that severed the most significant Davis family link between the

Old and the New South. No female representative of the Lost Cause would ever replace her. Winnie was a superstar of the nineteenth-century South, and her bond with the Confederate past and its war veterans was impossible to duplicate. Other young southern women were suggested as her replacement, including her older sister. These ideas were met with a harsh "emphatically no," however, from former Confederate general John B. Gordon, who had first christened Winnie the Daughter of the Confederacy.[35]

Winnie was an original: a unique combination of intellectual and woman of the people, American and European, southern and northern. Her image represented an odd fusion of ideals and fantasy as well as a bridge between the divides of North and South, the Old South and the New. The intellectual, sophisticated Daughter of the Confederacy, who had found her greatest happiness as a writer in New York City, remained a paradox to the end.

Epilogue

The Great-Great-Grandson of the Confederacy and the Daughter of New York

On a gorgeous early October day in 2012 I find myself at Beauvoir, the Jefferson Davis Home and Presidential Library in Biloxi, Mississippi. I am here to soak up the ambiance of the Gulf Coast home where Winnie spent so much time in her twenties. This raised Louisiana cottage was the site of her romance, the meeting between Fred and her parents to ask for her hand, and the final interview between Varina and Fred that terminated the couple's engagement.

The young lawyer would have arrived from Syracuse, New York, at Beauvoir Station on the edge of the property, hat and bags in hand. He would have made his way past Oyster Bayou—possibly spotting an exotic bird in flight—and then walked through Varina's prized rose gardens to reach his beloved Winnie.

I am awed by the inside of the house, as Fred himself must have been. Meticulously restored after Hurricane Katrina, the foyer ceilings boast gorgeous frescoes and plasterwork. An artwork originally displayed in the Vatican, chosen by Varina, hangs on one wall, and musical instruments such as a golden harp and a piano are prominently displayed. Winnie was known to serenade her parents and visitors to Beauvoir with her beautiful piano melodies in the front parlor. She and her sister, Maggie, both played the organ in the local Episcopal church when they stayed with their parents.[1]

I am here not only for the scenery but also to interview Bertram Hayes-Davis and his wife, Carol. Bertram is the great-great-grandson of Jefferson and Varina, the great-grandson of Margaret and Addison Hayes, and the grandson of Jefferson Addison Hayes-Davis. The former geologist who grew up in Colorado Springs is now the newest executive director of Beauvoir. Bertram is the last link in Winnie's story—the one who I hope can shed some light on her unusual life.

I wander a bit on the property, admiring the gorgeous lines of Beauvoir's raised cottage architecture—apparently, an adaptation of the style used by French settlers in the Caribbean to catch the cool ocean breezes.[2] I pass through a charming gift shop loaded with the southernisms that I miss as a Virginian living in the Midwest: a linen hand towel embroidered with a lobster and *Merry Christmas Y'all* next to a cookbook entitled *Gone with the Grits*. I am then ushered into the inner sanctum, the executive director's office.

Which is in a trailer.

Bertram Hayes-Davis smiles up at me. He is handsome, with thick white hair and a movie star smile. He looks eerily like the portraits I have seen in Colorado Springs of his great-grandfather Addison, known to the family as "Daddy Hayes."[3] His elegant and stylish wife, Carol, is a midwesterner from Ohio with a warm manner. Both are working together in said trailer while construction of the Presidential Library and staff offices is completed.

The library was to be open several weeks ago, but plans have been delayed by the unfortunate appearance of Hurricane Isaac. Determination and perseverance, however, are Davis family traits—and clearly part of Carol's heritage as well. The couple is not going to let a hurricane, or any other obstacle, hold them back from their plans for Beauvoir. "This is not what we signed up for," notes Carol, "but we are doing it for the right reasons—to carry out Varina's message for her."[4]

The couple graciously invites me into their world with an openness that I had not expected. They are busy today, just as they are every day here. Soon they will be greeting busloads of tourists, hosting a school event, and preparing for an evening cocktail party on-site. Even so, I feel I have their full attention when I ask them about Winnie, Margaret, Jefferson, and Varina.

I notice that despite the activity swirling around him on this particular day, Bertram still pauses to take a photo with a young boy on Beauvoir's back porch. The boy's family is clearly delighted and a bit stunned to encounter the great-great-grandson of Jefferson Davis mingling casually with visitors. They look as if they have seen a celebrity.

We spend lots of time talking over the next few days and eating delectable seafood at local restaurants White Cap Seafood and the Chimneys. We are united in our disappointment that the Chimney's famous coconut cake is not available the day we lunch there. Southern food enhances and facilitates our discussions about Winnie and her family.

What I find out is that Bertram's great-aunt Winnie could not escape the South, but his great-grandmother Margaret did. According to Bertram, Margaret's personality was quite unlike that of her people-pleasing younger sister: "I think Margaret was a much different person. She was born much earlier than Winnie and had been through a lot . . . Her love for the South and her family was intense, but she had created her own life in Colorado Springs. Maybe she had seen so much she needed to do something else."[5]

Now the generations have come full circle, with Bertram and Carol returning willingly to the South to preserve—and perhaps to change—the perception of the Davis legacy. They are custodians with a western-midwestern viewpoint and a commonsense approach to history.

Bertram and Carol enthusiastically explain their new vision for the historic site. Beauvoir will no longer be a monument to the Confederate soldier; it will be revamped according to Varina's stated wish that the property become a monument to Jefferson Davis. Carol confesses that she struggled with this concept until she began to understand that Varina wanted the public to be educated about her husband and all his achievements, not just the legacy of the Confederacy. Since moving to Mississippi, Carol reveals that she has been having dreams in which Varina visits her—perhaps the Davis matriarch is trying to give her advice on the direction Beauvoir needs to go post-Katrina.

Bertram, Carol, and I continue talking on the porch of the rebuilt Hayes cottage, where Margaret and her children used to stay when they visited Beauvoir. We sit in rocking chairs outside, luxuriating in the sunshine and sea breeze, with the glittering Gulf just across the street. Did Jefferson Davis finally get some real peace here at Beauvoir after all his struggles, both professional and personal? Bertram thinks so. Did Winnie? I think probably not. He was at the end of his life, while she was just beginning hers.

The Daughter of the Confederacy's bedroom lies just inside Beauvoir's front door and is dominated by her portrait as Queen of Comus at the

1892 New Orleans Mardi Gras. She is beautiful but projects that same melancholy air I noticed in the portrait of her I had seen in Virginia years ago. Her room boasts an ocean view and examples of her exquisite needlework. I can just imagine her sitting at her desk in this room working late into the night on her stories. Or perhaps writing love letters to Fred—all of which seem to have been destroyed by her mother or else lost to the winds of time.

Even in view of her comfortable life here and the cherished hours she spent with her aging father and mother—hours she deeply craved while in boarding school in Germany—I can see that the twenty-something Winnie was restless in this lovely but lonely place. Despite the railroad service and Beauvoir Station behind the property—which brought Fred, the Pulitzers, and even Oscar Wilde to visit—Beauvoir was an isolated location in the 1880s. You had to be determined to make your way here.

New York City proved to be a better place for Winnie to achieve her literary dream of writing and publishing her novels. Like her older sister, she tried to create her own identity outside of her southern heritage. While Winnie did achieve her dreams of writing and publishing her novels, she could not escape her status as Daughter of the Confederacy. In that respect Margaret was the One Who Got Away.

While many southerners still shy away from the history of the Confederacy and its related casualties, such as the broken engagement of Winnie Davis and Fred Wilkinson, Bertram emphatically does not. "History is one of the most important things we have in this country," he asserts, "and we need to make sure that we understand it, that we know all the reasons things occurred. I don't think it's difficult at all to talk about the War between the States."[6]

Perhaps the Davis family's southern mythology will be rejuvenated by the no-nonsense, can-do attitude of Beauvoir's newest director and his wife, who plan to cut through the crusty layers of "Lost Cause" mythology and examine Jefferson's life and career in its entirety. They feel the focus on his tenure as president of the Confederacy during the Civil War does not do justice to his other achievements.[7]

Most Americans do not realize that before he was elected president of the Confederacy, Jefferson was an army officer, a congressman, secretary of war under Franklin Pierce, and a two-term Mississippi senator. He was also a cultural force, helping to found the Smithsonian Institution and to design the United States Capitol building.[8]

Within this process Bertram and Carol will examine the Davis women as well: Winnie, Varina, Margaret, and Margaret's descendants. It is not just the physical structure of Beauvoir they are aiming to renovate. Understanding the spiritual, social, and personal structure of this most southern of families is integral to their vision for Beauvoir. Under their leadership the next chapter of the Davis and Hayes-Davis saga may prove to be its most revealing and its most exciting story yet.

While Bertram and Carol watch over and cultivate Beauvoir for the next generation in Mississippi, I get a sense that Winnie's spirit may rest elsewhere. New York became her true home, a place where she could relax, breathe, and blend in with the crowd.

The energy of the Theater District, where Winnie and Varina lived, must have suited her better than the languor and heat of the Gulf Coast. The literature, art, and culture of Manhattan drew her out of her shell and emboldened her to pursue her own literary career. It was here she became the best and truest version of herself.

Not more than a month after I visit Beauvoir, I find myself in New York City meeting a fellow biographer and dear friend for dinner. She suggests we eat at Un Deux Trois, a well-regarded French restaurant at 123 West 44th Street, located in what used to be the lobby of the Hotel Gerard, Winnie's second New York apartment. Located in the Theater District, the space is packed, filled with chic urbanites headed out to the latest Broadway show.

Before my friend arrives, I order a glass of Sancerre, close my eyes, and imagine I can hear Winnie's footsteps clicking across the parquet floor. I can see her in my mind's eye. She is wearing a tailored silk dress in her favorite dove gray color.

She sits down with me and laughs at the old southern myth that "poor Winnie Davis pined away and died because she had been forbidden to marry the Yankee."[9] She has been busy writing articles for Mr. Pulitzer and finishing up her latest novel. She indicates that we will meet another time, and she runs out the door to attend the theater, her gray eyes flashing with anticipation. The Daughter of the Confederacy, now the Daughter of New York, smiles and waves to me as she disappears into the crisp November night.

Acknowledgments

I have been working on this biography of Varina Anne "Winnie" Davis on and off since I was twenty-one years old. I am now forty-three, and throughout all that time, her tragic story has haunted me. When I moved to the Midwest four years ago, the allure of the South, with its dark, gothic postwar history, kept calling. Writing about Winnie has been a therapeutic way to stay connected with my southern past.

I am so grateful to those who supported me through this lengthy journey and believed in the power of Winnie's story. One of my Davidson College history professors, Dr. Sally McMillen, was the teacher who instilled in me a passion for women's history. Dr. McMillen's lectures about strong nineteenth-century southern women made a deep and lasting impression on me.

Dr. Lynda Lasswell Crist, editor of the Papers of Jefferson Davis at Rice University, has been an immensely valuable resource to me since my college days, when I first worked on Winnie for my undergraduate senior history thesis. The letters and newspaper and magazine snippets she sent me regarding Winnie and the Davis family kept me intrigued. I cannot thank her enough for her help and long-term involvement in this work.

I want to thank my good friend J.E.B. Stuart IV for his unending support and encouragement even when challenging obstacles appeared. His grace and diplomacy are things I will always admire. J.E.B. also introduced me to Bertram and Carol Hayes-Davis, both of whom could not have been more supportive of my work. They hosted me at Beauvoir multiple times, allowed me to look through their family papers, and gave me personal thoughts and insights on their family that made the story sing. Their clear vision for Beauvoir's museum and library, and for their family legacy, has been inspirational to me.

Bertram introduced me to another friend and museum colleague, Leah Witherow at the Pioneers Museum in Colorado Springs, the town where Margaret Davis and her family lived for many years. Leah is an amazing and dedicated curator who spent hours with me going through Hayes-Davis family scrapbooks until we found photographic evidence that Winnie had indeed visited her sister in Colorado in 1894.

Through Leah and Bertram I also was able to meet and talk to other descendants and relatives of the Davis family: energetic and enthusiastic Kathleen Fox-Collins, who drove me all over Colorado Springs and took me to the best used bookstore in town; and the lovely Marka Moser, who spent some time in Vail talking with me about the dynamics of her famous family. The insights that all these family members so graciously shared with me informed Winnie's story—which is also the story of the Davis family—in a rich and meaningful way.

A million thanks to my friends at Biographers International Organization (BIO): David Smith, "Librarian to the Stars," who in the blink of an eye found me all kinds of archival materials and sources in the northeastern United States and Midwest. Particular thanks go to David for locating Mary Craig Sinclair's unpublished "biography" of Winnie at the Lilly Library in Indiana. Thanks also to BIO president and founder Jamie Morris, author of *Pulitzer: A Life in Politics, Print, and Power*, who helped me find sources on Winnie's relationship with Joseph and Kate Pulitzer. And tremendous thanks to *Marmee and Louisa* author Eve LaPlante, who shared a family memoir with information about her relative and Winnie's fiancé, Alfred Wilkinson—known in Eve's family as "Uncle Fred." This information was a rare find and helped me flesh out Fred's side of the story.

Thanks also to Guy Gugliotta, author of the excellent book *Freedom's Cap: The United States Capitol and the Coming of the Civil War*, for his insightful comments and help regarding Jefferson Davis, his first marriage, and Jefferson's relationship with his father-in-law Zachary Taylor.

Many thanks to John Coski, Teresa Roane, and Drury Wellford at the Museum of the Confederacy in Richmond, Virginia, for their support, opinions, and excellent help with archival sources and photographs. Great thanks also go out to Erin Barnett and Claartje Van Dijk at the International Center of Photography in New York, who were both so gracious and helpful and met with me on short notice to discuss their 2012 exhibit on Jefferson Davis.

Thanks also to my friends at the United Daughters of the Confederacy in Richmond, Virginia: Lucy Steele and librarian Betty Luck, who helped me immensely with my research in the UDC files; and UDC president Jaime Likins for her support and interest in the Winnie project.

Thanks to my dear friend Diane Kiesel, also a Potomac author whose humor, advice, and support kept me from jumping off a cliff countless times during the writing process! Similar thanks go to Kay Smith, also a dear friend and an Iowa author, for reading various drafts of the Winnie chapters and offering excellent feedback. Also to authors Elizabeth Smartt, Ellen Brown, Jennifer Lyne, Kathleen Reid, Jane Hodges, and Betsy Connor Bowen whose help and advice set me on the right path. I cannot thank Richmond genealogist and my good friend Macon Willingham enough for her long-term help finding research bits for me from my original thesis that had fallen through the cracks as well for as helping me find new juicy tidbits on Winnie.

Thanks to my husband, Chris Lee, for his "tech support" and also his beautiful and haunting photographs of Winnie's grave and the White House of the Confederacy.

Thanks also to Dr. Michelle Krowl at the Library of Congress; Dr. Paul Levengood, Graham Dozier, and Nelson Lankford at the Virginia Historical Society; Sarah Kozma at the Onondaga Historical Association in Syracuse, New York; Colleen Thornton at the Town Clerk's Office in Narragansett, Rhode Island; Henry Arneth at Trinity College's Watkinson Library; Margaret Hrabe at the University of Virginia's Albert and Shirley Small Special Collections Library; and Xaris Martinez, doctoral student at the University of North Carolina. Thanks also to John Putnam for his research on the Davis family tree and to Deena Coutant for designing a readable and usable genealogical chart for my book. And thank you to Des Moines Art Center Curator Laura Burkhalter for her wonderful art lectures within our docent program. Her talks inspired me to examine images of women in nineteenth-century art more closely.

Immense thanks go to the University of Nebraska Press and Potomac Books team for efficiently shepherding me through the publication process with grace, enthusiasm, and humor. Bridget Barry did an elegant job of editing down the manuscript to a reasonable length and encouraging me to take out repetitive quotes and let my own voice come through. Thanks to her wonderful assistant Sabrina Sergeant who answered every question I had promptly and with good humor. Thanks to Kyle Simonsen and the art and design team for creating the most gorgeous cover for Winnie imaginable! Senior designer Annie Shahan's aesthetics were so reflective of my vision of what the cover and overall design should be. Thanks to my wonderful PR team: Jen Richards of OTRPR and Rosemary Vestal at UNP for being creative and thinking outside the box about Winnie. And thanks also to Elizabeth Gratch for her meticulous and thoughtful copyediting.

Finally, I dedicate this book to my mother, Anne Hardage, my maternal grandmother, Anne Purnell Heath, and my sister, Morgan Hardage Engel. They supported, cajoled, pushed, and cheered me on as I worked through the research, writing, travel, and the ups and downs of authorship. My mother in particular never let me forget that I could and should write this book. It is wonderful to finally reach the finish line!

Notes

FOREWORD

1. Letter from Varina Howell Davis, to Margaret Kempe Howell, May 22, 1864, Jefferson Davis Family Papers, Eleanor S. Brockenbrough Archives.
2. Thomason, *Jeb Stuart*, 133.

INTRODUCTION

Epigraph: "True to the Gray," quoted in Foster, *Ghosts of the Confederacy*, 30.

1. All the Executive Mansion descriptions come from Coski, *White House of the Confederacy*, 5, 9.
2. Coski, *White House of the Confederacy*, 5.
3. Coski, *White House of the Confederacy*, 9.
4. White House of the Confederacy tour, Richmond, April 2011.
5. Leveen, *Secrets of Mary Bowser*, reading group guide.
6. Johnson, *Pursuit*, 58.
7. Couling, *Lee Girls*, 116.
8. Edward M. Alfriend, "Social Life in Richmond during the War," *Cosmopolitan* (December 1891): 229–33 (available at www.mdgorman.com).
9. Alfriend, "Social Life in Richmond," 381.
10. Hendrick, *Statement of the Lost Cause*," 35.
11. Harrison, *Refugitta of Richmond*, 49.
12. Berkin, *Civil War Wives*, 161.
13. Chesnut, *Mary Chesnut's Civil War*, 85, 127.
14. Chesnut, *Mary Chesnut's Civil War*, 595.
15. Coski, *White House of the Confederacy*, 16.
16. *New York Times*, October 11, 1866.
17. "Jefferson Davis, Jr.," *Papers of Jefferson Davis* online, Rice University, http://jeffersondavis.rice.edu/JeffersonDavisJr.aspx.
18. *New York Times*, October 11, 1866.
19. *New York Times*, October 11, 1866.
20. White House of the Confederacy tour, Richmond, April 2011.
21. "Joseph Evan Davis," *Papers of Jefferson Davis* online, Rice University, http://jeffersondavis.rice.edu/JosephEvanDavis.aspx.
22. Cashin, *First Lady of the Confederacy*, 145–46.

1. A TRAGIC FALL

1. Couling, *Lee Girls*, 116.
2. Jones, *Rebel War Clerk's Diary*, 194–96.
3. Johnson, *Pursuit*, 53.
4. "Joseph Evan Davis," *Papers of Jefferson Davis* online, Rice University, http://jeffersondavis.rice.edu/JosephEvanDavis.aspx.
5. *Richmond Sentinel*, May 31, 1864, courtesy of *Papers of Jefferson Davis*, Rice University.
6. *Richmond Daily Dispatch*, May 2, 1864.
7. *Richmond Sentinel*, May 31, 1864.
8. *Richmond Sentinel*, May 31, 1864.
9. V. H. Davis, *Jefferson Davis*, 2:497.
10. Chesnut, *Mary Chesnut's Civil War*, 601.
11. Chesnut, *Mary Chesnut's Civil War*, 601.
12. Johnson, *Pursuit*, 57.
13. Harrison, *Refugitta of Richmond*, 123.
14. Strode, *Jefferson Davis*, 137.
15. Cashin, *First Lady of the Confederacy*, 68.
16. Berkin, *Civil War Wives*, 145–46.
17. Chesnut, *Mary Chesnut's Civil War*, 602.
18. Chesnut, *Mary Chesnut's Civil War*, 609.
19. Chesnut, *Mary Chesnut's Civil War*, 609.

2. MY NAME IS A HERITAGE OF WOE

1. Walter S. Griggs Jr., "James Ewell Brown Stuart: The General Who Sacrificed His Life to Save Richmond," *Richmond Guide* (Summer 2004).
2. Harrison, *Refugitta of Richmond*, 119.
3. Davis, Jeb Stuart, 409.
4. Thomason, *Jeb Stuart*, 500.
5. Jones, *Rebel War Clerk's Diary*, 206.
6. Jones, *Rebel War Clerk's Diary*, 206.
7. Thomason, *Jeb Stuart*, 501.
8. Davis, 412–13; Smith, *Life after J.E.B. Stuart*, 24–25.
9. Davis, 414.
10. Letter from Varina Howell Davis letter to Margaret Louisa Kempe, May 22, 1864, Jefferson Davis Family Papers, Eleanor Brockenbrough Archives.
11. Davis,.
12. Coski, *White House Pictorial Tour*, 31.
13. Rowland, *Varina Howell*, 367.
14. Rowland, *Varina Howell*, 506.
15. Letter from Varina Anne Davis to R. L. Hanes, April 22, 1895, Jefferson Davis Association, Rice University.

16. Chesnut, *Mary Chesnut's Civil War*, 786.
17. Chesnut, *Mary Chesnut's Civil War*, 663.
18. Catherine Lavender, "The Cult of Domesticity and True Womanhood," history class website, CUNY, www.library.csi.cuny.edu/dept/history/lavender/386/truewoman.html.
19. Crist et al., *Papers of Jefferson Davis*, 12:25.
20. Crist et al., *Papers of Jefferson Davis*, 12:197.
21. Swanson, *Bloody Crimes*, 3.
22. Swanson, *Bloody Crimes*, 5.
23. Jones, *Rebel War Clerk's Diary*, 465.
24. Lee, *Wartime Papers of Robert E. Lee*, 924.
25. Johnson, *Pursuit*, 43.
26. V. H. Davis, *Jefferson Davis*, 2:577.
27. V. H. Davis, *Jefferson Davis*, 2:577; Swanson, *Bloody Crimes*, 12.
28. Johnson, *Pursuit*, 19.
29. Johnson, *Pursuit*, 58.
30. Swanson, *Bloody Crimes*, 267.
31. Crist et al., intro. to *Papers of Jefferson Davis*, 12:vii.

3. ESCAPE, CAPTURE, AND FORT MONROE

Epigraph: Crist et al., *Papers of Jefferson Davis*, 12: 429–30.

1. Cashin, *First Lady of the Confederacy*, 157.
2. "The Evacuation and Burning of Richmond, Virginia," letter by Oscar F. Weisiger, May 29, 1865, relating to events of April 1865, Virginia Military Institute Archives, Civil War Collection, MS no. 00285.
3. Swanson, *Bloody Crimes*, 3.
4. Lankford, *Richmond Burning*, 242.
5. "The Fall of Richmond," *National Tribune*, October 4, 1890,www.mdgorman.com.
6. O'Reilly and Dugard, *Killing Lincoln*, 41.
7. Lankford, *Richmond Burning*, 164.
8. Tindal, "Confederate Treasure Train," 8.
9. Tindal, "Confederate Treasure Train."
10. Tindal, "Confederate Treasure Train," 10.
11. Chris James, "John Brown's Body," ". . . A Sour Apple Tree" blog, October 2, 2007, http://sourappletree.blogspot.com/2007/10/john-browns-body.html.
12. Swanson, *Bloody Crimes*, 95–100.
13. V. H. Davis, *Jefferson Davis*, 2:614–15.
14. Harrison, *Refugitta of Richmond*, 164.
15. Chesnut, *Mary Chesnut's Civil War*, 800.
16. Cashin, *First Lady of the Confederacy*, 161.
17. Johnson, *Pursuit*, 196.

18. Johnson, *Pursuit*, 202.
19. W. C. Davis, *Jefferson Davis*, 636; Johnson, *Pursuit*, 202.
20. Erin Barnett, assistant curator at the International Center of Photography (ICP), interview per email on February 28, 2013, regarding the ICP's exhibition *President in Petticoats! Civil War Propaganda in Photographs*, May 18–September 2, 2012.
21. Nina Silber, *The Romance of Reunion: Northerners and the South, 1835–1900* (Chapel Hill: University of North Carolina Press, 1993), 34.
22. W. C. Davis, *Jefferson Davis*, 645.
23. W. C. Davis, *Jefferson Davis*, 645.
24. Silber, "Intemperate Men," 299.
25. Ferrell, "Daughter of the Confederacy," 72.
26. LaCavera, *Varina Anne "Winnie" Davis*, 10.
27. Appleton and Boswell, *Searching for Their Places*, 146.
28. V. H. Davis, *Jefferson Davis*, 2:312.
29. Crist et al., *Papers of Jefferson Davis*, 12:17.

4. A FATAL ROMANCE

1. W. C. Davis, *Jefferson Davis*, 4–72; Strode, *Jefferson Davis*, 5–14; Beacroft, *Jefferson Davis*; Bleser, "Marriage of Varina Howell Davis and Jefferson Davis," 5–6; Rutherford, *Jefferson Davis*.
2. Rutherford, *Jefferson Davis*, 19.
3. Quoted in Rutherford, *Jefferson Davis*, 19.
4. W. C. Davis, *Jefferson Davis*, 84.
5. Cashin, *First Lady of the Confederacy*, 33–34; Gugliotta, *Freedom's Cap*, 42.
6. W. C. Davis, *Jefferson Davis*, 84.
7. Davis, *Cause Lost*, 11.
8. Hendrick, *Statesmen of the Lost Cause*, 23.
9. Kelly, with Smyer, *Best Little Stories, 267.*; De Leon, *Belles, Beaux and Brains of the 60's*, 68.
10. Cashin, *First Lady of the Confederacy*, 18–19.
11. Cashin, *First Lady of the Confederacy*, 11.
12. Cashin, *First Lady of the Confederacy*, 36.
13. Kelly, with Smyer, *Best Little Stories*, 268.
14. Bleser, "Marriage of Varina Howell Davis and Jefferson Davis," 7; Davis, *Man and His Hour*, 107.
15. Cashin, *First Lady of the Confederacy*, 38.
16. Scott, *Southern Lady*, 18.
17. Davis, *Cause Lost*, 9.
18. Gugliotta, *Freedom's Cap*, 44.
19. Gugliotta, *Freedom's Cap*, 45–47.
20. Davis, *Cause Lost*, 10.

21. Cashin, *First Lady of the Confederacy*, 55.
22. Tindall, "Jefferson Davis," 9.
23. Clay-Clopton and Sterling, *Belle of the Fifties*, 101.
24. Tindall, "Jefferson Davis," 10.
25. Tindall, "Jefferson Davis," 10; Beacroft, *Jefferson Davis*.
26. Johnson, *Pursuit*, 42.
27. W. C. Davis, *Jefferson Davis*, 303.
28. Cashin, *First Lady of the Confederacy*, 4.

5. SCANDAL AND SICKNESS

1. V. H. Davis, *Jefferson Davis*, 2:796.
2. Berkin, *Civil War Wives*, 195.
3. Berkin, *Civil War Wives*, 195.
4. Cashin, *First Lady of the Confederacy*, 171.
5. Wyatt-Brown, *House of Percy*, 169.
6. www.xroads.virginia.edu.
7. www.history.com/this-day-in-history/freedman's-bureau-created.
8. www.pbs.org/wgbh/amex/reconstruction.
9. V. H. Davis, *Jefferson Davis*, 2:805.
10. V. H. Davis, *Jefferson Davis*, 2:809–10.
11. Cashin, *First Lady of the Confederacy*, 172, 184–85.
12. Bleser, "Marriage of Varina Howell and Jefferson Davis," 25.
13. Strode, *Jefferson Davis*, 324.
14. Strode, *Jefferson Davis*, 328.
15. Bleser and Heath, "Clays of Alabama," 136.
16. Cashin, *First Lady of the Confederacy*, 191.
17. Cashin, *First Lady of the Confederacy*, 201.
18. Cashin, *First Lady of the Confederacy*, 201.
19. Cashin, *First Lady of the Confederacy*, 204.
20. Crist et al., *Papers of Jefferson Davis*, 12:xv.
21. Clay-Clopton and Sterling, *Belle of the Fifties*, 257–68; Cashin, *First Lady of the Confederacy*, 204.
22. V. H. Davis, *Jefferson Davis*, 814.
23. Cashin, *First Lady of the Confederacy*, 208.
24. Crist and Gibbs, *Papers of Jefferson Davis*, 13:110, 152.
25. Sarah Wollfolk Wiggins, "A Victorian Father: Josiah Gorgas and His Family," in Bleser, *In Joy and Sorrow* , 233.
26. Ferrell, "Daughter of the Confederacy," 70–71.

6. BOARDING SCHOOL BLUES AND THE DORSEY DILEMMA

Epigraph: Rev. Romulus Morris Tuttle, "Miss Winnie Davis, a Tribute," *Tuttle's Poems* (Dallas: W. M. Warlick, 1905), 4.

1. Cashin, *First Lady of the Confederacy*, 224–25.
2. *Confederate Veteran Magazine* 6 (January–December 1898): 466, Helen Walpole Brewer Library and Archives.
3. Cashin, *First Lady of the Confederacy*, 214.
4. *Confederate Veteran Magazine* 17 (January–December 1909): 419, Helen Walpole Brewer Library and Archives.
5. Crist and Gibbs, *Papers of Jefferson Davis*, 13:348.
6. Dolensky, "Daughters of Jefferson Davis," 319.
7. Crist and Gibbs, *Papers of Jefferson Davis*, 13:348.
8. Dolensky, "Daughters of Jefferson Davis," 317.
9. Dolensky, "Daughters of Jefferson Davis," 323–24.
10. Burr, "Jefferson Davis," 165.
11. Crist and Gibbs, *Papers of Jefferson Davis*, 13:119.
12. Berkin, *Civil War Wives*, 201.
13. Appleton and Boswell, *Searching for Their Places*, 158.
14. Strode, *Jefferson Davis*, 434.
15. Cashin, *First Lady of the Confederacy*, 217.
16. Cashin, *First Lady of the Confederacy*, 185.
17. LaCavera, *Varina Anne "Winnie" Davis*, 12,
18. Crist and Gibbs, *Papers of Jefferson Davis*, 13:376–77.
19. Strode, *Jefferson Davis*, 433.
20. Strode, *Jefferson Davis*, 434.
21. Strode, *Jefferson Davis*, 434.
22. Letter from Varina Howell Davis to Jefferson Davis, February 18, 1877, Karlsruhe, W. S. Hoole Special Collections.
23. Cashin, *First Lady of the Confederacy*, 217.
24. Ferrell, "Daughter of the Confederacy," 73.
25. Strode, *Jefferson Davis*, 451.
26. Letter from Varina Howell Davis to Jefferson Davis, February 18, 1877.
27. Letter from Varina Anne Davis to Varina Howell Davis, August 18, 1877, Karlshruhe, W. S. Hoole Library Special Collections.
28. Strode, *Jefferson Davis*, 438.
29. Letter from Varina Anne Davis to Varina Howell Davis, May 26, 1878, Karlsruhe, W. S. Hoole Library Special Collections.
30. Letter from Varina Anne Davis to Varina Howell Davis, May 26, 1878.
31. Dolensky, "Daughters of Jefferson Davis," 320.
32. Wyatt-Brown, *House of Percy*, 163.
33. Wyatt-Brown, *House of Percy*, 163.
34. "Sarah Anne Ellis Dorsey," *Papers of Jefferson Davis* online, Rice University, http://jeffersondavis.rice.edu/SarahDorsey.aspx.
35. Wyatt-Brown, *House of Percy*, 159.
36. Wyatt-Brown, *House of Percy*, 159–60.

37. Berkin, *Civil War Wives*, 204.
38. Letter from Margaret Addison Hayes to Varina Howell Davis, June 9, 1877, W. S. Hoole Special Collections Library.
39. Wyatt-Brown, *House of Percy*, 163.
40. Cashin, *First Lady of the Confederacy*, 222.
41. Cashin, *First Lady of the Confederacy*, 223.
42. Crist and Gibbs, *Papers of Jefferson Davis*, 13:538.
43. Crist and Gibbs, *Papers of Jefferson Davis*, 13:553.
44. LaCavera, *Varina Anne "Winnie" Davis*, 16.
45. Bleser, "Marriage of Varina Howell Davis and Jefferson Davis," 8.
46. Letter from Varina Anne Davis to Varina Howell Davis, Karlsruhe, September 27, 1877, W. S. Hoole Special Collections.
47. V. H. Davis, *Jefferson Davis*, 2:825–26.
48. Crist and Gibbs, *Papers of Jefferson Davis*, 13:432.
49. Wyatt-Brown, *House of Percy*, 163–64.
50. Letter from Margaret Addison Hayes to Varina Howell Davis, June 9, 1877.
51. Ross, *First Lady of the South*, 328; Wyatt-Brown, *House of Percy*, 164. (Ross says the garden party was in Winnie's honor.)
52. Thompson, *Beauvoir*.
53. Cashin, *First Lady of the Confederacy*, 228–29.
54. Thompson, *Beauvoir*.
55. Burr, "Jefferson Davis," 165.
56. W. C. Davis, *Jefferson Davis*, 685.
57. Hardin, *After the War*, 8.
58. Crist and Gibbs, *Papers of Jefferson Davis*, 13:569–70.
59. Davis, "American Girl Who Studies Abroad, First Paper"; and "American Girl Who Studies Abroad, Second Paper."

7. YELLOW FEVER

Epigraph: Letter from Varina Howell Davis to Jefferson Davis, June 20, 1875, in Crist and Gibbs, *Papers of Jefferson Davis*, 13:301.

1. Crist et al., *Papers of Jefferson Davis*, 12:146.
2. Clay-Clopton and Sterling, *Belle of the Fifties*, 262.
3. Clay-Copton and Sterling, *Belle of the Fifties*, 262.
4. Crist and Gibbs, *Papers of Jefferson Davis*, 13:228–29, 435.
5. V. H. Davis, *Jefferson Davis*, 2:826.
6. Ross, *First Lady of the South*, 327.
7. "Jefferson Davis, Jr.," *Papers of Jefferson Davis* online, Rice University, http://jeffersondavis.rice.edu/JeffersonDavisJr.aspx.
8. W. C. Davis, *Jefferson Davis*, 28–37; Crist and Gibbs, *Papers of Jefferson Davis*, 13:229.

9. *Confederate Veteran Magazine* (November 1909): 534, Helen Walpole Brewer Library and Archives.

10. Crist and Gibbs, *Papers of Jefferson Davis*, 13:515.

11. *Papers of Jefferson Davis* online, Rice University, www.jeffersondavis.rice/edu/resources.cfm_doc_id=1544.

12. Ross, *First Lady of the South*, 329.

13. Note from dean of faculty regarding Jefferson Davis Jr., n.d., Virginia Military Institute (VMI) Archives, Lexington.

14. "First Victim of Memphis Yellow-Fever Epidemic Dies," History.com, "This Day in History," August 13, 1878, www.history.com/this-day-in-history/first-victim-of-memphis-yellow-fever-epidemic-dies.

15. www.commericalappeal.com/news/2010/sep/11/yellow-fever-left-mark-on-memphis.

16. Crist and Gibbs, *Papers of Jefferson Davis*, 13:507.

17. Confederate Veteran.

18. Tennessee State Library and Archives, "Disasters in Tennessee," www.tn.gov/tsla/exhibits/disasters/epidemics.htm.

19. Cashin, *First Lady of the Confederacy*, 225.

20. Ross, *First Lady of the South*, 329–30.

21. Crist and Gibbs, *Papers of Jefferson Davis*, 13:514.

22. Faust, *This Republic of Suffering*, 17.

23. V. H. Davis, *Jefferson Davis*, 828.

24. Letter from Varina Howell Davis to Bessie Martin Dew, October 26, 1884, Helen Walpole Brewer Library and Archives.

25. Letter from Varina Howell Davis to Bessie Martin Dew, October 26, 1884.

26. Ross, *First Lady of the South*, 330.

27. Bessie Martin Dew, personal newspaper clippings collection, n.d., Helen Walpole Brewer Library and Archives.

28. Strode, *Jefferson Davis*, 490.

29. Ross, *First Lady of the South*, 330.

30. Strode, *Jefferson Davis*, 490.

31. Strode, *Jefferson Davis*, 493.

32. Strode, *Jefferson Davis*, 492–93.

33. Crist and Gibbs, *Papers of Jefferson Davis*, 13:422.

34. Tennessee State Library and Archives, "Disasters in Tennessee," www.tn.gov/tsla/exhibits/disasters/epidemics.htm.

35. Letter from Margaret Addison Hayes to Varina Howell Davis, June 9, 1877, W. S. Hoole Special Collections Library.

36. Strode, *Jefferson Davis*, 390.

37. Letter from Joel Addison Hayes to Varina Anne Davis, March 19, 1877, Bertram Hayes-Davis Private Collection.

38. Letter from Joel Addison Hayes to Varina Anne Davis, March 19, 1877.
39. Letter from Joel Addison Hayes to Varina Anne Davis, July 1, 1877, Bertram Hayes-Davis Private Collection.
40. Letter from Margaret Addison Hayes to Varina Anne Davis, December 18, 1879, Bertram Hayes-Davis Private Collection.
41. Letter from Margaret Addison Hayes to Varina Anne Davis, December 14, 1880, W. S. Hoole Special Collections Library.
42. Letter from Joel Addison Hayes to Varina Anne Davis, August 4, 1880, Bertram Hayes-Davis Private Collection.

8. PORTRAIT OF A LADY

1. W. C. Davis, *Jefferson Davis*, 678.
2. Ferrell, "Daughter of the Confederacy," 71.
3. Ferrell, "Daughter of the Confederacy," 73.
4. Ferrell, "Daughter of the Confederacy," 71.
5. Cashin, *First Lady of the Confederacy*, 235.
6. Alice Graham McCollin, "Clever Daughters of Clever Men," *Ladies' Home Journal*, December 1891, 12.
7. Letter from Varina Davis to Constance Cary Harrison, December 20, 1886, Harrison Family Papers, 1744–1930.
8. "The Home Life of Miss Winnie Davis," *Kansas City Times*, September 15, 1888.
9. Ross, *First Lady of the South*, 335-336.
10. Ross, *First Lady of the South*, 368.
11. *Richmond Times*, September 24, 1898.
12. W. C. Davis, *Jefferson Davis*, 684.
13. Baker, "Verner White," 423–24.
14. Baker, "Verner White," 423–24.
15. O'Brien, "Verner White," 222.
16. O'Brien, "Verner White."
17. Baker, "Verner White," 426.
18. Email from Colleen Beavers, head of Collections, Beauvoir, to the author, December 4, 2012.
19. Baker, "Verner White," 425.
20. LaCavera, *Varina Anne "Winnie" Davis*, 19
21. Ralph, "Mardi Gras at New Orleans," 285.
22. Williamson, *A Rage for Order*, 22.
23. Berkin, *Civil War Wives*, 209.
24. Ross, *First Lady of the South*, 340–41.
25. Swanson, *Bloody Crimes*, 390.
26. Ferrell, "Daughter of the Confederacy," 72.

9. DAUGHTER OF THE CONFEDERACY

Epigraph: Quoted in LaCavera, *Varina Anne "Winnie" Davis*, 71.

1. Foster, *Ghosts of the Confederacy*, 97.
2. Cox, *Dixie's Daughters*, 13.
3. Foster, *Ghosts of the Confederacy*, 135.
4. Hardin, *After the War*, 7–8.
5. Williamson, *Rage for Order*, 21.
6. Williamson, *Rage for Order*, 82.
7. Van der Heuvel, *Crowns of Thorns and Glory*, 250.
8. Foster, *Ghosts of the Confederacy*, 97.
9. Appleton and Boswell, *Searching for Their Places*, 146.
10. V. H. Davis, *Jefferson Davis*, 831.
11. Poppenheim et al., *History of the United Daughters of the Confederacy*, 1:2; LaCavera, *Varina Anne "Winnie" Davis*, 20; Oldendorf, "Lost Princess of the South," 2–3.

    There is some debate over where General Gordon first named Winnie the "Daughter of the Confederacy." Some sources give the location as West Point GA; some say Atlanta. I believe the most reliable sources are the UDC and Memorial Hall accounts, which claim West Point as the site of the event.
12. Davis, *Cause Lost*, 175.
13. Edwards, "Memories of Winnie Davis," 4, Jefferson Davis Family Papers, Eleanor Brockenbrough Archives.
14. Foster, *Ghosts of the Confederacy*, 136.
15. Foster, *Ghosts of the Confederacy*, 137.
16. Cashin, *First Lady of the Confederacy*, 290.
17. Letter from Margaret Davis Hayes to Varina Anne Davis, October 26, 1885, Colorado Springs CO, W. S. Hoole Special Collections Library.
18. Helen Clapesattle, *Dr. Webb of Colorado Springs* (Boulder: Colorado Associated University Press, 1984), 89.
19. Foster, *Ghosts of the Confederacy*, 97.
20. Poppenheim et al., *History of the United Daughters of the Confederacy*, 1:3.
21. Janney, *Burying the Dead but Not the Past*, 169.
22. Janney, *Burying the Dead but Not the Past*, 168; Poppenheim et al., *History of the United Daughters of the Confederacy*, 1:9.
23. Janney, *Burying the Dead but Not the Past*, 169.
24. Poppenheim et al., *History of the United Daughters of the Confederacy*, 1:42.
25. Poppenheim et al., *History of the United Daughters of the Confederacy*, 1:42; UDC database records, Richmond.
26. Applications for Membership, New York Chapter of the UDC of the State of New York, March 1897: Miss Jefferson Davis and Mrs. Varina Jefferson

Davis, UDC Files, Helen Walpole Brewer Library and Archives, Richmond.

27. Foster, *Ghosts of the Confederacy*, 172.

28. Cox, *Dixie's Daughters*, foreword.

29. Jamie Likins, president general of the UDC, 2012–14, with research help from UDC staff Amy Howard and Betty Luck, "Winnie Davis, 'Daughter of the Confederacy'" statement, July 27, 2013, Richmond.

30. Cita Cook, "The Lost Cause Legend about Winnie Davis, 'the Daughter of the Confederacy,'" in Klotter, *Human Tradition in the New South*, 4.

31. Ross, *First Lady of the South*, 336.

32. Letter from Varina Anne Davis to Gaston Robbins, April 10, 1887, Robbins Papers no. 4070, Southern Historical Collection.

33. Ferrell, "Daughter of the Confederacy," 73.

34. Burr, "Jefferson Davis," 165.

35. Keith Hardison, telephone interview by the author, from Biloxi MS, February 10, 1992.

36. W. C. Davis, *Jefferson Davis*, 685.

37. Scott, *Southern Lady*, 51.

10. LIFE IN A FISHBOWL

1. Williamson, *Rage for Order*, 20.

2. Ross, *First Lady of the South*, 349.

3. Cashin, *First Lady of the Confederacy*, 247.

4. Davis, "American Girl Who Studies Abroad, Second Paper," 6.

5. Davis, "American Girl Who Studies Abroad, First Paper," 9.

6. V. A. Davis, "American Girl Who Studies Abroad, First Paper," 9.

7. Letter from Varina Howell Davis to Constance Cary Harrison, December 20, 1886, Harrison Family Papers, 1744–1930, accession no. 2536, Albert and Shirley Small Special Collections Library.

8. V. A. Davis, "American Girl Who Studies Abroad, Second Paper," 6.

9. V. A. Davis, "American Girl Who Studies Abroad, Second Paper," 6.

10. V. A. Davis, "American Girl Who Studies Abroad, Second Paper," 6.

11. Morris, *Pulitzer*, 2.

12. Livingston, *Lilly*, 126.

13. Letter from Varina Howell Davis to Joseph Pulitzer, May 4, 1887, Joseph Pulitzer Papers.

14. Letter from Varina Anne Davis to Joseph Pulitzer, October 20, 1887, Joseph Pulitzer Papers.

15. Morris, *Pulitzer*, 259.

16. Morris, *Pulitzer*, 259.

17. Klotter, *Human Tradition in the New South*, 6.

18. Letter from Varina Howell Davis to Constance Cary Harrison, December 20, 1886, Harrison Family Papers.
19. Letter from Varina Howell Davis to Constance Cary Harrison, December 20, 1886.
20. W. C. Davis, *Jefferson Davis*, 685.
21. Letter from Varina Anne Davis to Charles Dudley Warner, December 23, 1885, Charles Dudley Warner Correspondence.
22. Letter from Varina Howell Davis to Charles Dudley Warner, December 26, 1886, Charles Dudley Warner Correspondence.
23. Letter from Varina Howell Davis to Charles Dudley Warner, December 26, 1886.
24 Cashin, *First Lady of the Confederacy*, 251–52.
25. Crist et al., *Papers of Jefferson Davis*, 12:234; Cashin, *First Lady of the Confederacy*, 252.
26. Ferrell, "Daughter of the Confederacy," 74; De Leon *Belles, Beaux and Brains of the 60's*, 68.
27. Davis, *Irish Knight of the Nineteenth Century*, 81.
28. Davis, *Irish Knight of the Nineteenth Century*, 45.
29. Davis, *Irish Knight of the Nineteenth Century*, 91.
30. Letter from Varina Howell Davis to Constance Cary Harrison, December 20, 1886.
31. "Miss Davis in New York: Many Ladies Watch," *Special Dispatch to the Washington Post*, November 7, 1886.
32. Letter from Varina Howell Davis to Bessie Martin Dew, December 29, 1886, Helen Walpole Brewer Library and Archives.
33. Letter from Varina Howell Davis to Bessie Martin Dew, December 29, 1886.

11. I WILL NEVER CONSENT!

1. Monsees, "How the Daughter of the Confederacy Almost Became a Daughter of New York."
2. "Miss Winnie Davis, the 'Child of the Confederacy,' Her Visit to Syracuse," *New Orleans Times-Picayune*, December 15, 1886.
3. "Miss Winnie Davis, the 'Child of the Confederacy.'"
4. Letter from Harry C. Durston, Secy., to Mrs. Fremont Older, January 24, 1950, Wilkinson (Emory) Family File.
5. *Syracuse Courier*, December 3, 1878, Wilkinson (Emory) Family File.
6. "Miss Winnie Davis, the 'Child of the Confederacy.'"
7. "Kaylan Historical Showcase, Wilkinson Romance," radio performance, WFBI, March 27, 1946, 1:30–1:45 p.m., Wilkinson (Emory) Family File.
8. "Kaylan Historical Showcase, Wilkinson Romance."
9. "Miss Winnie Davis in Syracuse," special dispatch to the *Washington Post*, November 22, 1886.

10. Letter from Varina Anne Davis to Joseph Pulitzer, December 29, 1886, Joseph Pulitzer Papers.
11. "Miss Winnie Davis in Syracuse."
12. Monsees, "How the Daughter of the Confederacy Almost Became a Daughter of New York."
13. Monsees, "How the Daughter of the Confederacy Almost Became a Daughter of New York."
14. "Kaylan Historical Showcase, Wilkinson Romance."
15. "A Notable Engagement," *Syracuse Standard*, April 17, 1890, Wilkinson (Emory) Family File.
16. LaPlante, *Marmee and Louisa*, 169.
17. Dorris, *Pardon and Amnesty under Lincoln and Johnson*, 278–312; Bleser, "Marriage of Varina Howell and Jefferson Davis," 23.
18. Powell, *Gone Are the Days*, 123.
19. Powell, *Gone Are the Days*, 138–39.
20. Powell, *Gone Are the Days*, 138.
21. "Kaylan Historical Showcase, Wilkinson Romance."
22. "Summer House is Memorial to Leader of the Jerry Rescue," *Syracuse Post Standard*, October 1, 1934, Wilkinson (Emory) Family File.
23. Williamson, *Rage for Order*, 23.
24. Keith Hardison, telephone interview by the author, from Biloxi MS, February 10, 1992.
25. "Miss Winnie Davis: The Young Woman who Is Best Known as the Daughter of the Confederacy," *The Washington Post*, February 13, 1887.
26. Ross, *First Lady of the South*, 356.
27. Letter from Varina Howell Davis to Kate Pulitzer, June 13, 1888, Joseph Pulitzer Papers.
28. Morris, *Pulitzer*, 271.
29. Ross, *First Lady of the South*, 355.
30. Monsees, "How the Daughter of the Confederacy Almost Became a Daughter of New York."
31. Letter from Varina Howell Davis to Maj. W. H. Morgan, September 1888, Davis and Family Papers, LC.
32. Letter from Varina Howell Davis to Maj. W. H. Morgan, September 1888.
33. Letter from Varina Howell Davis to Maj. W. H. Morgan, September 1888.
34. Letter from Varina Howell Davis to Maj. W. H. Morgan, September 1888.
35. W. C. Davis, *Jefferson Davis*, 685.
36. Letter from Varina Howell Davis to Maj. W. H. Morgan, September 1888.
37. Ross, *First Lady of the South*, 356.
38. Cashin, *First Lady of the Confederacy*, 262.
39. Monsees, "How the Daughter of the Confederacy Almost Became a Daughter of New York."

40. "Banking House Failures: Syracuse Excited over an Assignment: The House of Wilkinson and Co. Closes Its Doors Owing Nearly Half a Million—Assets Very Meagre," *New York Times*, December 11, 1884 (courtesy of Eve LaPlante).
41. LaPlante, *Marmee and Louisa*, 272.
42. LaPlante, *Marmee and Louisa*, 272.
43. Louisa May Alcott, quoted in LaPlante, *Marmee and Louisa*, 272.
44. Cashin, *First Lady of the Confederacy*, 261.
45. LaPlante, *Marmee and Louisa*, 249–50.
46. Letter from Varina Howell Davis to Maj. W. H. Morgan, September 1888.
47. Letter from Varina Howell Davis to Maj. W. H. Morgan, September 1888.
48. Cashin, *First Lady of the Confederacy*, 263.
49. "Notable Betrothal," *Syracuse Standard*, April 17, 1890, Wilkinson (Emory) Family File.
50. Silber, *Romance of Reunion*, 94.

12. ENGAGEMENT ISSUES

1. Ross, *First Lady of the South*, 358.
2. Monsees, "How the Daughter of the Confederacy Almost Became a Daughter of New York"; Ross, *First Lady of the South*, 358.
3. Foster, *Ghosts of the Confederacy*, 28.
4. Ross, *First Lady of the South*, 358.
5. Zimmerman, *Love Fiercely*, 113.
6. "The Daughter of the Confederacy," *New York Times*, October 20, 1889.
7. Letter from Varina Howell Davis to Gen. Jubal Early, May 5, 1883, Harrison Family Papers, 1744–1930, accession no. 2536, Albert and Shirley Small Special Collections Library.
8. Letter from Varina Howell Davis to Gen. Jubal Early, May 5, 1883.
9. Letter from Varina Howell Davis to Constance Cary Harrison, October 19, 1890, Harrison Family Papers, 1744–1930, accession no. 2536, Albert and Shirley Small Special Collections Library.
10. Ross, *First Lady of the South*, 336.
11. Melinda Beck, "Time for a Good Old-Fashioned Nervous Breakdown," *Wall Street Journal*, Health Journal, February 28, 2012, D2–3.
12. Gosling, *Before Freud*, 9.
13. Corn et al., *Women on the Verge*, 7.
14. Corn et al., *Women on the Verge*, 1.
15. Corn et al., *Women on the Verge*, 2.
16. Beck, "Time for a Good Old-Fashioned Nervous Breakdown," D3.
17. Monsees, "How the Daughter of the Confederacy Almost Became a Daughter of New York."
18. Kelly, "'Daughter of the Confederacy' Found Love with a Yankee," 82.

13. ITALIAN IDYLL

1. Morris, *Pulitzer*, 280.
2. Strode, *Jefferson Davis*, 563.
3. Strode, *Jefferson Davis*, 562.
4. "Winnie Davis in Paris," *Middletown Daily Press*, December 7, 1889.
5. "Winnie Davis in Paris."
6. V. H. Davis, *Jefferson Davis*, 930–31.
7. Letter from Varina Howell Davis to Maj. W. H. Morgan, March 9, 1890, Jefferson Davis Family Papers, 1795–1913, LC.
8. Ross, *First Lady of the South*, 366.
9. Letter from Varina Anne Davis to Varina Howell Davis, March 1, 1890, Jefferson Davis Family Papers, 1795–1913, LC.
10. Gabriel, *Art of Acquiring*, 21.
11. Letter from Varina Howell Davis to Maj. W. H. Morgan, (1889?), Jefferson Davis Family Papers, 1795–1913, LC.
12. Letter from Alfred Wilkinson to Varina Howell Davis, March 4, 1890, Jefferson Davis Family Papers, 1795–1913, LC.
13. Zimmerman, *Love Fiercely*, 113.
14. Cashin, *First Lady of the Confederacy*, 172–74, 46–48
15. Morris, *Pulitzer*, 309.
16. Morris, *Pulitzer*, 311.
17. Edwards, "Memories of Winnie Davis."
18. Gosling, *Before Freud*, 2.
19. Letter from Varina Anne Davis to Maj. W. H. Morgan, March [?], 1890, Jefferson Davis Family Papers, LC.

14. DEAR DIARY

Epigraph: Varina Anne Davis, dedication to Varina Howell Davis, *Italian Journal*, January 29–April 3, 1890, Jefferson Davis Family Papers, Eleanor S. Brockenbrough Archives.

1. John Coski, historian and vice president of research and publications, Museum of the Confederacy, Richmond, email to the author, August 30, 2011.
2. Coski, email to the author, August 30, 2011.
3. Varina Anne Davis, *Italian Journal*, diary entry from Friday, January 31, 1890, 1–2, Jefferson Davis Family Papers, Eleanor S. Brockenbrough Archives.
4. Davis, *Italian Journal*, 98.
5. Davis, *Italian Journal*, 3.
6. John Coski, historian and vice president of Research and Publications, Museum of the Confederacy, interview by the author, April 30, 2011, Richmond.

7. Davis, *Italian Journal*, 159, 225.
8. Davis, *Italian Journal*, 139.
9. Letter from Alfred Wilkinson to Varina Howell Davis, February 25, 1890, Jefferson Davis Family Papers, LC.
10. Varina Anne Davis, *Italian Journal*, 62.
11. Letter from Alfred Wilkinson to Maj. W. H. Morgan, March 1, 1890, Jefferson Davis Family Papers, LC.
12. Letter from Alfred Wilkinson to Varina Howell Davis, March 4, 1890, Jefferson Davis Family Papers, LC.
13. Letter from Alfred Wilkinson to Varina Howell Davis, March 4, 1890.
14. Davis, *Italian Journal*, 232.
15. Davis, *Italian Journal*, 233.
16. Alfred Wilkinson, letter to Varina Howell Davis, March 1, 1890.
17. Letter from Alfred Wilkinson to Varina Howell Davis, March 4, 1890.
18. Letter from Alfred Wilkinson to Varina Howell Davis, March 4, 1890.
19. Letter from Alfred Wilkinson to Varina Howell Davis, March 4, 1890.

15. A WORLD ON FIRE

1. "Winnie Davis to Be Married," *New York Times*, April 27, 1890.
2. Hardin, *After the War*, 15–16.
3. Letter from Varina Howell Davis to Gen. Jubal Early, April 20, 1890, Early Family Papers, 1764–1956, sec. 4, Virginia Historical Society (VHS).
4. Hardin, *After the War*, 15; Cashin, *First Lady of the Confederacy*, 271–72.
5. "A Coming Auspicious Event: And Some Kindly Meant but Perhaps Impertinent Newspaper Comment," *Rochester Herald*, April [?], 1890, Wilkinson (Emory) Family File.
6. *Troy Times*, April [?], 1890, OHA.
7. Monsees, "How the Daughter of the Confederacy Almost Became a Daughter of New York."
8. Sinclair, *Southern Belle*, 60.
9. Wilkinson memoir, 29.
10. Hardin, *Syracuse Landmarks*, 217.
11. Wilkinson memoir, 20.
12. Wilkinson memoir, 20.
13. Wilkinson memoir, 21.
14. "Wilkinson Homestead Totally Destroyed by Fire Thursday," *W Journal*, August 23, 1890, BLK 45D, Wilkinson (Emory) Family File.
15. Wilkinson memoir, 21.
16. "Explosion of Benzine," *Syracuse Journal*, August 23, 1890, BLK, 45D, Wilkinson (Emory) Family File.
17. Wilkinson memoir, 21.
18. Wilkinson memoir, 21.

19. "Explosion of Benzine."
20. Wilkinson memoir, 21.
21. Wilkinson, quoted in "Explosion of Benzine."
22. Wilkinson memoir, 22.
23. Ross, *First Lady of the South*, 370.
24. Ross, *First Lady of the South*, 370.
25. Cashin, *First Lady of the Confederacy*, 272.
26. "The Engagement Off: Mr. Wilkinson Not to Marry Winnie Davis," *Utica Globe*, October 18, 1890, Wilkinson (Emory) Family File.
27. Monsees, "How the Daughter of the Confederacy Almost Became a Daughter of New York."
28. Ross, *First Lady of the South*, 371.
29. Wilkinson memoir, 22.
30. Ross, *First Lady of the South*, 370.
31. Letter from Varina Howell Davis to Maj. W. H. Morgan, October 5, 1890, Jefferson Davis Family Papers, LC.
32. Letter from Varina Howell Davis to Maj. W. H. Morgan, October 5, 1890.
33. Wilkinson memoir, 22.

16. QUEEN OF A MYSTIC COURT

Epigraph: Sinclair, *Queen of a Mystic Court*, bk. 1.

1. "Romance Local Man with Davis Girl Hit in 1890," *Skaneatles (NY) Press*, January 6, 1961, Wilkinson (Emory) Family File.
2. "Romance Local Man with Davis Girl Hit in 1890."
3. "Romance Local Man with Davis Girl Hit in 1890."
4. Lynda Crist, ed., *Papers of Jefferson Davis* at Rice University, email to the author, October 10, 2012.
5. Monsees, "How the Daughter of the Confederacy Almost Became a Daughter of New York."
6. Scrapbook (CMLS) no. 29, Jefferson Davis Family Papers, Eleanor S. Brockenbrough Archives.
7. Scrapbook (CMLS) no. 29, Jefferson Davis Family Papers.
8. Rowland, *Varina Howell*, 507.
9. Edwards, "Memories of Winnie Davis," 6.
10. *Richmond Times*, September 24, 1898.
11. Evans, *Macaria*, intro., xviii.
12. Faust, "Altars of Sacrifice," 1218, 1211.
13. Faust, "Altars of Sacrifice," intro., xxi.
14. Faust, "Altars of Sacrifice," 1219.
15. Ross, *First Lady of the South*, 387–88.
16. Cashin, *First Lady of the Confederacy*, 273.
17. Cashin, *First Lady of the Confederacy*, 288.

18. LaCavera, *Varina Anne "Winnie" Davis*, 28.
19. Lily Jackson, "'Daughter of the Confederacy' and a Queen of Comus," Jefferson Davis Family Papers, Eleanor S. Brockenbrough Library.
20. D. R. McGuire, "When the Darling of the South Ruled Comus," *New Orleans Times Picayune*, February 25, 1938, 31, Jefferson Davis Scrapbook.
21. Mitchell, *All on Mardi Gras Day*, 103.
22. Martha M. Boltz, "The Civil War," *Washington Times Communities*, February 17, 2010.
23. Henri Schindler, *Mardi Gras Treasures: Jewelry of the Golden Age* (Gretna: Pelican Publishing, 2006), 15.
24. Sinclair, *Southern Belle*, 20–21.
25. Sinclair, *Queen of a Mystic Court*, bk. 1.
26. Sinclair, *Queen of a Mystic Court*, bk. 1.
27. Sinclair, *Queen of a Mystic Court*, bk. 1.
28. Sinclair, *Queen of a Mystic Court*, bk. 1.
29. McGuire, "When the Darling of the South Ruled Comus," 31; Sinclair, *Queen of a Mystic Court*, bk. 1.
30. Boltz, "Civil War."
31. Sinclair, *Southern Belle*, 54, 59.
32. Sinclair, *Southern Belle*, 58.
33. Sinclair, *Southern Belle*, 61; Sinclair, *Queen of a Mystic Court*, intro.
34. Sinclair, *Queen of a Mystic Court*, bk. 1.
35. Sinclair, *Queen of a Mystic Court*, bk. 1.
36. Sinclair, *Queen of a Mystic Court*, bk. 1.
37. Sinclair, *Queen of a Mystic Court*, bk. 1.
38. Sinclair, *Queen of a Mystic Court*, bk. 2.
39. Sinclair, *Southern Belle*, 59–60.
40. Sinclair, *Queen of a Mystic Court*, bk. 2.
41. Sinclair, *Queen of a Mystic Court*, bk. 2.
42. Sinclair, *Queen of a Mystic Court*, bk. 2.
43. Sinclair, *Queen of a Mystic Court*, bk. 2.
44. Sinclair, *Southern Belle*, 77, 75.
45. Sinclair, *Queen of a Mystic Court*, bk. 1.

17. NEW YORK, NEW WOMAN

Epigraph: Tuttle, "Miss Winnie Davis, a Tribute," *Tuttle's Poems*, 4.
1. Hardin, *After the War*, 20.
2. Sinclair, *Southern Belle*, 59.
3. Cashin, *First Lady of the Confederacy*, 273.
4. Cashin, *First Lady of the Confederacy*, 274.
5. Thomas Nelson Page, quoted in Silber, *Romance of Reunion*, 113.
6. Cashin, *First Lady of the Confederacy*, 279, 212.

7. Waugh, *Surviving the Confederacy*, 329.
8. Letter from Varina Davis to Mrs. A. McC. Kimbrough, November 12, 1894, Jefferson Davis Papers, LC.
9. Ross, *First Lady of the South*, 378.
10. Letter from Varina Howell Davis to Alice Graham Lanigan, June 6, 1891, Jim Davis, Private Collection, Richmond.
11. Cashin, *First Lady of the Confederacy*, 279.
12. Ross, *First Lady of the South*, 379.
13. Appleton and Boswell, *Searching for Their Places*, 155.
14. Zimmerman, *Love Fiercely*, 89.
15. Zacks, *Island of Vice*, 3.
16. Berkin, *Civil War Wives*, 214.
17. Harrison, *Refugitta of Richmond*, 198.
18. *New York City Directory*, vol. 110, July 1, 1897.
19. Cashin, *First Lady of the Confederacy*, 280.
20. *Women in Mourning*, 6 (catalog of the Museum of the Confederacy's corollary exhibition, November 14, 1984–January 6, 1986, Richmond).
21. Thomas, "Story of the Jefferson Davis Funeral Train."
22. *Richmond Dispatch*, May 30, 1893.
23. *Richmond Dispatch*, May 30, 1893.
24. Cashin, *First Lady of the Confederacy*, 277.
25. Archival photo of Varina Anne Davis, Margaret Addison Hayes, Joel Addison Hayes, and a friend, August 1894, Cripple Creek CO, Colorado Springs Pioneers Museum, Starsmore Center for Local History.
26. "Madeline Pollard Is in Colorado: She and the 'Daughter of the Rebellion' Are in the Same Town," *Greeley Tribune*, August 2, 1894, Colorado Historical Newspapers online, courtesy of the Colorado Springs Pioneers Museum.
27. Cashin, *First Lady of the Confederacy*, 288; Hardin, *After the War*, 18.
28. LaCavera, *Varina Anne "Winnie" Davis*, 31.
29. Klotter, *Human Tradition in the New South*, 8.
30. Varina Howell Davis, quoted in Klotter, *Human Tradition*, 9.
31. Davis, *Veiled Doctor*, 62.
32. Davis, *Romance of Summer Seas*, 4.
33. Davis, *Romance of Summer Seas*, 3.
34. Williamson, *Rage for Order*, 18.
35. Zimmerman, *Love Fiercely*, 153.
36. Fox, *Five Sisters*, 58.
37. Fox, *Five Sisters*, 60.
38. Zimmerman, *Love Fiercely*, 153.
39. Zheutling, *Around the World on Two Wheels*, 28.
40. Susan B. Anthony, quoted in Zheutling, *Around the World on Two Wheels*, 27.

41. Morris, *Pulitzer*, 338.
42. Varina Anne Davis, Will, February 11, 1898, Jefferson Davis Papers, LC.
43. Ross, *First Lady of the South*, 391.
44. Morris, *Pulitzer*, 344.

18. THE LAST CASUALTY OF THE LOST CAUSE

1. Letter from Varina Howell Davis to Constance Cary Harrison, September 7, 1898, Harrison Family Papers, 1744–1930, accession no. 2536, Albert and Shirley Small Special Collections Library.
2. Letter from Varina Howell Davis to Constance Cary Harrison, September 7, 1898.
3. *Richmond Dispatch*, September 20, 1898; Ross, *First Lady of the South*, 392.
4. Ross, *First Lady of the South*, 392.
5. Latimer, *Narragansett-by-the-Sea*, 55.
6. Latimer, *Narragansett-by-the-Sea*, 59.
7. Latimer, *Narragansett-by-the-Sea*, 51.
8. www.southcountymuseum.org/wth_Prominent_Visitors.html.
9. Letter from Varina Davis to Maj. W. H. Morgan, August 1, 1898, Jefferson Davis Papers, LC.
10. Letter from Varina Howell Davis to Constance Cary Harrison, September 7, 1898.
11. www.southcountymuseum.org/wth_Social Life.html.
12. Letter from Varina Howell Davis to Jefferson Hayes-Davis, September 8, 1898, Bertram Hayes-Davis Private Collection, Gulfport MS.
13. Letter from Varina Howell Davis to Constance Cary Harrison, September 7, 1898.
14. Cashin, *First Lady of the Confederacy*, 290.
15. Letter from Varina Howell Davis to Constance Cary Harrison, September 7, 1898.
16. Varina Anne Davis, quoted in Ferrell, "Daughter of the Confederacy," 84.
17. Strong, "Daughter of the Confederacy," 234–39.
18. *Richmond Dispatch*, September 20, 1898.
19. Return of Death, Varina Anne Jefferson Davis, September 18, 1898.
20. Gray and Bradley, "Medical History of Jefferson Davis"; reprinted in *Virginia Medical Monthly* 94 (January 1967): 4.
21. Gray and Bradley, "Medical History of Jefferson Davis," 3.
22. Resolution Letters, Telegrams, and Tributes to Varina Anne Davis, Jefferson Davis Family Papers, Eleanor S. Brockenbrough Archives; Cashin, *First Lady of the Confederacy*, 290.
23. *Narragansett Times*, September 23, 1898, Jefferson Davis Family Papers, Eleanor S. Brockenbrough Archives.
24. *New York City Directory*, 1898–99.

25. Martha M. Boltz, "New York Daughters of the Confederacy Honors 3 Davis Women," *Washington Times*, May 31, 1997, B3.
26. Return of Death, Varina Anne Jefferson Davis, September 18, 1898.
27. *Richmond Dispatch*, September 19, 1898, 1B.
28. Monsees, "How the Daughter of the Confederacy Almost Became a Daughter of New York."

19. DEATH AND THE MAIDEN

1. Funeral telegram, from Margaret Hayes-Davis to Varina Howell Davis, Jefferson Davis Collection, Jefferson Davis Family Papers, Eleanor Brockenbrough Archives.
2. *Richmond Dispatch*, September 23, 1898, Eleanor Brockenbrough Archives.
3. LaCavera, *Varina Anne "Winnie" Davis*, 33.
4. Boltz, "New York Daughters of the Confederacy Honors 3 Davis Women," *Washington Times*, May 31, 1997, B3, Helen Walpole Brewer Library and Archives.
5. Ferrell, "Daughter of the Confederacy," 72.
6. Bleser, "Marriage of Varina Howell Davis and Jefferson Davis," 38–39.
7. LaCavera, *Varina Anne "Winnie" Davis*, 36; *Richmond Dispatch*, September 24, 1898, VHS.
8. *Richmond Evening Leader*, September 24, 1898, Hobson Family Papers, 1776–1974, sec. 17, VHS.
9. *Richmond Dispatch*, September 24, 1898.
10. Loughridge and Campbell, *Women in Mourning Exhibition Catalog*, 14–15.
11. *Richmond Dispatch*, September 24, 1898.
12. *Richmond Dispatch*, September 24, 1898; LaCavera, *Varina Anne "Winnie" Davis*, 38.
13. Ross, *First Lady of the South*, 392.
14. Appleton and Boswell, *Searching for Their Places*, 144.
15. LaCavera, *Varina Anne "Winnie" Davis*, 41.
16. Poppenheim et al., *History of the United Daughters of the Confederacy*, 1:42.
17. "Winnie Davis," *UDC Magazine*, 16, Virginia State Library Archives, Richmond.
18. *A Walking Tour of St. Paul's*, brochure, St. Paul's Episcopal Church, Richmond, www.stpauls-episcopal.org.
19. *Walking Tour of St. Paul's*.
20. *Walking Tour of St. Paul's*.
21. *Richmond Dispatch*, September 24, 1898.
22. *Richmond Dispatch*, September 24, 1898.
23. Lankford, *Richmond Burning*, 13.
24. *Evening Leader*, September 24, 1898, Hobson Family Papers, 1776–1974, sec. 17, VHS.

25. Ross, *First Lady of the South*; Monsees, "How the Daughter of the Confederacy Almost Became a Daughter of New York"; Van der Heuvel, *Crowns of Thorns of Glory*, 258.
26. Monsees, "How the Daughter of the Confederacy Almost Became a Daughter of New York"; "Learn of Death of A. C. Wilkinson," *Syracuse Journal*, May 28, 1918, OHA.
27. *Richmond Dispatch*, September 24, 1898.
28. LaCavera, *Varina Anne "Winnie" Davis*, 45–47.
29. "Tribute of Respect to Miss Winnie Davis," Walter Barker Chapter, UDC no. 242, Macon MS, September 23, 1898, Helen Walpole Brewer Library and Archives.
30. Hardin, *After the War*, 21.
31. Letter from Varina Howell Davis to Chancellor Kimbrough, May 10, 1902, ALS, Kimbrough Papers, Mississippi Department of Archives and History, no. Z1210.
32. Cashin, *First Lady of the Confederacy*, 305.
33. *Confederate Veteran Magazine* 17 (January–December 1909): 420, Helen Walpole Brewer Library and Archives.
34. Bertram and Carol Hayes-Davis, interview by the author, October 3, 2012, Beauvoir, Biloxi MS; Hayes-Davis (Jefferson) Mississippi Legislative Act, 1890, Z2089.000, Mississippi Department of Archives and History.
35. Hardin, *After the War*, 20.

EPILOGUE

1. Docent-led tour of Beauvoir, October 3, 2012, Biloxi MS.
2. *Beauvoir: The Jefferson Davis Home and Presidential Library—History and Walking Tour Guide*. Biloxi MS: Beauvoir, 2008.
3. Bertram and Carol Hayes-Davis, interview by the author, October 3, 2012, Beauvoir, Biloxi MS.
4. Bertram and Carol Hayes-Davis, interview by the author, October 3, 2012.
5. Bertram and Carol Hayes-Davis, interview by the author, October 4, 2012, Beauvoir, Biloxi MS.
6. Emily Wagster Pettus, "For Miss., an Angst-Filled Civil War Anniversary," Associated Press, August 17, 2012, http://news.yahoo.com/miss-angst-filled-civil-war-anniversary-112249673.html.
7. Bertram and Carol Hayes-Davis, interview by the author, October 4, 2012.
8. Bertram and Carol Hayes-Davis, interview by the author, October 4, 2012; Beacroft, *Jefferson Davis*.
9. Sinclair, *Southern Belle*, 54.

Bibliography

PRIMARY SOURCES

Bertram Hayes-Davis Private Collection. Gulfport MS.

Charles Dudley Warner Correspondence. Watkinson Library. Trinity College, Hartford CT.

Davis Family photograph collection. Valentine Richmond History Center, Richmond VA.

Early Family Papers, 1764–1956. Sec. 4. Virginia Historical Society, Richmond.

Frederick Fillison Bowen Papers, 1863–1898. Sec. 1. Virginia Historical Society, Richmond.

Harrison Family Papers, 1744–1930. Accession no. 2536. Albert and Shirley Small Special Collections Library. University of Virginia, Charlottesville.

Helen Walpole Brewer Library and Archives. United Daughters of the Confederacy, Richmond VA.

Hobson Family Papers, 1776–1974. Sec. 17. Virginia Historical Society, Richmond.

James Branch Cabell Library. Special Collections and Archives. Manuscript Collections. Library of Virginia, Richmond.

Jefferson Davis Family Papers. Eleanor Brockenbrough Archives. Museum of the Confederacy, Richmond.

Jefferson Davis Family Papers. Manuscript Collection. Library of Congress, Washington DC.

Jefferson Davis Family Papers. W. S. Hoole Special Collections Library. University of Alabama, Tuscaloosa.

Jefferson Davis Scrapbook. Louisiana Room. Louisiana State University, Baton Rouge.

Joseph Pulitzer Papers. Special Manuscript Collections. Rare Book and Manuscript Library. Butler Library. Columbia University, New York.

Return of Death. Varina Anne Jefferson Davis, September 18, 1898. Certification of Vital Record. State of Rhode Island and Providence Plantations. Town Clerk's Office, Town Hall, Narragansett. Rhode Island State Archives.

Robbins Papers. No. 4070. Southern Historical Collection. Wilson Library. University of North Carolina, Chapel Hill.

Sinclair, Mary Craig. *Queen of a Mystic Court.* Bk. 1. Sinclair MS. Manuscript Department. Lilly Library. Indiana University, Bloomington.

Sprague, Mrs. Frances. Scrapbook. Mississippi Department of Archives and History, Jackson.

Starsmore Center for Local History. Colorado Springs Pioneers Museum, Colorado Springs.

Virginia Military Institute Archives. Civil War Collection. MS no. 00285. Lexington VA.

Wilkinson, Charlotte May. Memoir. MS. Private collection.

Wilkinson (Emory) Family. Richard and Carolyn Wright Research Center. Onondaga Historical Association, Syracuse NY.

SECONDARY SOURCES

Alfriend, Edward M. "Social Life in Richmond during the War." *Cosmopolitan*, December 1891, 229–33.

Appleton, Thomas H., Jr., and Angela Boswell, eds. *Searching for Their Places: Women in the South across Four Centuries.* Columbia: University of Missouri Press, 2003.

Ayers, Edward L. *Promise of the New South: Life after Reconstruction.* New York: Oxford University Press, 1993.

Baker, James Graham. "Verner White: Rediscovering a Neglected Texas Artist." *Southwestern Historical Quarterly* (April 2010): 422–36.

Barbee, Matthew Mace. "Matthew Fontaine Maury and the Evolution of Southern Memory." *Virginia Magazine of History and Biography* 120, no. 4 (2012): 372–93.

Beacroft, Percival, prod. *Jefferson Davis: An American President.* Documentary film. Freeport TX: Rosemont Pictures, 2008.

"Beauvoir, Home of Jefferson Davis." *Confederate Veteran* 35, no. 6 (June 1927): 216–17.

Berkin, Carol. *Civil War Wives: The Lives and Times of Angelina Grimké Weld, Varina Howell Davis, and Julia Dent Grant.* New York: Knopf, 2009.

Blaszczyk, Regina Lee. *The Color Revolution.* Cambridge MA: MIT Press, 2012.

Bleser, Carol K. "The Marriage of Varina Howell Davis and Jefferson Davis: 'I Gave My Best and All to a Girdled Tree.'" *Journal of Southern History* 65, no. 1 (February 1999): 3–40.

———, ed. *In Joy and Sorrow: Women, Family, and Marriage in the Victorian South.* New York: Oxford University Press, 1991.

Bleser, Carol, and Frederick M. Heath. "The Clays of Alabama: The Impact of the Civil War on a Southern Marriage." In Bleser, *In Joy and Sorrow.*

Burr, Frank A. "Jefferson Davis, the Ex-Confederate President at Home." *Philadelphia Enquirer*, July 10, 1881. Reprinted in *Tyler's Quarterly* 32 (1950–51): 163–80.
Cashin, Joan. *First Lady of the Confederacy: Varina Davis's Civil War*. Cambridge MA: Harvard University Press, 2006.
Chopin, Kate. *The Awakening*. Edited by Margaret Culley. New York: Norton, 1976.
Clay-Clopton, Virginia, and Ada Sterling. *A Belle of the Fifties: Memoirs of Mrs. Clay, of Alabama, Covering Social and Political Life in Washington and the South, 1853–66*. New York: Doubleday, Page, 1905.
Corn, Wanda, et al. *Women on the Verge: The Culture of Neurasthenia in Nineteenth Century America*. Published in conjunction with exhibition, Iris and B. Gerald Cantor Center for the Visual Arts at Stanford University, Board of Trustees of Leland Stanford Junior University, Stanford CA, 2004.
Coski, Ruth Ann. *The White House of the Confederacy: A Pictorial Tour*. Richmond: Museum of the Confederacy, 2001.
Couling, Mary P. *The Lee Girls*. Winston-Salem: John F. Blair, 1987.
Cox, Karen L. *Dixie's Daughters: The United Daughters of the Confederacy and the Preservation of Confederate Culture*. Gainesville: University Press of Florida, 2003.
"Daughter of the South." *Confederate Veteran Magazine* 6 (January–December 1898): 465–66.
Davis, Burke. *Jeb Stuart: The Last Cavalier*. Short Hills NJ: Burford Books, 1957.
Davis, Jefferson. *The Papers of Jefferson Davis*. Vol. 12: *June 1865–December 1870*. Edited by Lynda L. Crist, Suzanne Scott Gibbs, Brady L. Hutchison, and Elizabeth Henson Smith. Baton Rouge: Louisiana State University Press, 2008.
———. *The Papers of Jefferson Davis*. Vol. 13: *1871–1879*. Edited by Lynda L. Crist and Suzanne Scott Gibbs. Baton Rouge: Louisiana State University Press, 2012.
———. Rise and Fall of the Confederate Government. 1881. Reprint, New York: Da Capo, 1990.
Davis, Varina Anne Jefferson. "The American Girl Who Studies Abroad, First Paper." Originally published in *Ladies' Home Journal*, February 1892, 9. Courtesy of the Meredith Company, Des Moines IA.
———. "The American Girl Who Studies Abroad, Second Paper." Originally published in *Ladies' Home Journal*, March 1892, 6. Courtesy of the Meredith Company, Des Moines IA.
———. *An Irish Knight of the 19th Century: Sketch of the Life of Robert Emmet*. New York: John W. Lovell Company, 1888.
———. *A Romance of Summer Seas*. New York: Harper & Brothers, 1898.

———. *The Veiled Doctor*. New York: Harper & Brothers, 1895.
Davis, Varina Howell. *Jefferson Davis, Ex-President of the Confederate States of America: A Memoir by His Wife*. Vol. 2. 1890. Reprint, Baltimore: Nautical & Aviation Publishing Company, 1990.
Davis, William C. *The Cause Lost: Myths and Realties of the Confederacy*. Lawrence: University of Kansas Press, 1996.
———. *Jefferson Davis: The Man and His Hour*. New York: HarperCollins, 1991.
De Leon, Thomas Cooper. *Belles, Beaux and Brains of the 60's*. New York: G. W. Dillingham, 1909.
Dolensky, Suzanne T. "The Daughters of Jefferson Davis: A Study of Contrast." *Journal of Mississippi History* 51, no. 4 (November 1989): 313–40.
———. "Varina Howell, 1889 to 1906: The Years Alone." *Journal of Mississippi History* 47 no. 2 (May 1985): 90–109.
Dorris, Jonathan Truman. *Pardon and Amnesty under Lincoln and Johnson: The Restoration of the Confederates to Their Rights and Privileges, 1861–1898*. Chapel Hill: University of North Carolina Press, 1953.
Edwards, Harry Stillwell. "Memories of Winnie Davis." *Armstrong's Magazine* 4, no. 1 (January 1899): 3–6.
Evans, Augusta Jane. *Macaria; or, Altars of Sacrifice*. Edited by Drew Gilpin Faust. Baton Rouge: Louisiana State University Press, 1992.
Faust, Drew Gilpin. "Altars of Sacrifice: Confederate Women and the Narratives of War." *Journal of American History* 76, pt. 2 (March 1990): 1200–1228.
Ferrell, Charles Clifton. "The Daughter of the Confederacy: Her Life, Character and Writings." *Publications of the Mississippi Historical Society* (1899): 69–84.
Foster, Gaines M. *Ghosts of the Confederacy: Defeat, the Lost Cause, and the Emergence of the New South, 1865–1913*. New York: Oxford University Press, 1987.
Fox, James. *Five Sisters: The Langhornes of Virginia*. New York: Simon & Schuster, 2000.
Freeman, Douglas Southall. *Lee's Lieutenants: A Study in Command*. Vol. 1. New York: Scribner's, 1942.
Gabriel, Mary. *The Art of Acquiring: A Portrait of Etta and Claribel Cone*. Baltimore: Bancroft Press, 2002.
Gosling, F. G. *Before Freud: Neurasthenia and the American Medical Community: 1870–1910*. Urbana: University of Illinois Press, 1987.
Gray, Frederic W., MS, and Chester D. Bradley, MD. "The Medical History of Jefferson Davis." United Daughters of the Confederacy Files, Richmond. Reprinted in *Virginia Medical Monthly* 94 (January 1967): 19–23.
Gugliotta, Guy. *Freedom's Cap: The United States Capitol and the Coming of the Civil War*. New York: Hill & Wang, 2012.

Hardin, David. *After the War: The Lives and Images of Major Civil War Figures after the Shooting Stopped*. Chicago: Ivan R. Dee, 2010.

Hardin, Evamaria. *Syracuse Landmarks: An AIA Guide to Downtown and Historic Neighborhoods*. Syracuse: Onondaga Historical Association / Syracuse University Press, 1993.

Harrison, Constance Cary. *Refugitta of Richmond: The Wartime Recollections, Grave and Gay, of Constance Cary Harrison*. Edited by Nathaniel Cheairs Hughes Jr. and S. Kitrell Rushing. Knoxville: University of Tennessee Press, 2011.

Hendrick, Burton J. *Statement of the Lost Cause: Jefferson Davis and His Cabinet*. New York: Literary Guild of America, 1939.

Heuvel, Sean M., ed. *Life after J.E.B. Stuart: The Memoirs of His Granddaughter, Marrow Stuart Smith*. Lanham MD: Hamilton Books, 2011.

Janney, Caroline E. *Burying the Dead but Not the Past: Ladies' Memorial Associations and the Lost Cause*. Chapel Hill: University of North Carolina Press, 2008.

Johnson, Clint. *Pursuit: The Chase, Capture, Persecution, and Surprising Release of Confederate President Jefferson Davis*. New York: Citadel Press, 2008.

Kelly, C. Brian. "'Daughter of the Confederacy' Found Love with a Yankee, but the Couple's Happiness Became a Casualty of War." *Military History* 15, no. 6 (February 1999).

Kelly, C. Brian, with Ingrid Smyer. *Best Little Stories from the Civil War*. Naperville IL: Cumberland House, 2010.

Klotter, James C., ed. *The Human Tradition in the New South*. Lanham MD: Rowman & Littlefield, 2005.

LaCavera, Tommie Phillips, comp. and ed. *Varina Anne "Winnie" Davis: Daughter of the Confederacy*. Athens GA: Southern Trace Publishers, 1994.

Lankford, Nelson. *Richmond Burning: The Last Days of the Confederate Capital*. New York: Penguin Books, 2002.

LaPlante, Eve. *Marmee & Louisa: The Untold Story of Louisa May Alcott and Her Mother*. New York: Free Press, 2012.

Lattimer, Sallie. *Narragansett-by-the-Sea*. Charleston: Arcadia Publishing, 1997.

Leveen, Lois. *The Secrets of Mary Bowser*. New York: William Morrow, 2012.

Loughridge, Patricia R., and Edward D. Campbell Jr. *Women in Mourning Exhibition Catalog*. Richmond: Museum of the Confederacy, 1984. Published in conjunction with exhibition shown at the Museum of the Confederacy, November 14, 1984–January 6, 1986.

"Margaret Howell Davis Hayes." *Confederate Veteran Magazine* 17 (January–December 1909): 419–20.

McCollin, Alice Graham. "Clever Daughters of Clever Men." *Ladies' Home Journal*, December 1891, 12.

McSherry, Frank, Jr., Charles G. Waugh, and Martin Greenberg, eds. *Civil War Women: The Civil War Seen through Women's Eyes in Stories by Louisa*

May Alcott, Kate Chopin, Eudora Welty, and Other Great Women Writers. New York: Simon & Schuster, 1988.

Monsees, Anita. "How the Daughter of the Confederacy Almost Became a Daughter of New York." *Heritage* 7, no. 3 (January–February 1991): n.p.

Morris, James McGrath. *Pulitzer: A Life in Politics, Print, and Power*. New York: HarperCollins, 2010.

New York City Directory. Vol. 110. New York: Trow Directory & Booklanding Company, July 1897, 327.

O'Brien, Esse Forrester. "Verner White." *Art and Artists of Texas*. Dallas: Tardy Press, 1935.

Oldendorf, Keith N. "The Lost Princess of the South, Varina Anne 'Winnie' Davis." *Memorial Hall Foundation Newsletter* (Fall 1999).

Oliver, Julia. *Devotion: A Novel Based on the Life of Winnie Davis, Daughter of the Confederacy*. Athens: University of Georgia Press, 2006.

O'Reilly Bill, and Martin Dugard. *Killing Lincoln: The Shocking Assassination That Changed America Forever*. New York: Henry Holt, 2011.

Perry, John. *Mrs. Robert E. Lee: The Lady of Arlington*. Sisters OR: Multnomah Publishers, 2001.

Pickett, Lasalle Corbell. *Across My Path: Memories of People I Have Known*. 1916. Reprint, Freeport NY: Books for Libraries Press, 1970.

Poppenheim, Mary B., et al. *The History of the United Daughters of the Confederacy*. Vols. 1–2. Raleigh: Edwards & Broughton, 1955.

Powell, Alexander. *Gone Are the Days*. Boston: Little, Brown, 1938.

Ralph, Julian. "Mardi Gras at New Orleans." *Harper's Weekly*, March 19, 1892, 285.

Randall, Ruth Painter. *I Varina: A Biography of the Girl Who Married Jefferson Davis and Became the First Lady of the South*. Boston: Little, Brown, 1962.

Ross, Ishbel. *First Lady of the South: The Life of Mrs. Jefferson Davis*. New York: Harper, 1958.

Rowland, Eron Opha Moore. *Varina Howell, Wife of Jefferson Davis*. New York: Macmillan, 1927–31.

Rutherford, Mildred Lewis. *Jefferson Davis, the President of the Confederate States, and Abraham Lincoln, the President of the United States, 1861–1865*. Athens GA: United Daughters of the Confederacy, 1916.

Scott, Anne Firor. *The Southern Lady: From Pedestal to Politics, 1830–1930*. Chicago: University of Chicago Press, 1970.

Silber, Nina. "Intemperate Men, Spiteful Women, and Jefferson Davis." In *Divided Houses: Gender and the Civil War*, edited by Catherine Clinton and Nina Silber. New York: Oxford University Press, 1992.

———. *The Romance of Reunion: Northerners and the South, 1865–1900*. Chapel Hill: University of North Carolina Press, 1993.

Sinclair, Mary Craig. *Southern Belle*. New York: Crown Publishers, 1957.
Street, Julia. "Questions and Answers about New Orleans." *New Orleans Magazine* 34, no. 6 (March 2000): 346.
Strode, Hudson, ed. *Jefferson Davis: Private Letters, 1825–1889*. New York: Harcourt, Brace & World, 1966.
Strong, Leah A., ed. "The Daughter of the Confederacy." *Mississippi Quarterly* 20 (1966–67): 235–39.
Swanson, James. *Bloody Crimes: The Chase for Jefferson Davis and the Death Pageant for Lincoln's Corpse*. New York: HarperCollins, 2010.
Thomas, H. Edison. "The Story of the Jefferson Davis Funeral Train." Reprint of the article published in *L and N Magazine* (February 1955). United Daughters of the Confederacy Files, Richmond.
Thomason, John W., Jr. *Jeb Stuart*. Lincoln: University of Nebraska Press, 1994.
Tindall, Retta D. "The Confederate Treasure Train." UDC *Magazine* (October 2012): 8–14.
———. "Jefferson Davis Husband and Father." UDC *Magazine* (October 2011): 9–12.
Van der Heuvel, Gerry. *Crowns of Thorns and Glory: Mary Todd Lincoln and Varina Howell Davis, the Two First Ladies of the Civil War*. New York: Dutton, 1988.
Waugh, John C. *Surviving the Confederacy: Rebellion, Ruin, and Recovery—Roger and Sara Pryor during the Civil War*. New York: Harcourt, 2002.
Weidermeyer, Susan, and Amy Peltz, eds. *Impressionism, Fashion, and Modernity*. Chicago: Art Institute of Chicago, 2012. Published in conjunction with exhibitions shown at the Musée d'Orsay, Paris; Metropolitan Museum of Art, New York; and the Art Institute of Chicago.
Wiley, Bell Irvin. *Confederate Women*. Westport, Conn.: Greenwood Press, 1975.
Williamson, Joel. *A Rage for Order*. New York: Oxford University Press, 1986.
"Winnie Davis." UDC *Magazine* 11, no. 6 (June 1948): 16.
Woodward, C. Vann, ed. *Mary Chesnut's Civil War*. New Haven: Yale University Press, 1981.
Wyatt-Brown, Bertram. *The House of Percy: Honor, Melancholy, and Imagination in a Southern Family*. New York: Oxford University Press, 1994.
Zacks, Richard. *Island of Vice: Theodore Roosevelt's Doomed Quest to Clean Up Sin-Loving New York*. New York: Doubleday, 2012.
Zheutlin, Peter. *Around the World on Two Wheels: Annie Londonderry's Extraordinary Ride*. New York: Citadel Press, 2007.
Zimmerman, Jean. *Love, Fiercely: A Gilded Age Romance*. Boston: Houghton Mifflin Harcourt, 2012.

Index